THE RECOVERY OF THE SELF IN PSYCHOSIS

The Recovery of the Self in Psychosis details specific therapeutic approaches as well as considers how treatments can be individually tailored and adapted to help persons whose mental health challenges may be either mild or more severe. By focusing on basic elements of the experiences of persons diagnosed with psychosis and exploring the broader meanings these experiences have, each of these treatments offer distinctive ways to help persons define and manage their own recovery. The book includes measurable therapeutic processes, an empirically supported conceptual basis for understanding disturbances in self-experience and rich descriptions of the recovery process.

The Recovery of the Self in Psychosis moves beyond approaches which dictate what health is to persons with psychosis through education. It will be essential reading for all clinical psychologists and psychotherapists working with people diagnosed with psychosis.

Ilanit Hasson-Ohayon, PhD, is a rehabilitation psychologist and full professor at the department of psychology in Bar-Ilan University, Israel. She studies different psychological aspects of coping with illnesses, especially serious mental illnesses, and has been involved in practicing and supervising psychotherapy for over 20 years. She is an author of over 150 peer-reviewed papers and book chapters in the field of clinical-rehabilitation psychology.

Paul H. Lysaker, PhD, is a clinical psychologist at Richard L Roudebush VA Medical Center and a professor of clinical psychology at the Indiana University School of Medicine, USA. He has over 35 years of experience providing mental health treatment to adults diagnosed with serious mental illness. He has been active in clinical research for over 30 years and is an author of over 480 peer-reviewed papers related to wellness and recovery from serious mental illness.

THE INTERNATIONAL SOCIETY FOR PSYCHOLOGICAL AND SOCIAL APPROACHES TO PSYCHOSIS BOOK SERIES

Series editors: Anna Lavis and Andrew Shepherd

The International Society for Psychological and Social Approaches to Psychosis (ISPS) comprises a diverse range of individuals, networks and institutional members across more than twenty countries. Central to its ethos is that the perspectives of individuals with lived experience of psychosis, and their families and friends, are key to forging more inclusive understandings of, and collaborative therapeutic approaches to, psychosis.

With a core aim of promoting psychological and social approaches to psychosis, ISPS has a history stretching back more than five decades. During this time it has witnessed the relentless pursuit of primarily biological explanations for psychosis. This tide has been turning in recent years, with growing international recognition of a range of psychological, social, and cultural factors that have considerable explanatory traction and distinct therapeutic possibilities. Policymakers, treatment professionals, people with lived experience of psychosis, and family members are increasingly exploring interventions in which talking and listening are key ingredients. Psychosocially informed understandings and support frameworks are helpful for fostering and promoting personal recovery in the face of adverse psychotic experience. Recognising the humanitarian and therapeutic potential of these perspectives, ISPS embraces a wide spectrum of approaches from psychodynamic, systemic, cognitive, and arts therapies, to need-adapted and dialogical approaches, family and group therapies and residential therapeutic communities.

A further ambition of ISPS is to draw together diverse viewpoints on psychosis and to foster discussion and debate across the biomedical and social sciences, including establishing meaningful dialogue with practitioners and researchers who are more familiar with biological-based approaches. Such discussions are supported by growing evidence of the entanglement of genes and physiology with socio-cultural, environmental, and emotional contexts. This allows a consideration of mental distress as an embodied psycho-social experience that must be understood in relation to a person's life history and circumstances.

The ISPS book series seeks to capture these developments in the field by providing a forum in which authors with a variety of lived and professional experiences can share the significant value of their work. Complemented by international and national conferences and publication of the journal *Psychosis*, this series is central to the activities of ISPS and their global reach. It comprises books with a variety of empirical focuses and with differing experiential and disciplinary perspectives. Although diverse, the range of books combines intellectual rigour with accessibility to readers across the ISPS community. We aim for the series to be a resource for mental health professionals, for those developing and implementing policy, for academics in the social and clinical sciences, and for people whose interest in psychosis stems from personal or family experience.

To support its aim of advancing scholarship in an inclusive and interdisciplinary way, the series benefits from the advice of an editorial board whose members are drawn from across the ISPS community:

CBT for Psychosis
Process-orientated Therapies and the Third Wave
Caroline Cupitt

Personal Experiences of Psychological Therapy for Psychosis and Related Experiences
Peter Taylor, Olympia Gianfrancesco and Naomi Fisher

Attachment Theory and Psychosis
Current Perspectives and Future Directions
Katherine Berry, Sandra Bucci and Adam N. Danquah

The Recovery of the Self in Psychosis
Contributions from Metacognitive and Mentalization Based Oriented Psychotherapy
Ilanit Hasson-Ohayon and Paul H. Lysaker

Open Dialogue for Psychosis
Organising Mental Health Services to Prioritise Dialogue, Relationship and Meaning
Nick Putman and Brian Martindale

For more information about ISPS, email isps@isps.org or visit our website, www. isps.org.

For more information about the journal *Psychosis* visit www.isps.org/index.php/publications/journal

THE RECOVERY OF THE SELF IN PSYCHOSIS

Contributions from Metacognitive
and Mentalization Based Oriented
Psychotherapy

*Edited by Ilanit Hasson-Ohayon
and Paul H. Lysaker*

Routledge
Taylor & Francis Group

LONDON AND NEW YORK

First published 2021
by Routledge
2 Park Square, Milton Park, Abingdon, Oxon OX14 4RN

and by Routledge
605 Third Avenue, New York, NY 10158

Routledge is an imprint of the Taylor & Francis Group, an informa business

© 2021 selection and editorial matter, Ilanit Hasson-Ohayon and
Paul H. Lysaker; individual chapters, the contributors

The right of Ilanit Hasson-Ohayon and Paul H. Lysaker to be
identified as the authors of the editorial material, and of the
authors for their individual chapters, has been asserted in
accordance with sections 77 and 78 of the Copyright, Designs and
Patents Act 1988.

British Library Cataloguing-in-Publication Data
A catalogue record for this book is available from the British Library

Library of Congress Cataloging-in-Publication Data
A catalog record for this book has been requested

ISBN: 978-1-138-59819-5 (hbk)
ISBN: 978-1-138-59821-8 (pbk)
ISBN: 978-0-429-48650-0 (ebk)

Typeset in Times New Roman
by Apex CoVantage, LLC

CONTENTS

CONTRIBUTORS

Bargenquast Rebecca, Rebecca is a clinical psychologist, psychotherapist, and supervisor who currently runs her own private practice in Brisbane, Australia. Rebecca has extensive experience working with young people and adults who experience mental health difficulties. She has a special interest in psychotherapy for people diagnosed with a psychotic disorder with a focus on meaning-making and recovery-oriented approaches.

Beasley Rhianna, Psy.D., is a postdoctoral fellow at the Institute of Living, Hartford Hospital. She is interested in recovery-oriented approaches to psychosis.

Buck Kelly Dawn, is a Clinical Nurse Specialist who has over 35 years of experience in academia and clinical settings. She has worked for 15 years providing group and individual psychotherapy to adults with serious mental illness. She is an author of over 60 published papers. Her specific research and clinical interests involve intensive psychotherapy and metacognition in serious mental illness.

Debbané Martin, is Associate Professor and director of the Developmental Clinical Psychology Research Unit at the Faculty of Psychology and Educational Sciences, University of Geneva (Switzerland). He is also Senior Lecturer at the Research Department of Clinical, Educational, and Health Psychology, University College London (UK). His research activities focus on developmental psychopathology, examining the developmental roots of severe disorders in the psychosis or personality spectrum disorders. His team's scientific projects involve a number of different methodologies, including but not restricted to clinical measures and cognitive paradigms, as well as structural and functional neuroimaging. He is involved in a number of longitudinal projects following youth cohorts with clinical risk (schizotypy, borderline or antisocial traits) or genetic risk (22q11.2 Deletion syndrome) for severe psychopathology. Martin Debbané is a trained and licensed psychodynamic psychotherapist, acting as associate, supervisor and trainer in mentalization-based therapies at the Anna Freud Centre in London (UK), as well as in the francophone network for mentalization-based therapies.

Steven de Jong defended his PhD thesis on Metacognitive Reflection and Insight Therapy for persons with severe mental illness in 2018. He now divides his time between research and clinical work at Lentis Psychiatric Institute, in the Netherlands. His research interests are psychosis, the therapeutic alliance and metacognition.

Dimaggio Giancarlo, MD. a psychiatrist and psychotherapist, is a co-founding member of the Center for Metacognitive Interpersonal Therapy in Rome, Italy, and trainer for the Italian Society of Cognitive and Behaviour Psychotherapy (SITCC). His primary interest is in personality disorders. He has co-authored and edited seven books on psychopathology and psychotherapy, and more than 200 papers and book chapters in scientific journals. He is Editor-in-chief for the Journal of Clinical Psychology: In-Session, Associate Editor for Psychology and Psychotherapy and Senior Associate Editor for the Journal of Psychotherapy Integration and serves on the editorial board of the Journal of Personality Disorders.

Gumley Andrew is a Chartered Psychologist and Clinical Psychologist registered with the Health and Care Professions Council UK, and a Professor of Psychological Therapy, as well as a leading international researcher investigating psychological interventions for people with psychosis. Andrew developed and evaluated the first ever randomised controlled trial of Cognitive Behavioural Therapy for the prevention of relapse in people with Schizophrenia. Since then he has designed and lead randomised controlled trials of Cognitive Behavioural Therapy in people experiencing a range of mental health difficulties including young people at risk of developing psychosis, and individuals who have psychotic experiences which have not fully responded to Clozapine. He has been at the forefront of developing and piloting third wave interventions for psychosis, including Compassion Focused Therapy and Acceptance and Commitment Therapy, and has also undertaken extensive research into the importance of fear of recurrence as a block to recovery in people with psychosis. His research is funded by the National Institute of Health Research Health Technology Assessment (NIHR-HTA), Chief Scientist's Office (CSO) Scottish Government, UK Medical Research Council, the Danish Institute for Humanities Research, and NHS Greater Glasgow & Clyde.

Hamm Jay, is a clinical psychologist with research and practice interests in recovery-oriented treatments for persons with serious mental illness. He has an active clinical practice in a community mental health setting, in which he offers metacognitive-focused psychotherapy to adults diagnosed with serious mental illness and trains clinical staff and graduate students on recovery-oriented care. Dr. Hamm has authored over 25 articles and book chapters on phenomenology, recovery, metacognition, and psychotherapy for psychosis.

Hasson-Ohayon Ilanit, PhD, is a rehabilitation psychologist and full professor at the department of psychology in Bar-Ilan University, Israel. She studies different psychological aspects of coping with illnesses, especially serious mental illnesses, and has been involved in practicing and supervising psychotherapy for over 20 years. She is an author of over 150 peer-reviewed papers and book chapters in the field of clinical-rehabilitation psychology.

Igra Libby, is a Ph.D. student in Clinical Psychology at Bar-Ilan University, Israel. Her study is entitled "Metacognitive Reflection Insight Therapy: The role of metacognition, alliance and empathy in psychotherapy with persons who have a serious mental illness." Her main interests are the concepts of metacognition, alliance and empathy, and the role they play in the intersubjective encounter between client and therapist. Specifically, her Ph.D. focuses on Metacognitive Reflection Insight Therapy (MERIT) for persons with serious mental illness. She explores the factors that enable client and therapist to create congruence and shared meaning during the course of the treatment.

Korsbek Lisa, Ph.D. is a program manager on shared decision making in the mental health services of the Southern Region of Denmark. Before that she for more than ten years worked as a senior researcher at the Centre for Rehabilitation and Recovery in the Mental Health Services of the Capital Region of Denmark. She is educated in Comparative Literature with a master degree in the relationship between psychoanalysis and literature. She has lived experience of mental illness and recovery and she often uses this as a vantage point for a mixed perspective in her publications, contributing both with theoretical and research-based knowledge and with lived experience. In Denmark, Lisa Korsbek is associated with the work of promoting a recovery-oriented practice in the mental health services. She has published several studies and articles in Danish and English on recovery, recovery-oriented care, on shared decision and peer support, and on the narrative in psychoanalysis.

Lavi-Rotenberg Adi is a Ph.D. student in Clinical-Rehabilitation Psychology at Bar-Ilan University, Israel. Her study focuses on agency and perceived control among individuals coping with psychiatric and neurological conditions. Specifically, she is interested in examining identity aspects (self-stigma, concealment, shame and guilt) with relation to agency, and the possible links between those aspects and psychological outcome variables.

Leonhardt Bethany L., Psy D., HSPP, is a licensed clinical psychologist and an Assistant Professor of Clinical Psychology at the Indiana University School of Medicine. Dr. Leonhardt is a treatment team member of an early psychosis program, called the Prevention and Recovery Center at Eskenazi Health in Indianapolis, IN. Dr. Leonhardt provides supervision, clinical care, and conducts clinical research in the clinic. Her research interests include elucidating the role of integration in processes of and recovery from psychosis, as well as developing and adapting recovery oriented practices for individuals with early psychosis. Dr. Leonhardt is also part of IU Psychotic Disorders Program and collaborates on a range of clinical trials for the treatment of schizophrenia spectrum illnesses.

Lysaker Paul H., PhD, is a clinical psychologist at Richard L Roudebush VA Medical Center and a professor of clinical psychology at the Indiana University School of Medicine. He has over 35 years of experience providing mental health treatment to adults diagnosed with serious mental illness. He has been active in clinical research for over 30 years and is an author of over 480 peer-reviewed papers related to wellness and recovery from serious mental illness.

Mazor Yael, PhD, MSW, is a lecturer and researcher in the fields of Trauma, Post-traumatic Growth, Psychosis, and mental health Rehabilitation at the Hebrew University, Haifa University, Sapir academic college and School of rehabilitation and recovery at Uno academic college and MOH in Israel. Dr. Mazor is also a senior supervisor at multiple community rehabilitation organizations, has published several research papers, and specializes in Trauma informed rehabilitation, Posttraumatic Growth in mental illness, Psychosis and Trauma in mental health.

McGuire Nicola is a PhD student researching ways of improving psychosocial recovery from negative symptoms. Nicola is an MSc Global Mental Health graduate, former advocacy worker, and volunteer counsellor for persons surviving childhood trauma. Nicola is passionate about supporting other early career researchers interested in researching psychosis through community organisation.

McLeod Hamish J, is Director of the Doctorate in Clinical Psychology at the University of Glasgow, whose clinical career has focused on understanding and treating difficulties experienced by people with complex and persistent needs. His current research work is focused on developing, testing, and scaling up complex psychological interventions that address psychosocial barriers to recovery. This includes a particular focus on specific behavioural and emotional factors that interfere with recovery from psychiatric and neurological conditions. He has published over 40 peer reviewed articles and book chapters and is a collaborator on several randomized controlled trials examining psychological treatments for mental health problems.

O'Connor Kate, is a psychologist and clinical psychology registrar. She works in private practice in Brisbane, Australia. Kate graduated from her Masters of Clinical Psychology with distinction at Queensland University of Technology, after completing her thesis examining the utilisation of metacognitive narrative therapy for people with psychosis. Kate works from a psychoanalytic framework in her private practice, and has experience in the treatment of a diverse range of clinical presentations. She has a particular interest in issues relating to sense of self, and to love and intimacy within the therapeutic space. She has presented on this topic for her colleagues and continues to engage in training with the International Masterson Institute deepening her knowledge of disorders of self.

Ottavi Paolo, MD. Is a Clinical Psychologist, CBT Psychotherapist, certified Mindfulness Teacher, and Metacognitive Interpersonal Therapy Teacher and

Supervisor. He works especially with severe mental disorders such as Psychosis and Bipolar Disorders, Personality Disorders, and he applies Mindfulness in clinical contexts. He has published several contributions in international books and scientific magazines. He conceived and tested an innovative treatment for the social disabilities of schizophrenia: The Metacognition-Oriented Social Skills Training (MOSST), which has been recognized as an evidence-based treatment thanks to a randomized controlled trial published on Schizophrenia Bulletin in 2017. He designed and tested an original Mindfulness-based treatment for Personality Disorders: The Metacognitive-Interpersonal Mindfulness-Based Training for Personality Disorders (MIMBT-PD), whose preliminary results were published on the Journal of Nervous and Mental Disease in 2019. He is a co-author, together with G. Dimaggio, R. Popolo, and G. Salvatore, of the book Metacognitive Interpersonal Therapy: Body, Imagery and Change. Routledge, London, 2020.

Popolo Raffaele, psychiatrist and psychotherapist, is co-founding member of the Center for Metacognitive Interpersonal Therapy. Teacher of the Italian Society of Behavioral and Cognitive Therapy (SITCC). Trainer for the School of Specialization of Psychotherapy "StudiCognitivi", School of Psychotherapy "Humanitas" and "A.T. Beck's Institute". He is specialized in both clinical and research work on personality disorders and schizophrenia. He has written several papers published in national and international journals and chapters of books about the psychotherapeutic process and the pathology and treatment of schizophrenia and personality disorders, and in particular for persons with avoidant features.

Ridenour Jeremy, Dr. Ridenour is the associate director of admissions, the director of psychological testing, and a staff psychologist/psychoanalyst at the Austen Riggs Center. Dr. Ridenour completed his postdoctoral Fellowship at the Austen Riggs Center in June 2017. His research interests include the psychotherapeutic treatment of individuals with psychotic disorders with a particular focus in understanding how targeting mentalization (i.e. how people think about self and others) can be an important focus for recovery. He has written and presented on psychosis, paranoia, personality disorders, and psychological testing.

Roe David, Ph.D. is a licensed clinical psychologist, a Professor at the Department of Community Mental Health at the University of Haifa and director of the Center for Community Mental Health Research, Training, Services and Policy. His research focuses on the psychosocial processes of recovery from serious mental illness, stigma, routine outcome measurement (ROM), and the evaluation of interventions and services. His research has been funded by several local and international sources, including NIMH, Israeli Science foundation, The Israeli Ministry of Health, The Israel National Institute for Health Services Research and Health Policy, the Israeli National Insurance Institution and the Tauber and Rich foundations. Dr. Roe has published over 140 peer reviewed articles, 20 book chapters and co-authored three books. He serves as associate editor for the Journal of Mental Health, BMC psychiatry and Israel Journal of Psychiatry and is on the editorial board of Psychiatric Rehabilitation Journal, American Journal of Psychiatric Rehabilitation, Stigma and Health, Journal of Clinical Psychology, Psychosis and Social Welfare (Hebrew).

Salaminios George, is a PhD candidate at the Psychoanalysis Unit, Research Department of Clinical, Educational and Health Psychology, University College London. His doctoral project seeks to bridge classical psychoanalytic conceptualizations of psychotic processes with contemporary clinical research using a mentalization-based framework. He works as a research officer at the Early Years Parenting Unit, Anna Freud National Centre for Children and Families, and as an honorary psychodynamic psychotherapist at Camden and Islington NHS Foundation Trust.

Salvatore Giampaolo, MD. is a pscychiatrist and psychotherapist, and co-founding member of the Center for Metacognitive Interpersonal Therapy in Rome, Italy. His primary interest is the relationship between metacognitive processes and pathology and treatment of schizophrenia and of personality disorders, in particular paranoid personality disorders and personality disorders with dysregulated traits. He has coauthored the book *Metacognitive Interpersonal Therapy for Personality Disorders* and more than 100 papers in scientific journals. Dr. Salvatore has guest-edited many journal special issues on research and treatment for personality disorder. He is a trainer at the Humanitas – School of Psychotherapy in Rome.

Schweitzer Robert, is a Professor of Psychology at the Queensland University of Technology, in Brisbane, Australia. He is active as a clinician, teacher and researcher. He is committed to psychology as a human science, with research areas addressing the needs of people from refugee backgrounds, and psychotherapy process and outcome.

Vohs Jenifer L., Ph D., HSPP, is an Assistant Clinical Professor of Psychology in the Department of Psychiatry at IU School of Medicine and a member of the Indiana University (IU) Coordinated Specialty Care *Network* project for intervention in early psychosis at the Prevention and Recovery Center for Early Psychosis at Eskenazi Health in Indianapolis IN. Dr. Vohs is also active in a number of ongoing research projects with the IU Psychotic Disorders Program and in collaboration with the Assertive Community Treatment Center of Indiana and MERIT Institute, founded by Dr. Paul Lysaker. Her research publications reflect the breadth of her work, ranging from topics such as metacognition and negative symptoms in patients with schizophrenia to electrophysiological abnormalities in both humans and rodent models of psychopathology. She also serves as a clinical psychologist for the *Changing Health Outcomes through Integrated Care Excellence* (CHOICE) program at IU Health.

Yamin Amit, Ph.D., MSW, is a certified couples and family therapist and supervisor, and a certified supervisor in recovery-oriented mental health practice. She has extensive experience working with people who experience serious mental illness and with their families, and focuses on recovery-oriented approaches and narrative therapy. Dr. Yamin is engaged in implementation, training, and supervision of recovery-oriented interventions for people coping with mental illness and their families, as well as in implementing and supervising NAVIGATE program in Israel, which provides comprehensive treatment for people with first episode psychosis. She teaches at the Ono Academic College and at Tel-Aviv University.

Yanos Philip T., Ph.D. is a professor in the Psychology Department at John Jay College. He received his Ph.D. in clinical psychology from St. John's University in 1999 and completed a post-doctoral fellowship in Mental Health Services Research at Rutgers University in 2001. He has been a faculty member at John Jay since 2006 and was previously a faculty member at in the Department of Psychiatry of UMDNJ-New Jersey Medical School. Professor Yanos overriding professional goal is to help facilitate recovery from severe mental illness through research, direct clinical services, teaching, and mentoring/clinical supervision of professionals in training. Currently, a major research interest is the effect of stigma on the identity of people with severe mental illness (including self- or internalized stigma) and ways to address it through professional and peer-led means. He is the co-developer, with David Roe and Paul Lysaker of "Narrative Enhancement and Cognitive Therapy," a group-based treatment which aims to address the effects of internalized stigma among people with severe mental illness. He is the author of over 80 articles and book chapters.

THE ROLE OF METACOGNITION AND MENTALIZATION IN THE RECOVERY OF THE SELF

Introduction and overview

Ilanit Hasson-Ohayon and Paul H. Lysaker

Abstract: *Emerging evidence from studies on the subjective experience of recovery from psychosis indicates that mental health services need to move beyond seeking to reduce symptoms or promote skill acquisition. Wellness, as it is increasingly defined in terms of mental health, recognizes that services need to take into account the sense people make of the challenges they face and any resultant decisions about how they should best respond to these. Services are thus needed to support sense-making, including the ability to reflect upon and form an evolving and adaptive sense of oneself and one's place in the larger human community. In line with this, several different approaches to recovery-oriented psychotherapy and psychosocial rehabilitation are currently being developed for persons diagnosed with psychosis. Many of these approaches explicitly, or implicitly, use the terms metacognition, or mentalization, to describe the processes they target, in order to enable persons to form more integrated and diverse senses of self and others which would promote recovery. In this chapter we offer an introduction to an edited volume which not only presents a range of these kinds of therapies but also illustrates their potential to be useful in creating change and enhancing recovery for persons with a range of very different goals, abilities and challenges. To prepare the reader, we offer a description of the nature and evolution of the terms metacognition and mentalization, and discuss their theoretical links with health.*

The experience of psychosis cannot be reduced to any one set of symptoms, skill deficits, developmental experiences or even specific social or political challenges (Lysaker & Lysaker, 2010). Psychosis involves alterations to self-experience in which the previously held sense of self, and its trajectory over one's life, may be degraded or weakened, leaving a person less able to form an integrated idea of their past, emerging challenges or how to act as an agent in the world and to respond to these challenges (Lysaker & Klion, 2017). As suggested over a century ago by William James (1890), human experience is more than the experience of the world. Human beings also have self-experience or the experience of themselves experiencing the world. Self-experience is fundamentally a different kind of experience in contrast to an experience of an object we encounter. When human beings experience themselves experiencing the world, this is the experience of responding to the world and making interpretations and actions which are the basis for managing what is unfolding in the flow of life. It is also the basis for the experience of ourselves as having purposes, our relative position in the social world and self-complexity (Lysaker & Lysaker, 2017). In reference then to alterations to the sense of self in psychosis we are therefore concerned with the basic foundations of consciousness and subjectivity through which people continually experience their daily life (Moe & Docherty, 2013).

Challenges to the sense of self include disturbances in these basic foundations and have been documented in research on self-experience and psychosis. For example, studies have shown that persons with psychosis can have a degraded sense of self-clarity (Hasson-Ohayon et al., 2014) and reduced abilities to describe their own emotions (Fogley, Warman, & Lysaker, 2014). Based on this perspective, recovery from psychosis would seem for many to involve the reversal or amelioration of alterations to sense of self. The need to consider sense of self as a key aspect of recovery has important clinical implications. Among these is the likelihood that treatments that are primarily concerned with symptom remission and skill attainment such as cognitive behavioural therapy (CBT; e.g. Hagen, Turkington, Berge, & Gråwe, 2013) or others focused on the resolution of conflicts rooted in earlier experiences through psychoanalytical approaches (e.g. Robbins, 1993), may not be sufficiently well equipped to deal with these aspects of recovery. To address alterations to self-experience, interventions which involve processes and methods that support persons in recapturing the ability to experience an integrated sense of themselves and others within the flow of life are needed (Lysaker, Glynn, Wilkness, & Silverstein, 2010).

Spurred by reflections such as these, efforts have been underway for over a decade to develop psychosocial services, including group and individual psychotherapies, that can address alterations to self-experience among persons diagnosed with psychosis. While these therapies differ along many dimensions, they are alike in their goals to address clients as unique subjects, to promote sense-making of challenges related to a diagnosis of psychosis and other experiences of the self, and to enhance agency (Lysaker & Hasson-Ohayon, 2018). Each of these therapies also aspires to be broad enough to apply to persons with differing, needs, goals, abilities and challenges.

In this book, we explore one group of therapies focused on these issues. This set of therapies includes metacognitively and mentalization-oriented therapies which are primarily focused on supporting recovery by enhancing reflectivity in an intersubjective framework. To better establish the interconnections among these psychotherapies, we will begin this volume with a review of updated conceptualizations of recovery, metacognition, mentalization and intersubjectivity. This review of the literature is followed by a description of the chapters included in the book. Of note, given the natural space limitations that come with any printed volume, we have restricted our focus to treatments that have a significant intersubjective component. We thus have not been able to include a range of recovery-oriented treatments whose mechanisms may nevertheless be similar to those described. These include

Metacognitive Training (Moritz et al., 2014), Open Dialogue (Bergström et al., 2018), as well as clubhouse-based approaches (Tanaka, Davidson, & Craig, 2018). We therefore wish to acknowledge at the outset the need for future work to better elucidate the larger connections that exist within recovery-based care.

Psychosis and the self: barriers to health and achieving recovery

Since the end of the 19th and beginning of the 20th centuries, the loss of cohesive self-experience has been thought to play a central role in the interruption of a life that is often experienced in psychosis. Kraepelin (1896), Bleuler (1911) and Jaspers (1923) all referred to alterations in consciousness as an underlying feature of psychosis. Since then, similar observations have been made in the psychoanalytic literature (e.g. Searles, 1965), existential literature (e.g. Laing, 1960), phenomenological psychiatry (e.g. Stanghellini, 2000; Parnas & Handest, 2003), first-person accounts (e.g. Andresen, Oades, & Caputi, 2003) and empirical research (e.g. Hasson-Ohayon et al., 2014; Hasson-Ohayon, Goldzweig, Lavi-Rotenberg, Luther, & Lysaker, 2018; Lysaker, Dimaggio et al., 2018). Synthesizing this work, it has been suggested that for many persons diagnosed with psychosis, the ability to form integrated ideas about oneself and others is compromised. This may lead to difficulties in experiencing oneself as an agent who can reflect upon and respond to challenges and opportunities as they emerge in the world (Lysaker et al., 2020). One implication of this work is that recovery for many might involve a recapturing of the ability to form and use a cohesive and integrated sense of self and others as life unfolds. In other words, if a primary challenge to recovery is the loss of a previously held sense of self then recovery is likely to include the recapturing of that sense of self.

Of note, the construct of recovery has evolved considerably over the last few decades. The idea of recovery as involving social and personally meaningful changes first emerged in contrast to earlier models of psychosis which stressed that persons diagnosed with these conditions would most often experience deteriorating psychological and social function over time (c.f. Leonhardt et al., 2017; Roe, Mashiach-Eizenberg, & Lysaker, 2011; Silverstein & Bellack, 2008). Following longitudinal research demonstrating that the majority of persons diagnosed with serious mental illnesses are able to achieve a fully meaningful quality of life over time (Harding, Brooks, Ashikaga, Strauss, & Breier, 1987), and the survivors' movement that emphasized human rights and personal choices (Chamberlin, 1978), it was proposed that people with a diagnosis of psychosis can achieve, over time, a personally and socially meaningful life (c.f. Leonhardt et al., 2017). Further, the resolution of these challenges has been recognized to involve a broad multi-dimensional set of processes and outcomes (Leonhardt et al., 2017; van Weeghel, van Zelst, Boertien, & Hasson-Ohayon, 2019). Specifically, recovery has been suggested to involve a set of complementary objective and subjective aspects (Roe et al., 2011), which correspond to evaluations made by others and by the person respectively. Examples of objective aspects of recovery include symptom remission and the achievement of measurable behavioral milestones (Leonhardt et al., 2017). By contrast, subjective aspects of recovery are those that are directly connected to persons' experiences of themselves. As discussed by Anthony (1991), these are related to: "a deeply personal, unique process of changing one's attitudes, values, feelings, goals, skills, and/or roles. It is a way of living a satisfying, hopeful, and contributing life even with the limitations caused by illness" (p. 527).

Metacognition and mentalization as treatment approaches that could promote the recovery of a sense of self

As the experience of oneself experiencing the world, including one's purposes and place in the world, is by definition fundamentally subjective, the recapture of a subjective and reflective sense of self would necessarily be amongst the most subjective of all aspects of recovery and one of the most daunting to describe systematically. In an attempt to tackle the question of how psychosocial interventions might approach the issue of alterations to self-experience, it has been proposed that recovery-oriented treatments might address the processes which enable persons to form integrated and evolving ideas of themselves and others.

Metacognition and mentalization are two constructs which have been proposed to capture, in part, what allows human beings to have an integrated sense of themselves and others. Both constructs, along with the constructs of theory of mind and social cognition, are used to describe the processes which allow persons to think about one another (Pinkham et al., 2014). However, while social cognition abilities are focused on the capacity to make a correct judgement or inference about someone's emotional state or intentions, metacognition and mentalization refer to how well persons are able to integrate information into a larger sense of oneself and others (Fonagy, Gergely, & Jurist, 2018; Lysaker & Dimaggio, 2014).

The term metacognition was originally developed by Flavell (1979) on the basis of previous work in developmental and educational psychology (e.g. Vygotsky, 1931), to describe the myriad activities which allow persons to be aware of and reflect on their thoughts and experiences (Moritz & Lysaker, 2018). Notably, the current book adopts an integrative model of metacognition (Lysaker & Klion, 2017). This model attempts to further synthesize developments in the study of metacognition from studies of human development, cognitive psychology and constructivist psychology, as well as from general psychopathology, in order to describe the processes that enable persons to have available to them a sense of self and others. Importantly, these senses of self and others, which people can access and reflect on and which are the basis for action, are explicitly not perceptions of singular objects. The sense of self and others, which metacognition makes available, are formed within particular contexts by the integration of a broad range of embodied, cognitive, emotional and interpersonal experiences (Lysaker, Dimaggio et al., 2018). Moving away from metacognition as purely a cognitive phenomenon means that metacognition involves not only effortful reflection, but also an ongoing set of automatic activities. That is, people do not have a sense of themselves only when they effortfully summon or create one. Often our senses of who we are, and who others are, are simply present for us to think about.

To quantify metacognition, the integrative model proposes that it is a spectrum of experiences which range from the awareness of discrete and highly specific mental experiences (e.g. specific thoughts, emotions, or wishes) to a broader sense of the self and others that results from the synthesis of those discrete experiences (Hamm et al., 2012; Lysaker & Dimaggio, 2014; Lysaker & Hasson-Ohayon, 2014). In this model, both discrete and synthetic metacognitive acts are thought to influence one another. Our larger sense of self and other requires individual pieces of experience which can be later assembled. These individual pieces of experience are given meaning according to their context that is related to a larger sense of ourselves and others.

This conceptualization of metacognition has allowed it to be measurable as a progression of steps towards integration. To date most of this research has been carried out using the Metacognition Assessment Scale-Abbreviated (MAS-A; Lysaker et al., 2005), measuring metacognition as a multi-dimensional construct which is considered to be trait-like. This coding system was developed on the basis of Semerari et al.'s (2003) Metacognition Assessment Scale (MAS), a scale originally designed to detect changes within psychotherapy for adults with personality disorders. Following the MAS, the MAS-A divides metacognitive activities into four categories: 1. self-reflectivity, which refers to the comprehension of one's own mental states; 2. understanding others' minds, which refers to the comprehension of others' mental states; 3. decentration, which refers to the ability to take a non-egocentric view of the mind of others and recognize that others' mental states are influenced by a range of factors; and 4. Mastery, which refers to the ability to use complex metacognitive knowledge in order to cope with psychological problems. Unlike the MAS, the MAS-A considers the items of each scale as reflecting increasingly complex metacognitive acts, each calling for a greater level of integration than those before it. In this sense, each item of any of the four MAS-A scales is thought to reflect an ability that must be present at a basic level before the activities on the next level can be successfully carried out. The score for each subscale allows researchers to rate metacognitive functioning along a spectrum ranging from highly fragmented to highly integrated (Lysaker & Klion, 2017).

Similar to the concept of metacognition, the concept of mentalization also refers to a capacity to reflect upon the mental states of self and others, and includes processes that are both effortful and automatic (Ridenour, Knauss, & Hamm, 2018). However, whereas metacognition considers these forms of reflection as multi-determined, mentalization focusses on them as they occur in the context of an attachment relationship as well as the resultant ability to regulate one's affect (Brent & Fonagy, 2014). In most models of mentalization, disturbances in reflection occur generally in the context of disturbed attachment to caregivers and are related to a failure to regulate affect, leading to such emotional states that precludes reflection and thoughtful action.

In contrast to the more psychologically and constructivist-oriented background of the integrative model of metacognition, mentalization has a rich and more singular history based in psychoanalysis and, in particular, in the development of psychodynamic approaches to help adults diagnosed with borderline personality disorder. Following psychodynamic models of the development of the self, basic mentalization abilities are believed to develop within close and secure attachments to early caretakers. These attachments provoke and support mentalization, which is then acts as a buffer against stress and adversity later in life. When early attachments are disorganized, or riddled with anxiety, and are therefore not secure, persons are believed to become vulnerable to the loss of their mentalization abilities. Thus, in contrast to metacognitive theory, deficits in mentalization are believed to be state-like, and occur in response to situations that activate the experiences of insecure attachment, which then leads to a temporary state of emotional dysregulation (Fonagy, 2018).

Intersubjectivity, metacognition and mentalization

Returning to the issue of treatments that support the recovery of a sense of self, the integrative model of metacognition allows for the possibility that treatment could lead to improvements in metacognitive capacity, which could lead to the ability to recapture a sense of self acting as part of the foundation of recovery. For example, Metacognitive Reflection and Insight Therapy (MERIT, Lysaker & Klion, 2017), discussed in several of the chapters of this book (see Chapter 11; Chapter 7; Chapter 3), offers a set of eight key elements which should be enacted in a typical session resulting in the growth of metacognitive capacity. With greater metacognitive capacity, the experience of self and others is likely to become less fragmented and persons are better able to make sense of the challenges they face and to chart their own course to recovery. The same process could be described for Mentalization-Based Therapy, also discussed later in the book (Chapter 5; Chapter 2). In mentalization-based treatment, persons are supported to develop the ability to form more secure attachments, and then become able to develop the kinds of senses of self and others needed to find their way to a life which is personally meaningful to them.

While we have noted that metacognition and mentalization share much in common, including their reliance on automatic and effortful processes, they also share another key similarity which has bearing on how treatment might address alterations to self-experience. Specifically, the processes described by metacognition and mentalization are fundamentally intersubjective activities. For both models, any larger sense of self and others is always constructed, whether through the enhancement of metacognition or mentalization, with someone else either explicitly or implicitly in mind. Thus, representations of self and others always have meanings because of the actual or potential sharing of that sense (Hasson-Ohayon, Gumley, McLeod, & Lysaker, 2020).

Consistent with the ideas regarding intersubjectivity of Hasson-Ohayon, Kravetz, and Lysaker (2017), both metacognitive and mentalization approaches emphasize that addressing alterations to self-experience requires a sense of shared meaning, which can only occur via an empathic and respectful therapeutic relationship that encourages mutual exploration of each mind and narrative in the here-and-now. Thus, the therapist, regardless of whether the target is metacognitive or mentalization-based, always intervenes as a subject stimulating reflection of self and others and aims to understand something that is experienced as new to both client and therapist. Adopting a subjective presence requires that the therapist is aware of his or her own thoughts and emotions, which might include theoretical bias or stigma, and to continually reflect on the intersubjective dynamic in the session. For example, in response to a client's internalization of stigma, the therapist might react with a stigmatizing attitude or a complementary attitude, urging the client to resist self-stigma. Once therapists are aware of these possible dynamics, they can stimulate metacognition or mentalization, as tailored to the client's ability, and they can explore the client's thoughts and feelings towards the challenges that he or she faces.

Challenges for the self-experience and metacognitive-/ mentalization-based psychotherapeutic approaches

In summary, as understanding of recovery from psychosis has developed, awareness of a need for interventions which address subjective phenomena has grown, including alterations in sense of self and the ability to make sense of and respond to life. In parallel, the field has evolved and developed constructs such as metacognition and mentalization which have the potential to organize treatment around guidelines that support these kinds of subjective changes that are central to recovery from psychosis. But, how would this concretely occur in the real world? Clients presenting for psychotherapy do not arrive and simply ask for help with remedying alterations to their self-experience. They may announce that they suffer, but for vastly differing reasons. Some note oppression by stigma or destructive power differentials, and some come after experiencing different types of trauma. Others note that their lives are adversely affected by anomalous experiences, a history of trauma or lack of a deeper sense of connection with the human community. Others merely report that their lives, and the world they inhabit, have become confusing and unpredictable, and that they feel lost. Others come for treatment because someone else suggested or compelled them. Alterations to one's sense of self is an abstract idea that may, with time, come to be a helpful way to understand what is beneath these very real concerns; but then how do the treatments we have described above, treatments that are concerned with metacognition and mentalization within an intersubjective framework, proceed?

To explore this, the following chapters provide concrete descriptions of different applications of these ideas to help adults diagnosed with psychosis to recover a richer sense of themselves and make sense of the challenges they face, and so to move towards recovery. Several of the chapters are explicitly concerned with applying MERIT in different contexts. These include the chapters by Hamm and colleagues (Chapter 11) focused on helping people seeking to find a way to live with overwhelming histories of trauma; by Leonhardt and Vohs (Chapter 3) focused on helping those with recent experiences of psychosis who are trying to decide if in fact they really are facing psychiatric challenges; and by Buck and Lysaker (Chapter 7) which is focused on helping people reduce and possibly stop antipsychotic medication. McLeod and colleagues (Chapter 9) follow up on these ideas with an exploration of how the principles of MERIT could be used to address what are often called "negative symptoms", or the seeming loss of richness of motivation and volition. Bargenquast and colleagues (Chapter 6) address issues of transference and countertransference in a treatment that is guided by a set of metacognitive therapeutic principles to promote recovery. Other chapters are concerned with MBT. For instance, Salaminios and Debbané (Chapter 2) explore how MBT can be applied to help clients deal with phenomena associated with being at high risk of developing psychosis. Ridenour (Chapter 5) discusses how MBT procedures were implemented to help a client who presented with an overwhelming sense of confusion that could only be explained in ways that others might characterize as paranoid and which acted as a barrier to social connections. Salvatore and colleagues (Chapter 4) also focus on severe levels of disturbing anomalous experiences, but with a metacognitive approach that has close ties to schema therapy and related forms of cognitive therapy for persons experiencing persecutory delusions. Other chapters discuss treatment approaches that, while they are not explicitly focused on metacognition or mentalization, use reflective processes to support recovery. Hasson-Ohayon and colleagues (Chapter 10) discuss a group format of Therapeutic Alliance Focused Therapy (TAFT) that uses reflection on self and others in the group as part of the therapeutic processes. Roe and colleagues (Chapter 8) discuss Narrative Enhancement and Cognitive Therapy (NECT) to address self-stigma with mechanisms that are related to enhancing reflectivity within an intersubjective framework. Korsbek (Chapter 12) adds to the discussion on metacognitive and mentalization-based approaches a unique perspective on recovery as a necessarily intersubjective process called co-recovery. Finally, we offer some concluding thoughts about the larger place of this work as a whole within the history of the conceptualization and treatment of psychosis as well as its potential future directions.

By bringing together the application of metacognition and mentalization-based approaches, which are joined by their interest in intersubjectivity in different contexts and in response to different challenges to the recovery of the self, we particularly hope that practitioners can use this book to guide their work with persons with psychosis. It is our aspiration that this work will unlock for practitioners a way to think about their work and enable them to respond more meaningfully to the experiences of their clients. We hope to enhance the understanding of recovery as a recognizable human phenomenon, with commonalities we all share as human beings who seek to make meaning through our connections with others.

References

Andresen, R., Oades, L., & Caputi, P. (2003). The experience of recovery from schizophrenia: Towards an empirically validated stage model. *Australian & New Zealand Journal of Psychiatry, 37*(5), 586–594.

Anthony, W. A. (1991). Recovery from mental illness: The new vision of services researchers. Innovations and Research, *1*(1), 13–14.

Bergström, T., Seikkula, J., Alakare, B., Mäki, P., Köngäs-Saviaro, P., Taskila, J. J., . . . & Aaltonen, J. (2018). The family-oriented open dialogue approach in the treatment of first-episode psychosis: Nineteen-year outcomes. *Psychiatry Research, 270,* 168–175.

Bleuler, E. (1911). Dementia praecox or the group of schizophrenias. In G. Aschaffenburg (Ed.), *Manual of psychiatry*. Leipzig, Germany: Franz Deuticke.

Brent, B. K., & Fonagy, P. (2014). A mentalization-based treatment approach to disturbances of social understanding in schizophrenia. In P. H. Lysaker, G. Dimaggio, & M. Brune (Eds.), *Social cognition and metacognition in schizophrenia: Psychopathology and treatment approaches* (pp. 245–259). Gurgaon: Elsevier Science and Technology.

Chamberlin, J. (1978). *On our own: Patient-controlled alternatives to the mental health system.* New York: Hawthorne.

Flavell, J. H. (1979). Metacognition and cognitive monitoring: A new area of cognitive-developmental inquiry. *American Psychologist, 34*(10), 906.

Fogley, R., Warman, D., & Lysaker, P. H. (2014). Alexithymia in schizophrenia: Associations with neurocognition and emotional distress. *Psychiatry Research, 218*(1–2), 1–6.

Fonagy, P., Gergely, G., & Jurist, E. L. (Eds.). (2018). *Affect regulation, mentalization and the development of the self.* London: Routledge.

Hagen, R., Turkington, D., Berge, T., & Gråwe, R. W. (2013). *CBT for psychosis: A symptom-based approach.* London: Routledge.

Hamm, J. A., Renard, S. B., Fogley, R. L., Leonhardt, B. L., Dimaggio, G., Buck, K. D., & Lysaker, P. H. (2012). Metacognition and social cognition in schizophrenia: Stability and relationship to concurrent and prospective symptom assessments. *Journal of Clinical Psychology, 68*(12), 1303–1312.

Harding, C. M., Brooks, G. W., Ashikaga, T., Strauss, J. S., & Breier, A. (1987). The Vermont longitudinal study of persons with severe mental illness, II: Long-term outcome of subjects who retrospectively met DSM-III criteria for schizophrenia. *American Journal of Psychiatry, 144*(6), 727–735.

Hasson-Ohayon, I., Goldzweig, G., Lavi-Rotenberg, A., Luther, L., & Lysaker, P. H. (2018). The centrality of cognitive symptoms and metacognition within the interacting network of symptoms, neurocognition, social cognition and metacognition in schizophrenia. *Schizophrenia Research, 202,* 260–266. https://doi.org/10.1016/j.schres.2018.07.007.

Hasson-Ohayon, I., Gumley, A., McLeod, H., & Lysaker, P. H. (2020). Metacognition and intersubjectivity: Reconsidering their relationship following advances from the study of persons with psychosis. *Frontiers in Psychology, 11,* 567.

Hasson-Ohayon, I., Kravetz, S., & Lysaker, P. H. (2017). The special challenges of psychotherapy with persons with psychosis: Intersubjective metacognitive model of agreement and shared meaning. *Clinical Psychology & Psychotherapy, 24*(2), 428–440.

Hasson-Ohayon, I., Mashiach-Eizenberg, M., Elhasid, N., Yanos, P. T., Lysaker, P. H., & Roe, D. (2014). Between self-clarity and recovery in schizophrenia: Reducing the self-stigma and finding meaning. *Comprehensive Psychiatry, 55*(3), 675–680.

James, W. (1890). *The principles of psychology.* New York: Henry Holt and Company.

Jaspers, K. (1923). *General psychopathology* (3rd ed.). Berlin, Germany: Springer.

Kraepelin, E. (1896). *Psychiatry* (4th ed.). Leipzig, Germany: Barth.

Laing, R. D. (1960). *The divided self: An existential study in sanity and madness.* Harmondsworth: Penguin.

Leonhardt, B. L., Huling, K., Hamm, J. A., Roe, D., Hasson-Ohayon, I., McLeod, H. J., & Lysaker, P. H. (2017). Recovery and serious mental illness: A review of current clinical and research paradigms and future directions. *Expert Review of Neurotherapeutics, 17*(11), 1117–1130.

Lysaker, P. H., Carcione, A., Dimaggio, G., Johannesen, J. K., Nicolò, G., Procacci, M., & Semerari, A. (2005). Metacognition amidst narratives of self and illness in schizophrenia: Associations with neurocognition, symptoms, insight and quality of life. *Acta Psychiatrica Scandinavica, 112*(1), 64–71.

Lysaker, P. H., & Dimaggio, G. (2014). Metacognitive capacities for reflection in schizophrenia: Implications for developing treatments. *Schizophrenia Bulletin, 40*(3), 487–491.

Lysaker, P. H., Dimaggio, G., Hamm, J. A., Leonhardt, B. L., Hochheiser, J., & Lysaker, J. T. (2018). Disturbances in self-experience in schizophrenia: Metacognition and the development of an integrative recovery oriented individual psychotherapy. *Psychopathology, 52*, 135–142. https://doi.org/10.1159/000495297.

Lysaker, P. H., Glynn, S. M., Wilkness, S. M., & Silverstein, S. M. (2010). Psychotherapy and recovery from schizophrenia: A review of potential application and need for future study. *Psychological Services, 7*(2), 75–91.

Lysaker, P. H., & Hasson-Ohayon, I. (2014). Metacognition in schizophrenia: Introduction to the special issue. *The Israel Journal of Psychiatry and Related Sciences, 51*(1), 4.

Lysaker, P. H., & Hasson-Ohayon, I. (2018). Metacognition in serious mental illness: Implications for developing recovery oriented psychotherapies. In C. Cupitt (Ed.), *CBT for psychosis: Process-orientated therapies and the third wave.* ISPS Series Book. London: Routledge.

Lysaker, P. H., & Klion, R. E. (2017). *Recovery, meaning-making, and severe mental illness: a comprehensive guide to metacognitive reflection and insight therapy.* London: Routledge.

Lysaker, P. H., & Lysaker, J. T. (2010). Schizophrenia and alterations in self-experience: A comparison of 6 perspectives. *Schizophrenia Bulletin, 36*(2), 331–340.

Lysaker, P. H., & Lysaker, J. T. (2017). Metacognition, self-experience and the prospect of enhancing self-management in schizophrenia spectrum disorders. *Philosophy, Psychiatry and Psychology, 24*(2), 69–178.

Lysaker, P. H., Minor, K. S., Lysaker, J. T., Hasson-Ohayon, I., Bonfils, K., Hochheiser, J., & Vohs, J. L. (2020). Metacognitive function and fragmentation in schizophrenia: Relationship to cognition, self-experience and developing treatments. *Schizophrenia Research Cognition, 19*. https://doi.org/10.1016/j.scog.2019.100142.

Moe, A. M., & Docherty, N. M. (2013). Schizophrenia and the sense of self. *Schizophrenia Bulletin, 40*(1), 161–168.

Moritz, S., Andreou, C., Schneider, B. C., Wittekind, C. E., Menon, M., Balzan, R. P., & Woodward, T. S. (2014). Sowing the seeds of doubt: A narrative review on metacognitive training in schizophrenia. *Clinical Psychology Review, 34*(4), 358–366.

Moritz, S., & Lysaker, P. H. (2018). Metacognition – What did James H. Flavell really say and the implications for the conceptualization and design of metacognitive interventions. *Schizophrenia Research, 201*, 20–26.

Parnas, J., & Handest, P. (2003). Phenomenology of anomalous self-experience in early schizophrenia. *Comprehensive Psychiatry, 44*(2), 121–134.

Pinkham, A. E., Penn, D. L., Green, M. F., Buck, B., Healey, K., & Harvey, P. D. (2014). The social cognition psychometric evaluation study: Results of the expert survey and RAND panel. *Schizophrenia Bulletin, 40*(4), 813–823.

Ridenour, J., Knauss, D., & Hamm, J. A. (2018). Comparing metacognition and mentalization and their implications for psychotherapy for individuals with psychosis. *Journal of Contemporary Psychotherapy*, 1–7.

Robbins, M. D. (1993). *Experiences of schizophrenia: An integration of the personal, scientific, and therapeutic*. New York: Guilford Press

Roe, D., Mashiach-Eizenberg, M., & Lysaker, P. H. (2011). The relation between objective and subjective domains of recovery among persons with schizophrenia-related disorders. *Schizophrenia Research, 131*(1–3), 133–138.

Searles, H. (1965). *Collected papers on schizophrenia and related subjects*. New York: International University Press.

Semerari, A., Carcione, A., Dimaggio, G., Falcone, M., Nicolò, G., Procacci, M., & Alleva, G. (2003). How to evaluate metacognitive functioning in psychotherapy? The metacognition assessment scale and its applications. *Clinical Psychology & Psychotherapy, 10*(4), 238–261.

Silverstein, S. M., & Bellack, A. S. (2008). A scientific agenda for the concept of recovery as it applies to schizophrenia. *Clinical Psychology Review, 28*(7), 1108–1124.

Stanghellini, G. (2000). Vulnerability to schizophrenia and lack of common sense. *Schizophrenia Bulletin, 26*(4), 775–787.

Tanaka, K., Davidson, L., & Craig, T. J. (2018). Sense of clubhouse community belonging and empowerment. *International Journal of Social Psychiatry, 64*(3), 276–285.

van Weeghel, J., van Zelst, C., Boertien, D., & Hasson-Ohayon, I. (2019). Conceptualizations, assessments, and implications of personal recovery in mental illness: A scoping review of systematic reviews and meta-analyses. *Psychiatric Rehabilitation Journal, 42*(2), 169.

Vygotsky, L. S. (1931/1997). Genesis of higher mental functions. In R. W. Rieber (Ed.), *Collected works of L. S. Vygotsky* (Vol. 4, pp. 97–110). New York: Plenum. (Original work published 1931).

2

A MENTALIZATION-BASED TREATMENT FRAMEWORK TO SUPPORT THE RECOVERY OF THE SELF IN EMERGING PSYCHOSIS DURING ADOLESCENCE

George Salaminios and Martin Debbané

Abstract: *Mentalization-based treatment (MBT) is a psychodynamically oriented form of psychotherapy originally developed for the treatment of borderline personality disorder. The focus of MBT is on enhancing mentalizing, the imaginative capacity to reflect on the internal states (i.e. thoughts, feelings) underpinning one's own and others' behaviours. Disruptions in the capacity to use mental state information to understand oneself and others have been identified across the continuum of psychosis expression, from the premorbid and prodromal stages to its clinical forms. Recently, clinical adaptations of MBT for people diagnosed with psychosis have been reported in the literature. In this chapter we provide the conceptual framework to support the application of MBT to the recovery of the self in emerging psychosis during adolescence. We focus on adolescence as a critical period, during which robust mentalizing can help young people confronted with genetic and other risks for psychosis embark on interpersonal trajectories that contribute to sustaining the development of the self. We propose that among genetically predisposed individuals and in the context of early attachment difficulties, failures of the mentalizing processes to regulate increasing affective and bodily arousal in adolescence may lead to the perturbations in the sense of self seen as characteristic of psychosis. Against this background, we review clinical issues, as well as the core technical principles through which MBT can support the recovery of a coherent sense of self in young people faced with emerging psychosis.*

Introduction

Given the opportunity, every one of us can experience transient reality distortions akin to those observed in psychosis. For instance, experimentally induced sensory manipulation has been shown to generate both hallucinatory experiences and depersonalization phenomena in community samples (Caputo, 2010; Daniel & Mason, 2015; Tsakiris, Carpenter, James, & Fotopoulou, 2010). Similarly, some psychoactive drugs, such as amphetamines and LSD that create states of heightened sensory awareness, are known to produce transient psychotic symptoms

(Ham, Kim, Chung, & Im, 2017). Turning to everyday experience, it is safe to assume that when presented with unfamiliar situations that generate anxiety (i.e. walking in a quiet street at night and seeing two people approaching), every one of us is liable to engage in momentary paranoid thinking involving fear, suspiciousness and a mistrust of others (Freeman, 2007).

Sensory and affective experiences are constitutive of what we perceive as "real" and provide us with a first-person perspective of ourselves in the world. Thus, it is not surprising that when exposed to experimental conditions, or ambiguous situations that significantly alter the amount and novelty of sensory-affective signals, we become prone to experience difficulties in distinguishing between reality and imagination. Fortunately, we usually manage to recover from these experiences with relative ease. Situations that generate uncertainty and challenge our sense of reality trigger in us a search for meaning in an attempt to understand and regulate our self-experience. We may implicitly, or explicitly, ask ourselves: "Did I really hear someone calling my name, or am I just tired?" and "Are these people really following me, or are they just walking in the same direction as me?" In doing so, we turn to higher order cognitive processes (thinking about our thoughts and feelings) in an attempt to compensate for disruptions in our sensory system. By intuitively engaging in this reflective process about our thoughts and feelings we quickly become aware that the voices we heard were products of our own imagination, and that we may have misattributed others' intentions as malevolent because of our own anxiety. In essence, we recover our self-awareness, which provides us with an implicit sense of self-continuity in space (who we are in relation to others and the world) and in time (who we are now, who we have been in the past and who we will be in the future). This is relevant for work with people diagnosed with psychosis, whose lived experience is not phenomenologically defined by hallucinations or delusions, but by an enduring disturbance in establishing a basic sense of self (i.e. the sense of being the subject of one's own experiences) (Sass & Parnas, 2003; Stern, 1985). More specifically, the experience of psychosis fundamentally involves a profound breach in the self's ordinary "going-on-being" in the world, which can present in various forms, including a diminished sense of personal agency, a loss of temporal awareness, and perhaps most importantly, an undermined ability to genuinely relate to and be affected by others (Lysaker et al., 2018b). Indeed, individuals diagnosed with psychosis often report chronic and pervasive forms of self-alienation, loss of personal meaning and lack of social connectedness, despite symptomatic improvement following psychotherapeutic or pharmacological treatment (Hamm, Leonhardt, Ridenour, Lysaker, & Lysaker, 2018). This has led to an increasing interest in exploring the mental functions that can support the recovery of a basic sense of self in individuals living with psychosis (Lysaker et al., 2018b). The higher order psychological processes that help us sustain a coherent and stable self in the face of increasing sensory-affective complexity can, at least in part, come under the term *mentalizing* – that is, the imaginative capacity to understand the intentional mental states driving one's own and others' behaviours (Fonagy & Target, 1996).

Mentalizing represents a multidimensional construct that encompasses a number of processes associated with mental state understanding, such as theory of mind (ToM: inferring beliefs from others' behaviours), empathy (understanding and relating to the emotional states of others), mindfulness (emotional self-awareness) and self-monitoring (cognitive self-awareness) (for a discussion see Choi-Kain & Gunderson, 2008; Debbané et al., 2016b; Fonagy & Luyten, 2009). Good mentalizing entails the integration of these processes to construe a sensitive understanding of the internal imaginative states (i.e. thoughts, feelings) underpinning one's own and others' intentions, while acknowledging the ever-changing subjective nature of mental states (Fonagy, Gergely, Jurist, & Target, 2002; Fonagy & Luyten, 2009). As such, mentalizing enables us to form flexible and predictive representational models of human subjectivity in order to distinguish inner from external reality, sustain a coherent sense of self, and attenuate experiences of confusion and distrust within interpersonal relationships (Fonagy et al., 2002; Fonagy & Target, 1996).

Disruptions in the capacity to utilize mental state information to understand oneself and others have consistently been identified in people with long-standing psychotic experiences and in those presenting with first episode psychosis (FEP) (Brent & Fonagy, 2014). Critically, mentalizing difficulties appear to already be present during the early stages of emerging psychosis, among help-seeking adolescents manifesting sub-threshold symptoms consistent with the clinical high risk criteria (CHR) (Fusar-Poli et al., 2013), and in youths exhibiting non-clinical schizotypal personality traits (for a review see Debbané et al., 2016b). Yet, evidence indicates that mentalizing disruptions in the premorbid and prodromal phases of psychosis expression, during adolescence and early adulthood, do not constitute aetiologically causal factors for the development of what is later diagnosed as clinical psychosis (Piskulic et al., 2016). Rather, as we have previously argued, mentalizing may represent a key protective factor to (1) attenuate the trajectory of emerging psychosis in those at increased risk and (2) promote recovery in diagnosed individuals (Debbané et al., 2016b). Indeed, robust mentalizing during adolescence appears to preserve young people's ability to embark on critical developmental tasks entailing individuation and identity formation, as well as the initiation of peer and romantic relationships, all of which contribute to sustaining self-development in the context of emerging psychosis (Braehler & Schwannauer, 2012). Given that contemporary clinical research highlights the value of treating psychosis at its earliest stages, therapies targeting mentalizing difficulties can be applied preventively to support the development of the self in adolescents during the premorbid and prodromal phases of psychosis expression.

Mentalization-based treatment (MBT) is an integrative form of psychotherapy, originally designed to support the recovery of mentalizing in individuals suffering with borderline personality disorder (Bateman & Fonagy, 2010). Recently, clinical adaptations of MBT for people diagnosed with psychosis and individuals manifesting prodromal symptoms have been reported in the literature (Brent & Fonagy, 2014; Debbané et al., 2016a; Weijers et al., 2016). The conceptual framework upon which MBT is grounded specifically formulates a developmental model of the self, which is based on psychoanalysis, attachment theory and developmental psychology. In this chapter we provide the conceptual basis to support the application of MBT to the recovery of the self in emerging psychosis during adolescence.

To frame our subsequent discussion, we begin the first part of the chapter with a consideration of two key assumptions of the MBT framework: (1) the capacity to understand mental states emerges out of early attachment relationships and is inherently linked with the development of both the agentive and representational aspects of the self and (2) disturbances in early attachment relationships may disrupt the normative acquisition of mentalizing, causing enduring disturbances in the development of self-organization. From this basis we link the emergence of psychotic states in adolescence to the breakdown of mentalizing processes pertaining to the self. Specifically, we propose that psychotic phenomena, entailing the misattribution of mental states in oneself and others, represent failed compensatory attempts to sustain self-continuity in the context of sensory-affective uncertainty. We focus on adolescent development as a critical period during which failures of mentalizing processes to regulate increasing interpersonal stress may lead to difficulties in regulating self-experience and to the emergence of psychotic manifestations. Finally, we discuss the main technical principles through which MBT can support the recovery of a coherent self in young people confronted with emerging psychosis.

Becoming an agentive self: the acquisition of mentalizing within early attachment relationships

Within the mentalization-based approach, the capacity to represent mental states in oneself and others constitutes a developmental achievement linked closely to early attachment relationships (Fonagy et al., 2002). The quality of early attachment relationships provides children with an implicit expectation about the degree of physical safety and emotional support they will receive when approaching caregivers during states of physical and emotional distress (Bowlby, 1969). Most importantly, secure attachment enables young children to safely explore their caregiver's states of mind in order to find meaning and continuity in their self-experience (Fonagy & Target, 1997). A number of studies have shown that secure attachment is positively associated with the normative development of mentalizing processes such as ToM, emotion recognition and mindfulness (Fonagy, Redfern, & Charman, 1997; Sharp & Fonagy, 2008). The developmental model, supporting the links between early attachment, mentalizing and self-development, has been discussed in detail elsewhere (Fonagy et al., 2002; Fonagy & Target, 1997). Here we highlight some of its key aspects.

At the most basic level, infantile attachment-seeking behaviours (i.e. proximity seeking, clinging) are reciprocated by attuned caregivers via closely, but not perfectly, contingent physical actions (i.e. holding, soothing, feeding). For instance, when an infant in a state of distress cries or extends his or her arms, the caregiver will perceive their need to be fed, or their wish to be held, and respond accordingly. In doing so, the caregiver facilitates in the infant the emergence of a pre-reflective sense of agency, in that self-produced physical actions are experienced as functions that bring about goal-directed outcomes in the external environment (Csibra & Gergely, 1998). Repeated embodied interactions with caregivers affirm the reality and validity of infants' physiological arousal, thus allowing them to integrate their body-related experiences in order to scaffold a basic sense of themselves as separate human beings (Fonagy & Target, 1997; Fotopoulou & Tsakiris, 2017).

Although critical for the establishment of a basic sense of embodied selfhood, physical care alone is not sufficient to organize the range and complexity of infantile affective experiences (Fonagy & Campbell, 2017). When infants, or young children, experience complex affective states, for example what in adult representational terminology we would call "anxiety", their actual first-person experience is comprised of an overwhelming and confusing mixture of bodily signals coupled with largely implicit ideas and actions (Fonagy & Target, 1997). One can imagine the experience of an infant boy who wakes up alone in his cradle and does not immediately see his caregiver. In a state of intense helplessness, he may believe that his caregivers have disappeared and will never come back, an idea likely to generate a strong physiological stress-response as his survival relies upon their presence. In order to express this complex and overwhelming experience he may start crying uncontrollably in despair. Once the caregiver sees their child in this highly distressed state, they may proceed to soothe him by picking him up and holding him in their arms (conveying their embodied presence), but also by intuitively using their facial expression and tone of voice to mirror his affective state and convey a sensitive understanding of his experience. In doing so, the caregiver presents to the child an attuned yet slightly distorted reflection of his complex emotions, coupled with an implicit sense that these can be communicated and managed (*marked mirroring*). This highly intuitive dyadic interaction provides an experience of *containment* (Bion, 1962) that modulates the child's affective states and facilitates the capacity to mentally represent, give meaning to and take ownership of self-experience. Repeated experiences of mirroring complex emotions by caregivers enables children to find continuity in their affective experiences and internalize them as part of their self-regulatory repertoire. Thus, with the help of ordinary attuned parenting, children learn to use their minds (i.e. their mentalizing capacity) to regulate their affective states and provide for themselves the caregiving function originally afforded by their parental figures. Indeed, the quality of caregivers' mirroring during the first six months has been shown to influence children's capacity to regulate affect (Gergely, 2004). Furthermore, neuroscientific evidence indicates that as adults we recruit the same neural networks when engaging in parent-referential and self-referential reflective processing (Vanderwal, Hunyadi, Grupe, Connors, & Schultz, 2008), thus supporting the role of early affect-mirroring in self-development and mentalizing (Fonagy & Luyten, 2009).

Within the mentalization-based model, it is hypothesized that if the caregiver's mirroring responses are absent or grossly disconnected (e.g. laughing when the child is crying), the child may struggle to find meaning and continuity in their self-experience. Alternatively, if the mirroring is too exaggerated and imbued with the caregiver's own preoccupation (i.e. responding to the child's anxiety with a sense of panic), the child may experience their affective states as overwhelming and dangerous. In both cases, rather than internalizing a modulated mental representation of self-experience, the child will internalize the *perceived* attitude of the caregiver, either disconnecting from their affective and bodily states, or becoming overwhelmed by them (Fonagy & Target, 1997). Here we highlight the word *perceived* because genetic factors can influence how the child processes the caregiver's responses. Embodied and affective states that are not adequately mirrored by caregivers and/or mentally represented by children remain confusing, overwhelming and hard to regulate, and thus are prone to be experienced as alien to the self (Fonagy & Luyten, 2009). From this perspective, experiences of childhood neglect and trauma, which invariably entail aberrant mirroring responses, can be detrimental for self-development because they interfere with children's ability to "find" their embodied and psychological self in the minds of their caregivers. Furthermore, within abusive or neglectful caregiving relationships children may defensively inhibit their mentalizing capacity because reflecting on the caregiver's disturbing states of mind can be overwhelmingly painful (Chiesa & Fonagy, 2014). Instead, they may engage in preoccupied, avoidant or disorganized attachment behaviours (Liotti & Gumley, 2008), seeking to manage the caregiver's threatening states of mind, by controlling them, avoiding them or psychologically dissociating from them (Chisholm, 1996). Critically, however, their sense of implicit trust in what others conceal in their minds as well as their genuine curiosity to understand mental states (including their own) may both be severely compromised (Fonagy & Allison, 2014).

As we will discuss in the next section, among genetically predisposed individuals, mentalizing dysfunctions arising in the context of early attachment relationships may interact with adolescence-specific vulnerability factors, to augment the risk for the emergence of psychotic phenomena (Brent & Fonagy, 2014). Our aim is not to suggest that attachment relationships are causally associated with the development of what is later diagnosed as psychosis. Rather, we propose that attachment disturbances and mentalizing disruptions may signify the breakdown of resilience factors that could otherwise sustain self-continuity in adolescents faced with neurogenetic risk for psychosis.

Attachment, mentalizing and emerging psychosis

In this section we propose that the model presented earlier, linking attachment, mentalizing and self-development, may contribute to our understanding of the emergence and treatment of psychotic phenomena. We start our discussion with emerging evidence from contemporary neuroscience that is beginning to unveil the neurobiological systems through which early attachment relationships relate to psychosis vulnerability across development.

Attachment along the psychosis continuum

We have previously highlighted studies supporting at least five key neurobiological pathways for psychosis that relate to early attachment disturbances (Debbané et al., 2016b). In brief, attachment adversity during critical periods of neurodevelopment is linked to hyperactivation of the hypothalamic-pituitary-adrenal (HPA) stress-response system (Heim, Newport, Mletzko, Miller, & Nemeroff, 2008); increased dopamine synthesis and release in response to increased stress (Howes & Kapur, 2009; Strathearn, 2011); reduced oxytocin levels (Brent & Fonagy, 2014); chronic neuroinflammation (Kirkpatrick & Miller, 2013); and oxidative stress damage (Do, Cabungcal, Frank, Steullet, & Cuenod, 2009). Critically for self-development, each of these pathways appears to compromise the neurodevelopmental integrity of cortical brain regions that normally sustain the regulation of self-experiences, from basic sensory processing (i.e. filtering out irrelevant stimuli, assigning salience to stimuli, differentiating self from nonself-cues) to higher order mentalizing processes about self-generated contents (i.e. body states, thoughts, feelings) (Debbané et al., 2016b). This is important because, at the clinical level, a number of psychotic phenomena explicitly involve impaired self-awareness (Brent, Seidman, Thermenos, Holt, & Keshavan, 2014; Waters, Woodward, Allen, Aleman, & Sommer, 2010). For instance, auditory hallucinations have been associated with difficulties in monitoring the origin of one's own self-generated inner speech (Allen, Aleman, & Mcguire, 2007; Keefe, Arnold, Bayen, McEvoy, & Wilson, 2002). Similarly, delusions of alien control have been linked to impairments in monitoring the initiation and sensory consequences of self-produced physical actions (Blakemore, Oakley, & Frith, 2003). Concerning negative symptoms, the inability to understand and reflect on one's own affective states may be expressed symptomatically in the form of constricted affect. Thus contemporary neuroscience is beginning to unravel the complex matrix of associations linking adverse interpersonal experiences to perturbations in self-referential processing, characteristic of psychotic manifestations.

Further support for the developmental associations linking attachment and the process of psychotic pathogenesis can be found in the prodromal and premorbid phases of psychosis, among adolescents and young adults. Studies suggest that as many as 80% of young adults at clinical high risk for psychosis (CHR) demonstrate evidence of insecure attachment (Gajwani, Patterson, & Birchwood, 2013) and it appears that clinical outcomes for CHR adolescents relate to the level of insecure avoidant attachment styles at baseline (Quijada, Kwapil, Tizón, Sheinbaum, & Barrantes-Vidal, 2015). In non-help-seeking individuals, studies report significant associations between attachment avoidance and positive schizotypal expression (sub-threshold delusion and hallucination-like manifestations). Furthermore, both attachment avoidance and attachment anxiety correlate with expressions of negative schizotypy that include trait manifestations of social withdrawal, constricted affect and social anxiety (Berry, Band, Corcoran, Barrowclough, & Wearden, 2007; Sheinbaum, Bedoya, Ros-Morente, Kwapil, & Barrantes-Vidal, 2013). Overall, available literature supports the view that insecure attachment is linked to psychotic pathogenesis and clinical outcomes across the continuum of psychosis expression.

We do not presume that psychotic states are based solely on environmental/interpersonal factors, such as attachment adversity, acting in isolation. Indeed, insecure attachment as well as disruptions in the five attachment-based neurobiological pathways described earlier are not exclusive to psychosis. Similar pathways have also been implicated in the development of non-psychotic manifestations (Fonagy & Luyten, 2009; Tiwari & Gonzalez, 2018). What may be more specific to the experience of psychosis is how risk along these pathways can interact with, and amplify genetically based aberrations in the processing of sensory information. In the next section we propose that psychotic experiences in adolescence emerge out of disruptions in *embodied mentalizing* – the capacity to dynamically form higher order mental representations of sensory information coming from one's body (Debbané et al., 2016b; Luyten, van Houdenhove, Lemma, Target, & Fonagy, 2012).

An embodied mentalization framework for emerging psychosis in adolescence

Genetically based alterations in the detection, integration and processing of sensory signals constitute core features associated with the pathophysiology of psychosis (Greenwood et al., 2013). For example, impairments in sensory-motor gating (basic inhibitory processes of sensory input preventing cognitive fragmentation and sensory overload) represent well-known endophenotypes identified across the continuum of psychosis expression, and among first-degree relatives of people suffering with psychosis (Gottesman & Gould, 2003; Greenwood et al., 2013). As we described earlier, conditions that alter our capacity to regulate sensory and affective signals, and most importantly the bodily states that accompany them, challenge our sense of reality and compromise our implicit first-person experience of the world. This view is reflected in recent formulations from phenomenological approaches, which suggest that failures to regulate multi-sensory input may underpin basic forms of psychotic subjectivity, such as hyper-reflexivity (exaggerated attention to normally tacit phenomena pertaining to the self) and diminished self-affectation (diminution of the sense of personal agency) (Postmes et al., 2014).

Importantly, however, the capacity to construe mental representations of bodily and affective states, established in the context of embodied and mirroring interactions with caregivers during infancy, enables individuals to find meaning and continuity in their self-experience, notwithstanding its ambiguous, painful and, at times, seemingly unintelligible nature. According to this conceptualization, at-risk individuals with a sufficiently robust mentalizing capacity can attenuate the pathogenic effects of sensory processing impairments to sustain a coherent sense of selfhood anchored in time and space. In other words, and from a clinical point of view, the critical value of mentalizing in emerging psychosis may be to afford resilience and sustain self-continuity in the face of adverse sensory conditions

(Fonagy & Bateman, 2016). The example of phantom limb sensations can help us illustrate this point further. Individuals with phantom limb syndrome experience vivid sensory signals (primarily painful but also non-painful sensations) which generate the illusion that an amputated extremity is still present; yet they manage to remain aware that these sensations are not real (Ramachandran & Hirstein, 1998). We suggest that they are able do so, at least in part, because their implicit capacity to form mental representations of their self-experience has remained intact (i.e. they can reflect on the sensory consequences and most importantly the distressing affect associated with the experience of having an amputated extremity). As such, they manage to maintain a coherent self-structure (i.e. they are aware that they have lost an extremity that was once present, and they know that this knowledge is visible to others), without resorting to delusional or magical explanations of their sensory experience (e.g. that their extremity is still present but invisible to other people). Interestingly, concurrent lesions in prefrontal brain regions (which include key mentalizing networks) among individuals experiencing phantom limb sensations have been associated with visual-hallucinations pertaining to the amputated extremities (Ramachandran & Hirstein, 1998). The case of phantom limbs illustrates how subtle failures in low-level embodied regulation call for higher order psychological processes to attenuate the "realness" of aberrant sensory experience.

Returning to the pathogenesis of psychosis, we suggest that among genetically prone individuals, enduring alterations in the low-level processing of sensory-affective signals may interact with disruptions in higher order mentalizing systems (often arising in the context of early attachment disturbances) in a transactional process that compromises self-awareness and augments psychosis risk. Here we need to clarify that we employ the term "sensory-affective" to account for the un-mentalized sensory signals that underlie complex affective experiences (i.e. rage, fear, shame, despair). Within this framework, the construct of embodied mentalizing can be useful for our understanding of psychotic phenomena, specifically because it seeks to account for the dynamic cross-talk between low-level sensory signals and their mental representations through higher order psychological processes (Debbané et al., 2016b).

Developmentally, aberrant sensory states linked to psychosis often manifest during adolescence and are expressed within the domain of interpersonal relationships, which commonly evoke experiences of bodily and affective arousal (Fonagy, 2008). For instance, trait manifestations pertaining to social anhedonia (i.e. inability to experience pleasurable sensations within social situations) and social anxiety involve alterations in the processing of sensory-affective signals, so that even innocuous interpersonal experiences generate overwhelming distress (Blanchard, Horan, & Brown, 2001; Cohen, Najolia, Brown, & Minor, 2011). In the context of social anhedonia and social anxiety, difficulties in representing the mental states of oneself and others, to sustain self-awareness and downregulate the intensity of sensory-affective signals, can amplify the distress evoked within interpersonal situations. This may, in turn, lead to the emergence of clinically relevant outcomes such as interpersonal withdrawal, lack of intimacy, constricted affect and avolition, which signify maladaptive attempts to attenuate the overwhelming distress generated within social interactions (Gumley & Schwannauer, 2006).

Alternatively, or in conjunction, endophenotypic alterations in low-level sensory-gating regulation may generate states characterized by sensory overload, cognitive fragmentation and perceptual incoherence (Braff et al., 2001), in which normally tacit sensory-affective signals are experienced as novel, surprising and with an increased sense of realness. Although these sensory aberrations commonly remain latent during childhood, their potentiation through adolescence-specific vulnerability factors, such as bullying (Trotta et al., 2013) and cannabis use (Arseneault et al., 2002), together with other interpersonal experiences that lead to affective and bodily arousal, increase the risk for the emergence of clinically relevant manifestations. Failures to construe mental representations of these aberrant sensory states may result in experiences of overwhelming confusion where embodied signals, which normally sustain self-continuity, lose their meaning, become highly unpredictable and are perceived as external to the self (De Masi, Davalli, Giustino, & Pergami, 2015). Interestingly, clinical descriptions, pertaining to the phenomenology of the prodromal stages of psychosis, employ the concept of *delusional mood* to characterize a self-referential pre-psychotic state of diffuse and objectless anxiety about "something" that is not yet defined, but is always about to happen (Henriksen & Parnas, 2018). From a mentalization-based perspective, delusional mood may signify a dysfunction of embodied mentalizing, where sensory-affective signals coming from one's body (the diffuse anxiety) fail to be harnessed with one's mind (thus the anxiety remains undefined and objectless). In essence, bodily signals may signify the presence of a very real and often painful feeling, but the disruption of higher order mentalizing processes prevents the individual from knowing what this feeling is and why it is present. In order to escape the intolerable uncertainty linked with these states of fragmentation, and to regain a minimal sense of self-continuity, individuals may engage in a form of dis-embodied "hyper-mentalizing" (Sharp et al., 2013), where sensory-affective signals coming from one's body are discarded to attenuate their distressing effect. Instead, delusional explanations of self-experiences, decoupled from shared reality with others and impervious to contradictory sensory evidence, are developed and held with rigid certainty, offering a *psychic retreat* (Steiner, 2003) from the intensity of un-mentalized sensory-affective signals. Although this retreat to delusional thinking patterns often entails profound distress characterized by feelings of fear and persecution, the threat to the self is no longer nameless, or experienced as originating from one's own mind, but is instead organized around objects in the external world. In other words, delusional states afford a false sense of cohesion that temporarily reduces the anxiety of fragmentation linked to states of overwhelming affect, albeit at the grave cost of mental and relational isolation (De Masi, 2018; Evans, 2018; Steiner & Harland, 2011).

Importantly from our developmental perspective, when the sensory-affective aberrations linked to psychosis emerge during early development, they may contribute to undermine the normative elaboration of mentalizing processes and further increase psychosis vulnerability, even in the absence of overt attachment adversity (Debbané & Barrantes-Vidal, 2014; Debbané et al., 2016b). For instance, young children or adolescents who avoid interpersonal contact in the context of social anxiety, may deprive themselves of the opportunity to have their affective states reflected, or "mirrored", by close others, thereby disrupting their capacity to construe second-order representations of their self-experience (Ballespí, Pérez-Domingo, Vives, Sharp, & Barrantes-Vidal, 2018). Similarly, children who experience difficulties in inhibiting sensory stimuli may struggle to relate to and make use of the mirroring responses offered by others within attachment relationships. Indeed, among people suffering with psychosis, aberrations in sensory-gating functions, which typically reach full maturity during early childhood, have been associated with decreased performance in mentalizing tasks assessing social-cue perception (Wynn, Sergi, Dawson, Schell, & Green, 2005). In essence, the process of psychotic pathogenesis actively inhibits the capacity to form emotional links with others, which in turn severely undermines the developmental capacity to think about, reflect on and regulate one's own emotional experiences (Bion, 1959). We are thus suggesting that suboptimal mentalizing functions, often found in the context of difficulties in early attachment relationships, may combine with an underlying endophenotypic trait liability in a developmental transactional process that converges towards what is diagnosed as clinical psychosis.

Before proceeding to discuss the clinical implications of this framework in more detail, we first reiterate two key points that we hope can be discerned from the previous paragraphs: (1) at its core, psychosis does not represent an "affectless" condition and should not be clinically treated as such. On the contrary, we believe that the experience of psychosis is characterized by states of overwhelming un-mentalized affect that threaten the very integrity of the self; and (2) psychotic phenomena (i.e. delusions, hallucinations, odd behaviours, blunted affect) commonly entail the breakdown of mentalizing processes pertaining to the self (the capacity to reflect on one's own thoughts and feelings). These signify failed compensatory attempts to attenuate the intensity of sensory-affective signals and regain a minimal sense of self-continuity. We believe that, in order to support the genuine recovery of the self in emerging psychosis, psychotherapeutic treatments need to first and foremost help individuals construct a mental representation of themselves as thinking and feeling beings (Fonagy, 2000). Treatments that are primarily focused on the elimination of specific symptoms, or seek to "train" individuals into altering maladaptive thinking patterns may be insufficient to support genuine meaning-making and the recovery of a coherent sense of self (Hamm et al., 2018).

In line with classical psychoanalytic conceptualizations (Bion, 1959; Steiner, 2003; Lucas, 2013; Evans, 2018), we suggest that individuals confronted with psychosis are caught in an unresolved inner conflict, between engaging with a reality that entails unbearable emotional states that threaten to overwhelm the self, and shielding the self into a delusional system that involves the collapse of genuine relations with the world and with others. According to our perspective, recovering self-continuity in the face of challenging sensory-affective uncertainty requires the construction of a higher order reflective process, though which painful states can be thought about (i.e. mentalized) and adequately regulated. In this sense, interpersonal contact, including psychotherapeutic contact, can be both threatening and protective for young people faced with emerging psychosis. It is threatening because attachment to others can stimulate painful sensory-affective signals that threaten the integrity of the self; yet it is protective because the minds of others can be used to mirror, reflect and mentally represent the individual's felt experience.

A mentalization-based treatment (MBT) framework for emerging psychosis in adolescence: from theory to clinical practice

According to our model of psychosis development, articulated within an MBT framework, psychotic phenomena entailing aberrant mentalizing can be conceptualized as failed attempts to establish a minimal sense of self-continuity in the face of sensory-affective uncertainty. Fonagy et al. (2002) suggest that, in order to manage the distressing nature of painful emotional states, individuals with impaired mentalizing may turn to "pre-mentalistic" modes of self-organization (the teleological, psychic equivalence and pretend modes). These modes represent ordinary stages of self-development in infancy and early childhood, antedating the emergence of mentalizing and the establishment of a coherent self-structure. However, experiences of bodily and affective arousal, particularly within interpersonal relationships, can lead to the re-emergence of the pre-mentalizing modes of functioning beyond childhood. Indeed, as we will illustrate, psychotic phenomena reflect exaggerated forms of pre-reflective modes of self-organization. We proceed to discuss how these modes may manifest across typical development, as well as in the phenomenology of psychotic symptoms.

The *teleological mode* (Fonagy & Bateman, 2006) refers to the most basic form of self-organization, in which internal states in the self and others can only be understood in terms of their physical consequences, such as behaviours and actions. For instance, infants can only come to recognize their embodied states (i.e. hunger) and experience the care of their parents through contingent physical actions (i.e. feeding). Similarly, adults during moments of stress may feel the need to seek physical signs of affection (i.e. feeling cared for only when hugged). In essence, teleological mode functioning entails the loss of the capacity to imaginatively envisage abstract "inner states" in oneself and others. In extreme forms of teleological mode functioning, individuals diagnosed with psychosis may engage in overt physical actions and seemingly unintelligible behaviours as means to experience and communicate their internal states. For example, an individual may start spinning around in order to concretely represent a sense of confusion, or light a fire to express a state of intense anger. Within the psychotherapy setting, which typically arouses interpersonal stress, individuals suffering with psychosis may look for physical clues to discern the mental states of their clinician. For example, an increase in the number of books on the therapist's desk may be perceived concretely as a sign that the therapist's mind is too full to listen to the client. Furthermore, people suffering with psychosis can make mental state inferences on the basis of the therapist's body language (i.e. the therapist momentarily looking away from the client being taken as a sign of disinterest). Similarly, cancelled sessions or even silences during the session may be particularly painful, because they can be concretely experienced by clients with psychosis as signs that the therapist is physically "disappearing".

The *psychic equivalence mode* (Fonagy & Target, 1996) refers to a type of self-organization in which one's thoughts and feelings are taken as unequivocally real and the ability to consider alternative perspectives of one's own internal experience is lost. In psychic equivalence the differentiation between internal and external reality ceases to exist, and the subjective nature of mental states is denied. For instance, young children commonly believe that their private knowledge is shared by external others; what they know or feel inside becomes isomorphic to external reality. Turning to adult relationships, feelings of jealousy often signify psychic equivalence functioning, as one person assumes that they "know" what is in the other's mind. Although in non-clinical states these phenomena are transient and the capacity to mentalize self-experience can be promptly recovered, in psychosis psychic equivalence functioning becomes increasingly pervasive. Paranoid delusional ideation represents a prototypical example of psychic equivalence because beliefs about others' intentions are held with absolute conviction (i.e. they do not constitute possibilities but certainties). For example, a young person who makes random eye contact with someone on the street may become convinced that others are spying on her. In the context of psychotherapy, the clinician's inquisitive stance may be perceived concretely by individuals diagnosed with psychosis as an intention to "get inside their head", or to "steal their thoughts". Similarly, the therapist's interventions may be experienced as attempts to insert unwanted thoughts into their minds. In essence, what the person is feeling inside becomes entangled with the intentional mental states of others, signifying a loss of self-other boundaries. Ideas of reference also entail psychic equivalence functioning, as the opacity of other people's mental states is denied (i.e. a conviction that people on the radio are directly addressing oneself).

Finally, in the *pretend mode* of self-organization (Fonagy & Target, 1996), mentalizing activity becomes decoupled from present perceptual and affective content, and the capacity to genuinely reflect on internal experiences and communicate them within interpersonal relationships is disrupted. While engaged in playing, children may know that their imaginary experience is not isomorphic to external reality, however they remain unaware of the possible links between their internal states and external reality. Beyond childhood, individuals may demonstrate pretend mode functioning when they engage in elaborate dialogues about their internal states, which remain devoid of genuine reflection and affective content. Similarly, individuals suffering with psychosis can engage in vague hyperreflexive modes of discourse during psychotherapy that leave the clinician with a sense of meaninglessness and confusion. Importantly, pretend mode functioning can become so pervasive that it can appear on the surface as genuine mentalizing.

For instance, it is not uncommon for individuals who are admitted to in-patient units in delusional states to present in the initial assessment with a calm, seemingly rational attitude that defies the presence of any emotional problems. In these instances, feelings of confusion, doubt and suspicion evoked in clinicians may alert them to consider that the client is actively dissociating from the reality and impact of his/her painful self-experience (Lucas, 2013).

Although the pre-mentalizing modes of functioning represent early forms of self-organization, they significantly disrupt the elaboration of adaptive affect-regulation strategies, increase interpersonal distress and further compromise the capacity to distinguish between reality and imagination. Most importantly, they disrupt genuine relatedness with others and undermine the capacity to find meaning in one's own experiences, both of which constitute the very essence of a fulfilling life. As we discuss in the next section, adolescence represents a critical period during which the breakdown of mentalizing processes in the context of increased interpersonal stress can lead to the re-emergence of pre-mentalizing modes of functioning and the development of psychotic manifestations.

Adolescence, mentalizing and psychosis risk

On the basis of clinical insights (Fonagy & Luyten, 2016), we suggest that among those who are at risk for psychosis, disruptions in embodied mentalizing become particularly marked during adolescence, which is characterized by the widening of interpersonal relationships, together with biopsychological changes that profoundly modify young peoples' position in the domains of sexuality and aggression (Laufer & Laufer, 1995). Although prior to adolescence affective states related to sexuality and aggression are less integrated into one's sense of agency, their potentiation through adolescent development confronts young people with novel possibilities; procreation and potentially causing harm through one's aggression. This creates a challenge for mentalizing during adolescence, as embodied states associated with experiences of unprecedented intensity in sexual and aggressive arousal remain without fully regulated mental representations, in contrast to other forms of affective states which have been consistently mirrored throughout childhood (Fonagy, 2008; Fonagy & Allison, 2016; Target, 2007). This makes intense sensory-affective states in adolescence liable to poorly regulated thought and behaviour, especially in the context of interpersonal stress (Fonagy & Luyten, 2016). Under favourable circumstances, adolescents with relatively robust mentalizing capacities use the minds of their peers, and other trustworthy adults, to further elaborate their ability to form mental representations of self-experience, and integrate their sexual and aggressive states in their developing self-structure.

However, children who have experienced difficulties in early attachment relationships encounter the emotional storms of adolescence with a potentially undermined mentalizing capacity (Ensink et al., 2015). For these adolescents, engagements with intense feelings pertaining to aggression and sexuality, and most importantly, with the bodily states that accompany them, may produce equally intense distress, leading to further disruptions of mentalizing and the re-emergence of pre-mentalizing modes of self-organization.

In this context, the process of mentalization-based psychotherapeutic work with adolescents at the premorbid and prodromal phases of emerging psychosis would focus on fostering embodied mentalizing, that is, the capacity to form mental representations of sensory signals coming from one's body, in order to understand one's feelings in relation to oneself and others. According to this perspective, and in line with the format and core principles of MBT in its application with adolescents suffering with personality disorders (Rossouw & Fonagy, 2012), the psychotherapist's role involves identifying and mirroring the client's felt experience and affective states, as they unfold within the therapeutic relationship and beyond. The frequency of the sessions can vary depending on the treatment programme, with most outpatient MBT programs for adolescents offering once weekly individual psychotherapy for a period of 18 months, combined with once monthly family sessions when possible. In the next section we present the main MBT principles that, we believe, can support the recovery of self-awareness and self-continuity in the face of emerging psychosis during adolescence.

Basic principles of MBT

In this section we summarize the main technical principles common to MBT approaches applied to different clinical populations. The aim of MBT is first and foremost to enhance mentalizing. As such, the MBT therapist is not engaged into altering maladaptive thinking patterns or bringing about behavioural change. Rather, in line with metacognitive approaches to psychotherapy (Hasson-Ohayon, Kravetz, & Lysaker, 2017; Lysaker et al., 2018a), the focus during MBT sessions remains on creating an intersubjective narrative construction space which fosters in clients the capacity to think about their emerging thoughts and feelings. However, contrary to metacognitive approaches, and in keeping with its psychoanalytic heritage, MBT adopts a developmentally informed approach by clinically addressing the links between attachment relationships, mentalizing functions and affecting regulation processes. More specifically, in MBT the goal of enhancing mentalizing within the psychotherapy setting primarily relies on the recapitulation of early attachment dynamics within the client-therapist relationship (Brent, 2009). This is important because it is in the context of attachment relationships that mentalizing originally develops, or becomes disrupted (Brent, 2009). In essence, MBT works by establishing an attachment relationship with the client, which inherently evokes affective states, while continuously engaging the client in a reflective process about those states. Although the MBT therapist seeks to help individuals reflect on their states of mind across different interpersonal situations, including those that occur outside the session, we believe that repairing "in the moment" mentalizing ruptures, when these occur within the client-therapist relationship, constitutes one of the most important elements of the treatment.

The overall objective in MBT is to help people reflect on how they think and feel about themselves and others, as well as how distortions in understanding themselves can lead to maladaptive experiences. We suggest that in the treatment of young people faced with emerging psychosis, this can be achieved through the use of the following clinical principles: (1) adopting a therapeutic stance which promotes mentalizing; (2) focusing on affective experiences and mirroring these in the session; and (3) enhancing embodied mentalizing.

First of all, the therapeutic stance in MBT seeks to convey that mental states are complex and subjective in nature. This is particularly important because adolescents who are at risk for psychosis may demonstrate rigid certainty when inferring the mental states of others (psychic equivalence functioning). By adopting a not-knowing stance and demonstrating genuine curiosity about the client's mental states, their thoughts and feelings, the therapist seeks to stimulate curiosity in the client about their own mind. This is highly relevant for young people who have defensively inhibited their curiosity about mental states in the context of childhood abuse and neglect. The therapist takes on a fairly active role, by encouraging the person to reflect on their interpersonal experiences, including experiences of the therapy session. This includes engaging in active questioning about the person's state of mind across different interpersonal contexts, and most importantly within the here-and-now of the psychotherapeutic encounter. The aim is to create an atmosphere of curious exploration and investigation about mental states. In terms of the therapist's interventions, as a general principle these need to remain short, simple and calibrated to the client's mentalizing capacity. Given that increased arousal, evoked within the therapeutic relationship, is likely to disrupt the elaboration of mentalizing, less complex interventions are often needed to promote a sense of safety and understanding in the client (Brent & Fonagy, 2014).

Most importantly perhaps, the focus during MBT sessions consistently stays on young persons' affective states, rather than on their behaviour or symptoms. Because individuals diagnosed with psychosis, or at-risk adolescents, experience difficulties in understanding mental states, in contrast to classical psychoanalytic technique, deep interpretations of unconscious conflicts, or links between early experiences and current behaviours (no matter their perceived accuracy), are usually avoided (Brent & Fonagy, 2014; Target, 2016). Instead, the main task of the therapist is to make affect the joint topic of attention during the session. More specifically, the therapist attempts to help the person recognize and verbalize what they are feeling, as well as reflect on what happened right before these feelings emerged (Target, 2016). Through this continuous willingness to "receive", sensitively reflect and label the client's mental states (marked mirroring), the therapist seeks to create a trusting relationship, where non-mentalizing concrete explanations of behaviour can be reconceived by the client in terms of opaque and complex states of mind. In essence, everything that is in the young person's mind can be talked about and reflected on in the therapy. By increasing their awareness of their own and other people's minds, young people faced with emerging psychosis can start using their thoughts, instead of concrete physical actions (as in teleological mode), to regulate and communicate their affective experiences.

As we noted in the previous sections, confrontations with highly distressing affective states in the context of psychotic pathogenesis during adolescence can lead to aberrant bodily and perceptual experiences. When these manifest during the session, the therapist should sensitively direct the young person's attention into thinking about the "internal states" that may underpin them (i.e. fostering embodied mentalizing). This often involves supporting young people to find words to express affective states, and make links between specific feelings and bodily or perceptive experiences. By reinvesting aberrant bodily and perceptive experiences with affective meaning, clients can develop a more coherent view of their self-experience, which can in turn strengthen their sense of self-continuity. Importantly, however, young people will commonly try to avoid becoming aware of, and reflecting on, potentially painful internal states. They may instead engage in hyper-reflexive convoluted descriptions of their experiences (pretend mode functioning), or offer concrete, matter-of-fact and delusional explanations about them (psychic equivalence functioning). One should remain alert to the fact that these mentalizing ruptures represent signs of high arousal. Therefore, the MBT therapist should try to intervene in order to clarify elements that seem odd, or disconnected, and inquire about possible feelings that may underpin them. For instance, when confronted with psychic equivalence functioning, the therapist should attempt to sensitively challenge rigid states of mind and introduce the possibility of alternative perspectives where one's experience can become the source of curious exploration. Similarly, when the young person functions in pretend mode, the therapist should engage in active questioning about their affective states, maintain the focus of the narrative on the here-and-now and refrain from offering long, intellectualized interventions about their self-experience. Because affective arousal in the context of emerging psychosis will often manifest within the domain of bodily-action (rather that in narrative), the clinician must be sensitive to subtle embodied signs (i.e. slowing of speech, avoiding eye contact, increased incoherence, flat affective tone) and make these the focus of discussion when they manifest within the session. For example, the therapist may say: "It seems to me that you are talking a bit less than usual today. I am wondering what is in your mind when you were silent", or "I am noticing that you are looking around the room and I am curious about what goes through your mind when you are looking around". In doing so, the therapist seeks to help clients recognize the links between embodied signals and intentional mental states, as well as implicitly convey that affective states can be communicated and managed within the intersubjective narrative space of the therapy setting. Through this process, the young person is encouraged to discover their embodied and psychological self within the mind of the therapist, in order to give meaning, find self-continuity and take ownership of their self-experiences (a process very similar to the marked mirroring of affective experience in early childhood).

This is by no means a simple task. The therapist confronted with emerging psychosis has to first help the young person reflect on and contain the disturbing nature of psychotic manifestations. When these emerge in the session, they are prone to generate anxiety and confusion not only in the client, but in the therapist too. In order to retain the mentalizing stance, the therapist has to engage with a continuous process of self-reflection (use his/her own mentalizing capacity) that will help to understand and regulate the emotional impact that the young person's communications and symptomatic manifestations may generate. By managing to remain curious about the affective states that underpin psychotic phenomena, the therapist can "survive" the client's attempts to dissociate from the awareness of painful inner states and implicitly communicate that the minds of others can be used to generate personal meaning. In other words, by recognizing the person as an intentional agent and by showing concern about inner states, the therapist can stimulate in them a sense of agency and concern about their own inner states.

Importantly, however, as the person's capacity for reflective functioning increases, overwhelmingly painful sensory-affective states related to feelings of depression, anxiety and shame (often about the experience of psychosis itself) may come to fore (Evans, 2018; Steiner, 2003). Therapists should maintain the mentalizing stance in order to help young people regulate these feelings and gradually integrate them into their developing self-structure. Although the emergence of these painful affective states often signifies the recovery of a more coherent self-structure, if the capacity to mentalize is not stable enough, they can lead to further disruptions in mentalizing, the intensification of psychotic phenomena and potentially the termination of treatment. In these cases, family MBT sessions can be used to engage the family into sustaining a reflective process about the young person's experience outside the sessions, which can allow the treatment to continue. Similarly, good communication between the therapist and other mental health professionals involved in the young person's psychiatric care can help establish a sufficiently strong external setting that can support the containment of painful affective states and provide a sense of safety in the young person. We believe that the support of the family and other mental health professionals can significantly enhance the chances for positive outcomes in the psychotherapeutic treatment of adolescents confronted with emerging psychosis.

Conclusion

The main focus of this chapter was to offer the conceptual basis to support the application of MBT to the recovery of self in emerging psychosis. Overall, we suggest that psychotherapeutic interventions focusing on mentalizing can help individuals sustain resilience against rigid and delusional thinking patterns in the face of neurogenetic or other risk for psychosis. Indeed, recent empirical evidence highlights the protective role of mentalizing along the developmental continuum of psychosis expression. For example, Braehler and Schwannauer (2012) reported that the level of mentalizing capacity, assessed using narrative methodologies, moderates adaptation and individuation processes in adolescents recovering from a first episode of psychosis. In the premorbid stage of psychosis, Bartels-Velthuis, Blijd-Hoogewys, and Van Os (2011) reported that in sample of young adolescents who experienced non-clinical hallucinations within the previous five years, the risk for the development of secondary delusional ideation was lower for those with higher ToM scores. More recently, Peters et al. (2016) found that a sample of individuals who experienced non-clinical auditory hallucinations reported better mindfulness skills compared to individuals diagnosed with psychosis and non-voice-hearing subjects. These studies indicate that robust mentalizing may represent a factor that protects at-risk individuals from the psychopathological effects of emerging psychosis. Furthermore, these findings support the use of MBT as a preventative treatment to enhance mentalizing and sustain self-development in young people who present with sub-clinical psychotic manifestations, prior to the development of clinically diagnosable symptoms.

Although clinical trials assessing the effectiveness of MBT in the treatment of emerging psychosis during adolescence have yet to be conducted, recent studies have shown the feasibility of MBT for individuals diagnosed with psychosis (Lana et al., 2015; Weijers et al., 2016), as well as its effectiveness in the treatment of adolescent conditions that often include comorbid psychotic symptoms (Rossouw & Fonagy, 2012). We believe that even when MBT is not offered as a treatment modality in its own right, mental health professionals involved in the care of adolescents who experience psychotic symptoms, whether working in psychiatry, nursing or social work, can use the affect-based framework offered by MBT in their attempts to understand what these young people are going through. These attempts can often generate meaningful therapeutic outcomes because they provide young people with a strong sense of being present in others' minds.

References

Allen, P., Aleman, A., & Mcguire, P. K. (2007). Inner speech models of auditory verbal hallucinations: Evidence from behavioural and neuroimaging studies. *International Review of Psychiatry*, *19*(4), 407–415.

Arseneault, L., Cannon, M., Poulton, R., Murray, R., Caspi, A., & Moffitt, T. E. (2002). Cannabis use in adolescence and risk for adult psychosis: Longitudinal prospective study. *BMJ*, *325*(7374), 1212–1213.

Ballespí, S., Pérez-Domingo, A., Vives, J., Sharp, C., & Barrantes-Vidal, N. (2018). Childhood behavioral inhibition is associated with impaired mentalizing in adolescence. *PLoS One*, *13*(3), e0195303.

Bartels-Velthuis, A. A., Blijd-Hoogewys, E. M., & Van Os, J. (2011). Better theory-of-mind skills in children hearing voices mitigate the risk of secondary delusion formation. *Acta Psychiatrica Scandinavica*, *124*(3), 193–197.

Bateman, A., & Fonagy, P. (2010). Mentalization based treatment for borderline personality disorder. *World Psychiatry*, *9*(1), 11–15.

Berry, K., Band, R., Corcoran, R., Barrowclough, C., & Wearden, A. (2007). Attachment styles, earlier interpersonal relationships and schizotypy in a non-clinical sample. *Psychology and Psychotherapy: Theory, Research and Practice*, *80*(4), 563–576.

Bion, W. R. (1959). Attacks on linking. *The International Journal of Psychoanalysis*, *40*, 308–315.

Bion, W. R. (1962). *Learning from experience*. London: Karnac.

Blakemore, S.-J., Oakley, D. A., & Frith, C. (2003). Delusions of alien control in the normal brain. *Neuropsychologia*, *41*(8), 1058–1067.

Blanchard, J. L., Horan, W. P., & Brown, S. A. (2001). Diagnostic differences in social anhedonia: A longitudinal study of schizophrenia and major depressive disorder. *Journal of Abnormal Psychology*, *110*(3), 363.

Bowlby, J. (1969). *Attachment and loss: Attachment*. New York: Basic Books.

Braehler, C., & Schwannauer, M. (2012). Recovering an emerging self: Exploring reflective function in recovery from adolescent-onset psychosis. *Psychology and Psychotherapy: Theory, Research and Practice*, *85*(1), 48–67.

Braff, D. L., Geyer, M. A., Light, G. A., Sprock, J., Perry, W., Cadenhead, K. S., & Swerdlow, N. R. (2001). Impact of prepulse characteristics on the detection of sensorimotor gating deficits in schizophrenia. *Schizophrenia Research*, *49*(1–2), 171–178.

Brent, B. K. (2009). Mentalization-based psychodynamic psychotherapy for psychosis. *Journal of Clinical Psychology*, *65*(8), 803–814.

Brent, B. K., & Fonagy, P. (2014). A mentalization-based treatment approach to disturbances of social understanding in schizophrenia. In P. H. Lysaker, G. Dimaggio, & M. Brune (Eds.), *Social cognition and metacognition in schizophrenia: Psychopathology and treatment approaches* (pp. 245–259). Gurgaon: Elsevier Science and Technology.

Brent, B. K., Seidman, L. J., Thermenos, H. W., Holt, D. J., & Keshavan, M. S. (2014). Self-disturbances as a possible premorbid indicator of schizophrenia risk: A neurodevelopmental perspective. *Schizophrenia Research*, *152*(1), 73–80.

Caputo, G. B. (2010). Strange-face-in-the-mirror illusion. *Perception*, *39*(7), 1007.

Chiesa, M., & Fonagy, P. (2014). Reflective function as a mediator between childhood adversity, personality disorder and symptom distress. *Personality and Mental Health*, *8*(1), 52–66.

Chisholm, J. S. (1996). The evolutionary ecology of attachment organization. *Hu Nat*, *7*(1), 1–37.

Choi-Kain, L. W., & Gunderson, J. G. (2008). Mentalization: Ontogeny, assessment, and application in the treatment of borderline personality disorder. *American Journal of Psychiatry*, *165*(9), 1127–1135.

Cohen, A. S., Najolia, G. M., Brown, L. A., & Minor, K. S. (2011). The state-trait disjunction of anhedonia in schizophrenia: Potential affective, cognitive and social-based mechanisms. *Clinical Psychology Review*, *31*(3), 440–448.

Csibra, G., & Gergely, G. (1998). The teleological origins of mentalistic action explanations: A developmental hypothesis. *Developmental Science*, *1*(2), 255–259.

Daniel, C., & Mason, O. J. (2015). Inducing psychotic-like experiences: The role of schizotypy. In O. J. Mason & G. Claridge (Eds.), *Schizotypy: New dimensions* (pp. 147–162). London & New York: Routledge.

Debbané, M., & Barrantes-Vidal, N. (2014). Schizotypy from a developmental perspective. *Schizophrenia Bulletin*, *41*(suppl_2), S386–S395.

Debbané, M., Benmiloud, J., Salaminios, G., Solida-Tozzi, A., Armando, M., Fonagy, P., & Bateman, A. (2016a). Mentalization-based treatment in clinical high-risk for psychosis:

A rationale and clinical illustration. *Journal of Contemporary Psychotherapy, 46*(4), 217–225.

Debbané, M., Salaminios, G., Luyten, P., Badoud, D., Armando, M., Tozzi, A. S., Fonagy, P., & Brent, B. K. (2016b). Attachment, neurobiology, and mentalizing along the psychosis continuum. *Frontiers in Human Neuroscience, 10.*

De Masi, F. (2018). The unconscious and psychosis: Some considerations on the psychoanalytic theory of psychosis. In *Key papers on borderline disorders* (pp. 109–141). London & New York: Routledge.

De Masi, F., Davalli, C., Giustino, G., & Pergami, A. (2015). Hallucinations in the psychotic state: Psychoanalysis and the neurosciences compared. *The International Journal of Psychoanalysis, 96*(2), 293–318.

Do, K. Q., Cabungcal, J. H., Frank, A., Steullet, P., & Cuenod, M. (2009). Redox dysregulation, neurodevelopment, and schizophrenia. *Current Opinion in Neurobiology, 19*(2), 220–230.

Ensink, K., Normandin, L., Target, M., Fonagy, P., Sabourin, S., & Berthelot, N. (2015). Mentalization in children and mothers in the context of trauma: An initial study of the validity of the Child Reflective Functioning Scale. *British Journal of Developmental Psychology, 33*(2), 203–217.

Evans, M. (2018). Catch 22: The inflammatory nature of insight. *Psychoanalytic Psychotherapy, 32*(4), 335–350.

Fonagy, P. (2000). Attachment and borderline personality disorder. *Journal of the American Psychoanalytic Association, 48*(4), 1129–1146.

Fonagy, P. (2008). A genuinely developmental theory of sexual enjoyment and its implications for psychoanalytic technique. *Journal of the American Psychoanalytic Association, 56*(1), 11–36.

Fonagy, P., & Allison, E. (2014). The role of mentalizing and epistemic trust in the therapeutic relationship. *Psychotherapy, 51*(3), 372.

Fonagy, P., & Allison, E. (2016). Psychic reality and the nature of consciousness. *The International Journal of Psychoanalysis, 97*(1), 5–24.

Fonagy, P., & Bateman, A. W. (2006). Mechanisms of change in mentalization-based treatment of BPD. *Journal of Clinical Psychology, 62*(4), 411–430.

Fonagy, P., & Bateman, A. W. (2016). Adversity, attachment, and mentalizing. *Comprehensive Psychiatry, 64*, 59–66.

Fonagy, P., & Campbell, C. (2017). What touch can communicate: Commentary on "mentalizing homeostasis: The social origins of interoceptive inference" by Fotopoulou and Tsakiris. *Neuropsychoanalysis, 19*(1), 39–42.

Fonagy, P., Gergely, G., Jurist, E. L., & Target, M. (2002). *Affect regulation, mentalization and the development of the self.* London: Routledge.

Fonagy, P., & Luyten, P. (2009). A developmental, mentalization-based approach to the understanding and treatment of borderline personality disorder. *Development and Psychopathology, 21*(4), 1355–1381.

Fonagy, P., & Luyten, P. (2016). A multilevel perspective on the development of borderline personality disorder. *Developmental Psychopathology, 1–67.*

Fonagy, P., Redfern, S., & Charman, T. (1997). The relationship between belief-desire reasoning and a projective measure of attachment security (SAT). *British Journal of Developmental Psychology, 15*(1), 51–61.

Fonagy, P., & Target, M. (1996). Playing with reality I. *The International Journal of Psycho-analysis, 77*(2), 217.

Fonagy, P., & Target, M. (1997). Attachment and reflective function: Their role in self-organization. *Development and Psychopathology*, *9*(4), 679–700.

Fotopoulou, A., & Tsakiris, M. (2017). Mentalizing homeostasis: The social origins of interoceptive inference. *Neuropsychoanalysis*, *19*(1), 3–28.

Freeman, D. (2007). Suspicious minds: The psychology of persecutory delusions. *Clinical Psychology Review*, *27*(4), 425–457.

Fusar-Poli, P., Borgwardt, S., Bechdolf, A., Addington, J., Riecher-Rossler, A., Schultze-Lutter, F., . . . & Yung, A. (2013). The psychosis high-risk state: A comprehensive state-of-the-art review. *JAMA Psychiatry*, *70*(1), 107–120. https://doi.org/10.1001/jamapsychiatry.2013.269.

Gajwani, R., Patterson, P., & Birchwood, M. (2013). Attachment: Developmental pathways to affective dysregulation in young people at ultra-high risk of developing psychosis. *British Journal of Clinical Psychology*, *52*(4), 424–437.

Gergely, G. (2004). The role of contingency detection in early affect–regulative interactions and in the development of different types of infant attachment. *Social Development*, *13*(3), 468–478.

Gottesman, I. I., & Gould, T. D. (2003). The endophenotype concept in psychiatry: Etymology and strategic intentions. *American Journal of Psychiatry*, *160*(4), 636–645.

Greenwood, T. A., Swerdlow, N. R., Gur, R. E., Cadenhead, K. S., Calkins, M. E., Dobie, D. J., . . . & Lazzeroni, L. C. (2013). Genome-wide linkage analyses of 12 endophenotypes for schizophrenia from the Consortium on the Genetics of Schizophrenia. *American Journal of Psychiatry*, *170*(5), 521–532.

Gumley, A., & Schwannauer, M. (2006). *Staying well after psychosis: A cognitive interpersonal approach to recovery and relapse prevention*. Chichester, UK: John Wiley & Sons.

Ham, S., Kim, T. K., Chung, S., & Im, H.-I. (2017). Drug abuse and psychosis: New insights into drug-induced psychosis. *Experimental Neurobiology*, *26*(1), 11–24.

Hamm, J. A., Leonhardt, B. L., Ridenour, J., Lysaker, J. T., & Lysaker, P. H. (2018). Phenomenological and recovery models of the subjective experience of psychosis: Discrepancies and implications for treatment. *Psychosis*, *10*(4), 340–350.

Hasson-Ohayon, I., Kravetz, S., & Lysaker, P. H. (2017). The special challenges of psychotherapy with persons with psychosis: Intersubjective metacognitive model of agreement and shared meaning. *Clinical Psychology & Psychotherapy*, *24*(2), 428–440.

Heim, C., Newport, D. J., Mletzko, T., Miller, A. H., & Nemeroff, C. B. (2008). The link between childhood trauma and depression: Insights from HPA axis studies in humans. *Psychoneuroendocrinology*, *33*(6), 693–710.

Henriksen, M. G., & Parnas, J. (2018). Delusional mood. In G. Stanghellini et al. (Eds.), *The Oxford handbook of phenomenological psychopathology*. Oxford University Press.

Howes, O. D., & Kapur, S. (2009). The dopamine hypothesis of schizophrenia: Version III – the final common pathway. *Schizophrenia Bulletin*, *35*(3), 549–562.

Keefe, R. S., Arnold, M. C., Bayen, U. J., McEvoy, J. P., & Wilson, W. H. (2002). Source-monitoring deficits for self-generated stimuli in schizophrenia: Multinomial modeling of data from three sources. *Schizophrenia Research*, *57*(1), 51–67.

Kirkpatrick, B., & Miller, B. J. (2013). Inflammation and schizophrenia. *Schizophrenia Bulletin*, *39*(6), 1174–1179.

Lana, F., Marcos, S., Mollà, L., Vilar, A., Pérez, V., Romero, M., & Martí, J. (2015). Mentalization based group psychotherapy for psychosis: A pilot study to assess safety, acceptance and subjective efficacy. *International Journal of Psychology and Psychoanalysis*, *1*(007).

Laufer, M., & Laufer, M. (1995). *Adolescence and adolescent breakdown: A psychoanalytic view*. New Haven, CT: Yale University Press. Reprinted, London: Karnac.

Liotti, G., & Gumley, A. (2008). An attachment perspective on schizophrenia: The role of disorganized attachment, dissociation and mentalization. In A. Moskowitz, I. Schäfer, & M. J. Dorahy (Eds.), *Psychosis, trauma and dissociation: Emerging perspectives on severe psychopathology* (pp. 117–133). New York: Wiley-Blackwell.

Lucas, R. (2013). *The psychotic wavelength: A psychoanalytic perspective for psychiatry*. London: Routledge.

Luyten, P., van Houdenhove, B., Lemma, A., Target, M., & Fonagy, P. (2012). A mentalization-based approach to the understanding and treatment of functional somatic disorders. *Psychoanalytic Psychotherapy*, *26*(2), 121–140.

Lysaker, P. H., Dimaggio, G., Hamm, J. A., Leonhardt, B. L., Hochheiser, J., & Lysaker, J. T. (2018a). Disturbances in self-experience in schizophrenia: Metacognition and the development of an integrative recovery-oriented individual psychotherapy. *Psychopathology*, 1–8.

Lysaker, P. H., Hamm, J. A., Vohs, J., Kukla, M., Pattison, M. L., Leonhardt, B. L., & Lysaker, J. T. (2018b). Understanding the course of self-disorders and alterations in self-experience in schizophrenia: Implications from research on metacognition. *Current Psychiatry Reviews*, *14*(3), 160–170.

Peters, E., Ward, T., Jackson, M., Morgan, C., Charalambides, M., McGuire, P., . . . & Garety, P. A. (2016). Clinical, socio-demographic and psychological characteristics in individuals with persistent psychotic experiences with and without a "need for care". *World Psychiatry*, *15*(1), 41–52.

Piskulic, D., Liu, L., Cadenhead, K. S., Cannon, T. D., Cornblatt, B. A., McGlashan, T. H., . . . & Walker, E. F. (2016). Social cognition over time in individuals at clinical high risk for psychosis: Findings from the NAPLS-2 cohort. *Schizophrenia Research*, *171*(1–3), 176–181.

Postmes, L., Sno, H., Goedhart, S., Van Der Stel, J., Heering, H., & De Haan, L. (2014). Schizophrenia as a self-disorder due to perceptual incoherence. *Schizophrenia Research*, *152*(1), 41–50.

Quijada, Y., Kwapil, T. R., Tizón, J., Sheinbaum, T., & Barrantes-Vidal, N. (2015). Impact of attachment style on the 1-year outcome of persons with an at-risk mental state for psychosis. *Psychiatry Research*, *228*(3), 849–856.

Ramachandran, V. S., & Hirstein, W. (1998). The perception of phantom limbs. The DO Hebb lecture. *Brain: A Journal of Neurology*, *121*(9), 1603–1630.

Rossouw, T. I., & Fonagy, P. (2012). Mentalization-based treatment for self-harm in adolescents: A randomized controlled trial. *Journal of the American Academy of Child & Adolescent Psychiatry*, *51*(12), 1304–1313. e1303.

Sass, L. A., & Parnas, J. (2003). Schizophrenia, consciousness, and the self. *Schizophrenia Bulletin*, *29*(3), 427–444.

Sharp, C., & Fonagy, P. (2008). The parent's capacity to treat the child as a psychological agent: Constructs, measures and implications for developmental psychopathology. *Social Development*, *17*(3), 737–754.

Sharp, C., Ha, C., Carbone, C., Kim, S., Perry, K., Williams, L., & Fonagy, P. (2013). Hypermentalizing in adolescent inpatients: Treatment effects and association with borderline traits. *Journal of Personality Disorders*, *27*(1), 3–18.

Sheinbaum, T., Bedoya, E., Ros-Morente, A., Kwapil, T. R., & Barrantes-Vidal, N. (2013). Association between attachment prototypes and schizotypy dimensions in two independent non-clinical samples of Spanish and American young adults. *Psychiatry Research, 210*(2), 408–413.

Steiner, J. (2003). *Psychic retreats: Pathological organizations in psychotic, neurotic and borderline patients*. London: Routledge.

Steiner, J., & Harland, R. (2011). Experimenting with groups in a locked general psychiatry ward. *Psychoanalytic Psychotherapy, 25*(1), 16–27.

Stern, D. N. (1985). *The interpersonal world of the infant: A view from psychoanalysis and developmental psychology*. London: Karnac Books.

Strathearn, L. (2011). Maternal neglect: Oxytocin, dopamine and the neurobiology of attachment. *Journal of Neuroendocrinology, 23*(11), 1054–1065.

Target, M. (2007). Is our sexuality our own? A developmental model of sexuality based on early affect mirroring. *British Journal of Psychotherapy, 23*(4), 517–530.

Target, M. (2016). Mentalization within intensive analysis with a borderline patient. *British Journal of Psychotherapy, 32*(2), 202–214.

Tiwari, A., & Gonzalez, A. (2018). Biological alterations affecting risk of adult psychopathology following childhood trauma: A review of sex differences. *Clinical Psychology Review, 66*, 69–79.

Trotta, A., Di Forti, M., Mondelli, V., Dazzan, P., Pariante, C., David, A., . . . & Murray, R. M. (2013). Prevalence of bullying victimisation amongst first-episode psychosis patients and unaffected controls. *Schizophrenia Research, 150*(1), 169–175.

Tsakiris, M., Carpenter, L., James, D., & Fotopoulou, A. (2010). Hands only illusion: Multisensory integration elicits sense of ownership for body parts but not for non-corporeal objects. *Experimental Brain Research, 204*(3), 343–352.

Vanderwal, T., Hunyadi, E., Grupe, D. W., Connors, C. M., & Schultz, R. T. (2008). Self, mother and abstract other: An fMRI study of reflective social processing. *Neuroimage, 41*(4), 1437–1446.

Waters, F., Woodward, T., Allen, P., Aleman, A., & Sommer, I. (2010). Self-recognition deficits in schizophrenia patients with auditory hallucinations: A meta-analysis of the literature. *Schizophrenia Bulletin, 38*(4), 741–750.

Weijers, J., ten Kate, C., Eurelings-Bontekoe, E., Viechtbauer, W., Rampaart, R., Bateman, A., & Selten, J.-P. (2016). Mentalization-based treatment for psychotic disorder: Protocol of a randomized controlled trial. *BMC Psychiatry, 16*(1), 191.

Wynn, J. K., Sergi, M. J., Dawson, M. E., Schell, A. M., & Green, M. F. (2005). Sensorimotor gating, orienting and social perception in schizophrenia. *Schizophrenia Research, 73*(2–3), 319–325.

3

ADAPTING METACOGNITIVE REFLECTION AND INSIGHT THERAPY FOR EARLY PSYCHOSIS (MERIT-EP)

A focus on insight and recovery of the self

Bethany L. Leonhardt and Jenifer L. Vohs

Abstract: *There is now mounting evidence that intervening early in the course of psychosis (EP) is related to improved outcomes. However, attaining these positive outcomes requires addressing unique barriers to engaging an EP population. The challenges specific to engaging individuals with EP include two key factors: impaired insight and threats to personal recovery. An adapted version of Metacognitive Reflection and Insight Therapy (MERIT) has been created to address the unique barriers to engaging individuals with EP, referred to as MERIT-EP. The adaptation of MERIT-EP and case examples from a randomized clinical trial are presented and discussed.*

Introduction

In recent years, there has been a growing recognition of the need to intervene earlier in the experience of psychosis in order to mitigate some of the deleterious effects of experiencing prolonged psychosis (Mueser et al., 2015). Early psychosis (EP) refers to individuals within five years following an initial experience of psychosis. While this certainly can include a large age range, EP tends to refer to individuals in early adulthood and thus this chapter will focus on this age range. This early phase is a time in which individuals are often not only grappling with serious challenges, but also navigating young adulthood and attempting to understand what psychosis means in the context of their unique lives. Individuals with EP are particularly vulnerable to not recognizing their potential for recovery, which could increase the likelihood of experiencing prolonged dysfunction; efforts to intervene early and attend to the specific needs associated with EP are rapidly expanding (Dixon et al., 2015). Specifically, recovery-oriented treatment has been identified as central to intervention in EP (Browne et al., 2017; Dixon et al., 2015), with many models of care for EP emphasizing shared decision making and flexibility in the core tenets of specialized EP care, offering a range of services to facilitate each individual's unique recovery process (Mueser et al., 2015).

The growing international movement towards providing intervention early in the course of psychosis has led to EP specific programmes (Maio, Graham, Vaughan,

Haber, & Madonick, 2015; Neale & Kinnar, 2017). Individual clinics may differ slightly in structure and implementation, but largely these programmes consist of a team-based approach to provide a range of services to those with EP, including individual and group psychotherapy, family interventions, peer support, medications, and supported employment/education specialist services. These programmes have been shown to be effective in promoting personal recovery for individuals with EP as well as in decreasing the use of acute services by this population (Kane et al., 2015).

Particular challenges in early psychosis

Despite positive outcomes of the early intervention model of care for individuals with EP, there remain unique challenges to working with this population. One such challenge is engagement in services, as individuals with EP have unique characteristics that can make them particularly difficult to engage (Dixon, Holoshitz, & Nossel, 2016). Several factors are thought to be related to why an EP population is difficult to engage, including impaired insight, or awareness of illness, and the impact of receiving a serious diagnosis on personal recovery during early adulthood (Eisenstadt, Monteiro, Diniz, & Chaves, 2012; Myers, Bhatty, Broussard, & Compton, 2017; Windell, Norman, Lal, & Malla, 2015; Tait, Birchwood, & Trower, 2003). Such a diagnosis may make individuals with EP more likely to reject treatment outright as attending treatment confirms that they do suffer from a mental health condition (Doyle et al., 2014). We will examine each of these factors associated with impaired engagement in EP, and will then outline how an adapted version of Metacognitive Reflection and Insight Therapy (MERIT, Lysaker & Klion, 2017) referred to as MERIT-EP (Vohs et al., 2018) may address barriers to engagement and help individuals with EP move toward personal recovery.

Impaired insight in early psychosis

Impaired insight has long been identified as a potential barrier to recovery for individuals who experience serious mental illness, as it is linked to a range of poor outcomes (Kurtz, Olfson, & Rose, 2013; Vohs et al., 2015) and poorer engagement in treatment (Dixon et al., 2016; Lincoln, Lüllmann, & Rief, 2007). Recent work has elaborated on what it means to have poor insight, proposing an integrated model of insight that describes the concept as more than acceptance of a diagnosis, or an "illness label". Instead it has been conceptualized as a failure to integrate information about one's own life and psychiatric challenges into a consensually valid account (Vohs, George, Leonhardt, & Lysaker, 2016). As Vohs and colleagues (2016) have described, impaired insight is not a lack of awareness about reality, as individuals with impaired insight can still possess awareness in other domains of life. Instead, individuals with impaired insight have failed to form a nuanced, integrated understanding of the complex circumstances that led to their experience of psychiatric difficulty and to then make decisions about how to respond to such difficulties (Lysaker, Clements, Placak Hallberg, Knipschure, Wright, 2002; Lysaker et al., 2018).

The idea that individuals with EP are particularly susceptible to difficulty in integrating new and often distressing experiences into their account of their unique lives is consistent with this contemporary, integrated model of insight (Leonhardt et al., 2017; Leonhardt, Ratliff, & Vohs, 2018). The description of the integrated model of insight put forth by Vohs and colleagues (2016) suggests that poor insight likely reflects a number of contributing factors, including: anomalous experiences (e.g. symptoms) which are difficult to make sense of; abnormalities in brain function and hence neurocognitive deficits, which limit the ability to access and process the information necessary to compose insight; disturbed meta-cognition (higher order cognitive processes, such as self and other reflectivity, decentration and mastery, all of which are foundational in the coherent integration of experience); social cognitive deficits, which can interfere with the integration of social information; and stigma which may render integration painful and destructive (Vohs et al., 2016). Such a model not only identifies many potential pathways to insight but also suggests that, like all forms of human meaning making, insight involves complex processes, which may be facilitated or hampered by a range of factors.

Further, the overlap between insight and self-stigma, or internalized negative beliefs about mental illness, is essential to consider in models of insight; as work in this area has demonstrated that insight may be less about awareness and more about an attitude toward mental illness (Hasson-Ohayon, 2018). This has been found to be particularly true with adolescent populations (Hasson-Ohayon, 2018), and has important considerations for those with EP, as psychosis typically begins during life stages in which identity is being formed and internalized stigma can certainly impact the view of the self. Thus, a young adult experiencing psychosis may deny having a mental illness as a way to reject a potentially stigmatizing and damaging label.

Impaired insight can be a barrier to recovery throughout the course of psychosis, but impaired insight is often greater for those in the early phase (Vohs et al., 2015). When EP populations have been studied specifically, it has been shown that poor insight in EP is linked with poorer treatment engagement (Compton, 2005; Doyle et al., 2014) and poorer outcomes (Drake et al., 2007). Moreover, studies have shown poor insight to be associated with a number of other factors thought to impede personal recovery, such as recovery style (Thompson, McGorry, & Harrigan, 2003; Windell et al., 2015), poorer social relationships (Dębowska, Grazwa, & Kucharska-Pietura, 1998; Lysaker et al., 2013) and difficulty in functioning in important life roles, such as work (Erickson, Jaafari, & Lysaker, 2011).

Making sense of the complexity of psychotic experiences and their sequelae is difficult at any life stage, but may be particularly challenging during a first episode, which often occurs as an individual is still forming their identity. This challenge heightens the likelihood that individuals with EP will struggle to form a meaningful account of their experience of psychosis and integrate it into their burgeoning sense of self as they transition into adulthood. Interventions for impaired insight will fall short when drawn from a medical model of insight, which refers to insight as inability to accept a particular fact, to see an experience as mental illness, or to see the need for medication (Lysaker et al., 2018). This is not to say that some individuals do not find relief and utility in a diagnosis or benefit from medication, but rather the issue with a medicalized view of insight is that it involves an expert trying to convince the individual of an explanation of their experience without incorporating the individual's point of view. This model tends to privilege the provider's point of view regarding what an experience is (i.e. mental illness) over that of the person experiencing it (i.e. people are trying to harm me). Clearly, interventions carried out in this manner are also at risk of undermining an individual's path toward personal recovery. Thus, any interventions aimed at improving insight in EP must account for a sense of personal recovery, and assist persons to make sense of confusing or frightening experiences, and navigate the stigma that could potentially derail attempts to live a personally fulfilling life (Hasson-Ohayon, 2018; Lysaker et al., 2018).

Personal recovery in early psychosis

Personal recovery has many definitions in the literature, but most identify five common factors that contribute to a sense of personal recovery: connectedness, identity as more than someone with a mental health condition, hope, meaning making, and a sense of empowerment to make decisions about one's own life (Connell, Schweitzer, & King, 2015; Leonhardt et al., 2017). Recovery is not something that can be given to an individual, as individuals must be active agents in their recovery. Similar to individuals with prolonged psychosis, recovery has been shown to be possible for a majority of individuals with EP, and individuals with EP also describe that recovery is multi-faceted and about more than just symptom remission (Windell, Norma, & Malla, 2012). While many individuals who experience serious mental health conditions struggle to gain and maintain a sense of recovery, individuals with EP seem to be in a particularly vulnerable phase of life in terms of personal recovery for two key reasons; impact upon identity during a developmental phase in life and impact upon social connections.

Regarding identity, the onset of psychosis can have deleterious effects upon one's sense of identity during early adulthood. Early adulthood is a fraught time for most people, regardless of mental health status, as young people work to figure out different aspects of their identities and make plans for the next phase of life. The frightening and often disorientating experiences that can accompany an initial psychotic break often impact how individuals see themselves (O'Keeffe et al., 2018). For example, some individuals have questioned whether it is possible for them to achieve their dreams following the disruption of psychosis. Additionally, many young people with EP struggle to make sense of the overwhelming and confusing experiences associated with the onset of psychosis, a step that seems essential to integrating the experience of psychosis into a complex view of oneself and resisting stigmatizing views. A qualitative study, with individuals with EP, showed that having made a meaningful interpretation of psychosis, a stronger sense of self, and strengthened relationships with others were essential factors in improving personal recovery (Connell et al., 2015). Dynamics within familial relationships and a desire to establish individuation can also be impacted in EP. Many individuals with EP, especially those at a younger age when experiencing the onset of psychosis, still live at home, or move back in with their parents after experiencing a psychotic break, which can add stress to familial relationships (Lal et al., 2019).

Social relationships are also deleteriously impacted with the onset of psychosis, which can have particularly devastating effects during a particularly social time in life. Some individuals lose their friends, and are left feeling socially isolated or different from their peers, questioning if they will be able to find a romantic partner or a friend to spend time with (Gajwani, Larkin, & Jackson, 2018). Social withdrawal and a loss of relationships directly affect the sense of connectedness, a key aspect of personal recovery (Connell et al., 2015). Loss of social relationships and perceptions of social isolation are related to increased hopelessness and risk for suicide attempts in EP, and perhaps unsurprisingly, increased social connection is related to better rates of recovery (Connell et al., 2015; Gajwani et al., 2018; Jordan et al., 2018).

Adapting MERIT for EP

Thus far, we have made the case that both the integrated model of impaired insight and personal recovery (connectedness, hope, identity, meaning making, and empowerment) are vital considerations for engaging individuals with EP. Moreover, both involve the ability to make sense of one's experiences and integrate this information into a nuanced, flexible account; such acts require metacognitive capacity and hence suggest that metacognition is a vital treatment target. Metacognition refers to a range of mental activities, from discrete to synthetic, in which individuals develop an increasingly nuanced and complex understanding of self and others, and use that understanding to respond to the psychosocial challenges that they face (Semerari et al., 2003). Lysaker and Klion (2017) have formalized a guidebook for targeting metacognition in psychotherapy, referred to as Metacognitive Reflection and Insight Therapy (MERIT), which is discussed earlier in the introduction chapter to this volume (Chapter 1). MERIT was adapted by Vohs and colleagues (2018) for an EP population to specifically target insight in EP in the Midwestern United States. The adapted version of MERIT, MERIT-EP, was developed from a small randomized clinical trial in which 20 individuals with EP were randomized to receive either MERIT-EP or treatment as usual (TAU).

Findings from a randomized controlled trial of MERIT-EP

All procedures were reviewed and approved by the Institutional Review Board of Indiana University. All participants consented to the study procedures before being enrolled in the study. To protect confidentiality, we have systematically altered details of cases that are presented. Individuals enrolled in an early psychosis clinic as part of a larger community mental health centre were screened if they were within five years of the onset of a primary psychotic illness, between the ages of 18–35, and did not have a primary substance use disorder. They were included as participants only if they demonstrated impaired insight, measured by two widely accepted measures of insight in psychosis, the PANSS (Kay, Fiszbein, & Opler, 1987) insight item and the SUMD (Amador et al., 1993). Ten participants were randomized to receive MERIT-EP and ten received TAU. Sessions were held in an early psychosis outpatient clinic, were conducted weekly, and were 45–50 minutes long.

MERIT-EP was found to be both feasible and acceptable, as the majority of participants completed MERIT-EP delivered as part of routine clinic practice. Of the ten randomized to MERIT-EP, two individuals were asked to leave the study due to continual boundary violations with their therapist, including inappropriate sexual behavior that did not improve after several attempts to address it in sessions. One other individual randomized to MERIT-EP had an extended break in the course of his therapy, but did eventually complete all 24 sessions. Thus, even without counting the individual who completed with a break, the study suggests a 70% acceptance rate. All individuals in the TAU group completed the study.

Regarding the primary outcome of insight, the PANSS insight item, analysis demonstrated a positive interaction between time and treatment status $(F(1,16) = 4.32, p = .05, p\eta2 = .2)$, supporting the superiority of MERIT-EP over TAU. The treatment interaction reflects a greater than 1-point difference for the PANSS insight item in the treatment group only, hence representing a clinically significant reduction from an average of moderately impaired insight to only minimally impaired insight. The other insight measure used, the SUMD, yielded consistent findings, with a non-statistically significant trend for a positive interaction between treatment group and time $(F(1,16) = 3.2, p = .09, p\eta2 = .18)$. These data provide preliminary evidence supporting the use of MERIT-EP to improve insight in young individuals.

MERIT-EP adaptations

As an adaptation of MERIT, MERIT-EP not only included the eight elements of MERIT, but also required three key modifications for an EP population. First, MERIT-EP included a focus on exploring narratives around the onset of illness to address poor insight in EP and exploring the impact that stigma about mental illness may have had on sense of self and identity. Second, given the difficulty of engaging this population, there was additional focus on building the therapeutic alliance. Finally, there were additional efforts made to promote capacity to understand the perspectives of others, given that the metacognitive profile of EP shows that this ability is significantly impacted when compared to individuals with prolonged psychosis (Vohs et al., 2015). We will now describe these adaptations further with examples from the study.

Focus on narratives around onset of illness

As noted above, all participants enrolled in the study met criteria for impaired insight, a common and important issue in EP, as participants could not integrate their experiences of psychosis into their understanding of their own lives, and often denied, or failed to recognize the consequences of some of their experiences. Participants varied in their desire to discuss the onset of psychosis. Importantly, MERIT-EP stays within the spirit of MERIT and is a non-directive approach in which the individual chooses the topics of conversation. However, if onset of illness was never discussed in the larger conversation about participants and their lives, therapists would notice this and ask the participant why this topic or period of time was not part of the conversation. This intervention was offered not to force participants to talk about a topic they were unwilling to, but to promote reflectivity around a participant's reluctance to think about this part of life. Often, participants would describe discomfort around remembering this part of their lives, for fear these experiences would emerge again. Other reasons included fear that the therapist would judge the participant as "crazy" or not in touch with reality, or would label the participant with a mental health diagnosis. A final theme that often emerged was a desire on the participant's part to view their psychosis as a one-time occurrence, and not something that they continued to experience.

Central to all of these reasons offered by participants, for why reflecting on these experiences with another person was difficult, seemed to be how these experiences impact one's sense of identity, including stigmatizing beliefs about mental illness. What does it mean to have experienced psychosis? Does this put me in a particular category of someone who has a mental health diagnosis? Will these experiences come back if I think about them? What does this mean for my personal goals (for example graduating from college, working in a particular field, having a family)? Therapists offered interventions to explore these topics and ideas around the participant's unique identity as more than someone who experienced psychosis, but also as a talented musician, an avid film enthusiast, and a son. Therapists explored themes of stigma with participants, including psychosis occurring as part of a continuum of human experience rather than an experience that somehow marked them as "ill" or "incompetent". This conversation was often quite powerful and was a contrast to other etiological explanations participants had been given about psychosis. Participants often viewed psychotic experiences as a sign of otherness, and thought that symptoms were a sign that they were damaged. The alternative continuum model offered participants hope and helped them to see psychosis as a human reaction, increasing their sense of agency and potential to overcome such experiences.

When narratives around the onset of illness were discussed, therapists offered interventions to promote reflectivity about the historical events surrounding these experiences and personal meaning making of these experiences. Specifically, therapists did not focus on symptoms, unless they emerged as something significant to the participant. Instead, therapists encouraged participants to reflect on the circumstances occurring in their lives and to integrate psychotic experiences into their understandings of their own unique lives. For example, one participant described feeling increasingly paranoid and uncomfortable around other people during the last year of high school, and attributed this to a secret group targeting and torturing him. The therapist offered interventions to explore the circumstances in his life around this time as well as his experience of feeling persecuted by others and eventually discovered that during high school the participant's family member had been shot. The participant and therapist explored his grief and distrust that came from losing a loved one in a violent manner and reflected on how this impacted the participant's view of himself and others. Over time, the participant was able to integrate this autobiographical detail, and his internal experience of it, into his understanding of feeling distrustful of the world.

In another example, a participant was describing a recent change in herself, noting that she did not want to go out and be social in the way that she had done before. The therapist inquired about this change, asking the participant to reflect on when this change had occurred and what the narrative events were around the time of this change. The participant identified coming to treatment as one of the events that led her to not want to be as social, and the therapist offered interventions to explore how involvement in mental health treatment and a change in social habits were related. They explored together themes of stigma, including how the participant's view of herself had changed after experiencing psychosis, as well as how she thought she would be perceived by others. The participant also reflected on aspects of her psychosis that made her not want to be around people, as she noted she often felt "paranoid" and had a hard time figuring out the intentions of other people.

Focus on building the therapeutic relationship

Given the difficulty of engaging individuals with EP in services (Dixon et al., 2016), MERIT-EP included a particular focus on building the therapeutic relationship. Like any approach to psychotherapy, therapeutic alliance is a key element of MERIT. Thus, attending to the therapeutic relationship was not an addition for MERIT-EP, but instead there were specific considerations for engaging young individuals in early phases of illness. These included; attending to and discussing stigma associated with mental health labels, attending to the complexities of identity in early adulthood and the impact of experiencing psychosis during this time, and engaging in creative methods to make participants more comfortable with engaging in therapy. For example, one participant described discomfort with the standard therapy set up (sitting in chairs and talking) and through inquiry about other ways the participant interacted with others, the therapist learned that the participant was an avid chess player and spent time playing chess with her family. The participant and therapist agreed to have their conversations over a chess board, and the participant taught the therapist how to play. The rest of the sessions were then conducted during games of chess. Other examples of creative methods included watching music videos a participant was interested in and structuring conversations around the music, or engaging a participant around his interest in fantasy sports leagues.

In each of these examples, it seemed important for the therapist to interact with or be curious about some part of the participant's life outside of illness identity. Many times, these creative attempts to engage participants seemed to disrupt the idea that the therapist was "in charge" and often participants were active in teaching therapists about these activities. MERIT provides a flexible framework and one that encourages therapist creativity; thus these examples are not outside of the normal MERIT framework. However, the types of creative approaches employed for engaging young people, at the early stages of psychosis, may need to pay particular attention to issues of power and demonstrate willingness on the part of the therapist to listen and be collaborative rather than the authority.

Addressing deficits with understanding the minds of others

Related to forming relationships with others, MERIT-EP included an adaptation to specifically address the impairments that individuals with EP have in understanding the internal states of others and being able to make guesses about the intentions and desires of other people. Vohs and colleagues (2015) found that individuals with EP had similar metacognitive profiles to individuals with more prolonged psychosis, which include significant deficits, when compared to individuals with other mental health diagnoses, on self-reflectivity, understanding the minds of others, decentration, defined as seeing the world outside of oneself, and mastery, or the ability to use knowledge of self and others to respond to psychological problems. Individuals with EP scored similarly to individuals with prolonged psychosis on all four domains of metacognition, but did show significant deficits in understanding the minds of others relative to those with prolonged psychosis. These deficits would impact many of the factors discussed above, including forming a therapeutic alliance and insight.

To address deficits in understanding of others, therapists had to continually assess the participants' levels of awareness of the mind of the other and offer interventions appropriate to the participants' ability. Because participants tended to experience greater difficulty on this ability than other populations, therapists had to present basic ideas about other people having their own mental activities, and attempting to help participants differentiate between the mental activities of others. Often, therapists used themselves as examples, talking about when their thoughts differed from the participants' thoughts or outlining the mental activity in their minds as the session unfolded. For example, one therapist often shared with a participant when something the participant was saying was making the therapist have a particular memory.

Therapists also addressed low understanding of the mind of others by offering interventions to stimulate participants to think about the internal states of significant others in their lives. It was not uncommon for this to be a new idea to participants, as many of them had not considered the internal states of others in their lives. It may be that there is a developmental aspect to this capacity, as it seems congruent with normal development as an adult to realize that one's own parents (or other perceived authority figures) have their own unique lives that impact their desires, reactions, behaviors, and so on. For example, a therapist asked the participant what he thought a narrative event (moving to a new city) was like for his mother. The participant struggled to form ideas about what moving was like for his mother and could only reflect on the experience from his own point of view. The therapist discussed her own experiences with moving and was able to scaffold some ideas about what this experience may have been like for his mother. The participant was then able to join the therapist in thinking about his mother in a more complex way.

Conclusions

As increasing evidence builds that intervening early in the course of psychosis is related to improved outcomes, there is a need to develop and adapt treatments to address the unique challenges of working with individuals with EP. Such individuals represent a unique population from those with a more prolonged psychosis as they are, by definition, earlier in their phase of psychosis and also are often at a different developmental stage in life. This can pose difficulties in engaging individuals with EP in treatment, particularly as individuals with EP often resist treatment, since engagement in treatment implies that their experience of psychosis is in fact serious and may not be a singular event. This is an understandable desire, that young people would be reluctant to accept mental health labels and strive to believe that psychosis may never return and interrupt their lives again – which is certainly possible and happens in a number of cases. However, for some individuals with EP, psychosis does return, and the individuals in this situation often have poor insight and face particular barriers to establishing personal recovery due to threats to self-identity that are posed by experiencing the onset of a serious mental illness during a time of individuation and burgeoning autonomy; as well as difficulties with integrating experiences of psychosis into their understandings of themselves and their unique lives.

Any treatment that is offered to individuals with EP must address these barriers and assist persons to make meaning of confusing and emotionally charged experiences, in a way that resists stigmatizing accounts of mental illness, promotes a return to a fulfilling life, and assists them in understanding and connecting in adaptive and meaningful ways with others. As we have outlined above, MERIT-EP has been adapted for individuals with EP to specifically address these key barriers to engagement as well as to assist persons with EP to move toward personal recovery in the face of the onset of a serious mental illness. The flexibility of MERIT as an intervention, and the specific adaptations for early psychosis, offer a potentially powerful way for EP clinics to effectively and meaningfully engage individuals and help them move toward personal recovery.

References

Amador, X. F., Strauss, D. H., Yale, S. A., Flaum, M. M., Endicott, J., & Gorman, J. M. (1993). Assessment of insight in psychosis. *American Journal of Psychiatry, 150*(6), 873–879.

Browne, J., Penn, D. L., Meyer-Kalos, P. S., Mueser, K. T., Estroff, S. E., Brunette, M. F., . . . & Kane, J. M. (2017). Psychological well-being and mental health recovery in the NIMH RAISE early treatment program. *Schizophrenia Research, 185,* 167–172.

Compton, M. (2005). Barriers to initial outpatient treatment engagement following first hospitalization for a first episode of nonaffective psychosis: A descriptive case series. *Journal of Psychiatric Practice, 11*(1), 62–69.

Connell, M., Schweitzer, R., & King, R. (2015). Recovery from first episode psychosis and recovering self: A qualitative study. *Journal of Psychiatric Rehabilitation, 38*(4), 359–364.

Dębowska, G., Grazwa, A., & Kucharska-Pietura, K. (1998). Insight in paranoid schizophrenia—Its relationship to psychopathology and premorbid adjustment. *Comprehensive Psychiatry, 39*(5), 255–260.

Dixon, L. B., Goldman, H. H., Bennett, M. E., Wang, Y., McNamara, K. A., Mendon, S. J., . . . & Essock, S. M. (2015). Implementing coordinated specialty care for early psychosis: The RAISE Connection Program. *Psychiatric Services, 66*(7), 691–698.

Dixon, L. B., Holoshitz, Y., & Nossel, I. (2016). Treatment engagement of individuals experiencing mental illness: Review and update. *World Psychiatry, 15*(1), 13–20.

Doyle, R., Turner, N., Fanning, F., Brennan, D., Renwick, L., Lawlor, E., & Clarke, M. (2014). First-episode psychosis and disengagement from treatment: A systematic review. *Psychiatric Services, 65,* 603–611. https://doi.org/10.1176/appi.ps.201200570.

Drake, R. J., Dunn, G., Tarrier, N., Bentall, R. P., Haddock, G., & Lewis, S. W. (2007). Insight as a predictor of the outcome of first-episode nonaffective psychosis in a prospective cohort study in England. *The Journal of Clinical Psychiatry, 68*(1), 81–86.

Eisenstadt, P., Monteiro, V. B., Diniz, M. J., & Chaves, A. C. (2012). Experience of recovery from a first episode psychosis. *Early Intervention in Psychiatry, 6*(4), 476–480. https://doi.org/10.1111/j.1751-7893.2012.00353.x.

Erickson, M. A., Jaafari, N., & Lysaker, P. H. (2011). Insight and negative symptoms as predictors of functioning in a work setting in patients with schizophrenia. *Psychiatry Research, 189,* 161–165.

Gajwani, R., Larkin, M., & Jackson, C. (2018). "What is the point of life?": An interpretive phenomenological analysis of suicide in young men with first episode psychosis. *Early Intervention in Psychiatry, 12*(6), 1120–1127. https://doi.org/10.1111/eip.12425.

Hasson-Ohayon, I. (2018). Overlap and distinction between measures of insight and self stigma. *Psychiatry Research, 266,* 47–64.

Jordan, G., MacDonald, K., Pope, M. A., Schorr, E., Malla, A. K., & Iver, S. N. (2018). Positive changes experienced after a first episode of psychosis: A systematic review. *Psychiatric Services, 69*(1), 84–89. https://doi.org/10.1176/appi.ps.201600586.

Kane, J., Robinson, D., Schooler, N., Mueser, K., Penn, D. L., & Rosenheck, R. A. (2015). Comprehensive versus usual community care for first episode psychosis: 2 year outcomes form NIMH RAISE early treatment program. *The American Journal of Psychiatry, 173*(4), 362–372.

Kay, S. R., Fiszbein, A., & Opler, L. A. (1987). The positive and negative syndrome scale (PANSS) for schizophrenia, *Schizophrenia Bulletin, 13*(2), 261–276.

Kurtz, M. M., Olfson, R. H., & Rose, J. (2013). Self-efficacy and functional status in schizophrenia: Relationship to insight, cognition and negative symptoms. *Schizophrenia Research*, *145*(1–3), 69–74.

Lal, S., Malla, A., Marandola, G., Theriault, J., Tibbo, P., Manchanda, R., . . . & Banks, N. (2019). "Worried about relapse": Family members' experiences and perspectives of relapse in first episode psychosis. *Early Intervention in Psychiatry*, *13*(1), 24–29.

Leonhardt, B. L., Huling, K., Hamm, J. A., Roe, D., Hasson-Ohayon, I., McLeod, H., & Lysaker, P. H. (2017). Recovery and serious mental illness: A review of current clinical and research paradigms and future directions. *Expert Review of Neurotherapeutics*, *17*(11), 1117–1130.

Leonhardt, B. L., Ratliff, K. L., & Vohs, J. L. (2018). Recovery in first episode psychosis: A case study of metacognitive reflection and insight therapy (MERIT). *American Journal of Psychotherapy*, *71*(4), 128–134.

Lincoln, T. M., Lüllmann, E., & Rief, W. (2007). Correlates and long-term consequences of poor insight in patients with schizophrenia. A systematic review. *Schizophrenia Bulletin*, *33*(6), 1324–1342. https://doi.org/10.1093/schbul/sbm002.

Lysaker, P. H., Clements, C. A., Placak Hallberg, C., Knipschure, S. J., & Wright, D. E. (2002). Insight and personal narratives of illness in schizophrenia. *Psychiatry*, *65*, 197–206.

Lysaker, P. H., & Klion, R. E. (2017). *Recovery, meaning- making, and severe mental illness: A comprehensive guide to metacognitive reflection and insight therapy* (1st ed.). New York, NY: Routledge. https://doi.org/10.4324/9781315447001.

Lysaker, P. H., Hamm, J. A., Vohs, J., Kukla, M., Pattison, M., Leonhardt, B. L., & Lysaker, J. T. (2018). Understanding the course of self-disorders and alterations in self experience in schizophrenia: Implications from research on metacognition. *Current Psychiatry Reviews*, *14*(3), 160–170.

Lysaker, P. H., Vohs, J., Hillis, J. D., Kukla, M., Popolo, R., Salvatore, G., & Dimaggio, G. (2013). Poor insight into schizophrenia: Contributing factors, consequences and emerging treatment approaches. *Expert Review of Neurotherapeutics*, *13*(7), 785–793.

Maio, M., Graham, P., Vaughan, D., Haber, L., & Madonick, S. (2015). Review of international psychosis programmes and a model to overcome unique challenges to the treatment of early psychosis in the United States. *Early Intervention in Psychiatry*, *9*, 1–11.

Mueser, K. T., Penn, D. L., Addington, J., Brunette, M. F., Gingerich, S., Glynn, S. M., . . . & Kane, J. M. (2015). The NAVIGATE program for first episode psychosis: Rationale, overview, and description of psychosocial components. *Psychiatric Services*, *66*(7), 680–690.

Myers, N., Bhatty, S., Broussard, B., & Compton, M. T. (2017). Clinical correlates of initial treatment disengagement in first-episode psychosis. *Clinical Schizophrenia & Related Psychoses*, *11*(2), 95–102. https://doi.org/10.3371/CSRP.MYBH.103114.

Neale, A., & Kinnar, D. (2017). Early intervention in psychosis services. *British Journal of General Practice*, *67*(661), 370–371. https://doi.org/10.3399/bjgp17X692069.

O'Keeffe, D., Sheridan, A., Kelly, A., Doyle, R., Madigan, K., Lawlor, E., & Clarke, M. (2018). Recovery in the real world: Service user experiences of mental health service use and recommendations for change 20 years on from a first episode psychosis. *Administrative Policy of Mental Health*, *45*(4), 635–648. https://doi.org/10.1007/s10488-018-0851-4.

Semerari, A., Carcione, A., Dimaggio, G., Falcone, M., Nicolò, G., Procacci, M., & Alleva, G. (2003). How to evaluate metacognitive functioning in psychotherapy? The metacognition assessment scale and its applications. *Clinical Psychology & Psychotherapy, 10*(4), 238–261.

Tait, L., Birchwood, M., & Trower, P. (2003). Predicting engagement with services for psychosis: Insight, symptoms and recovery style. *British Journal of Psychiatry, 182,* 123–128.

Thompson, K., McGorry, P. D., & Harrigan, S. M. (2003). Recovery style and outcome in first-episode psychosis. *Schizophrenia Research, 62*(1–2), 31–36. https://doi.org/10.1016/S0920-9964(02)00428-0.

Vohs, J. L., George, S., Leonhardt, B. L., & Lysaker, P. H. (2016). Impairments in insight and reflectivity in schizophrenia: Correlates, consequences and developing treatment approaches. *Expert Review of Neurotherapeutics, 22,* 1–12.

Vohs, J. L., Leonhardt, B. L., James, A. V., Francis, M. M., Breier, A., Mehdiyoun, N., . . . & Lysaker, P. H. (2018). Metacognitive reflection and insight therapy for early psychosis: A preliminary study of a novel integrative psychotherapy. *Schizophrenia Research, 195,* 428–433. https://doi.org/10.1016/j.schres.2017.10.041.

Vohs, J. L., Lysaker, P. H., Liffick, E., Francis, M. M., Leonhardt, B. L., James, A., . . . & Breier, A. (2015). Metacognitive capacity as a predictor of insight in first-episode psychosis. *Journal of Nervous and Mental Disease, 203,* 372–378.

Windell, D. L., Norman, R., Lal, S., & Malla, A. (2015). Subjective experiences of illness recovery in individuals treated for first-episode psychosis. *Social Psychiatry and Psychiatric Epidemiology, 50*(7), 1069–1077. https://doi.org/10.1007/s00127-014-1006-x.

Windell, D. L., Norman, R., & Malla, A. K. (2012). The personal meaning of recovery among individuals treated for a first episode of psychosis. *Psychiatric Services, 63*(6), 548–553. https://doi.org/10.1176/appi.ps.201100424.

4

THE PROCESS OF RECOVERY OF SENSE OF SELF IN THE FACE OF PERSECUTORY DELUSIONS AND HOSTILITY

Giampaolo Salvatore, Paolo Ottavi, Raffaele Popolo and Giancarlo Dimaggio

Abstract: *People with psychosis who hold a persecutory delusion (PD) may think that others are focusing their attention on them, with malevolent intentions and plots. Such beliefs may result in significant suffering and social life disruption. The most well-known intervention for PDs is cognitive behavioural therapy, in which the main goals are to reduce stigma, help clients question their delusional attributions and reduce sustaining factors such as repetitive thinking. The merits of these approaches notwithstanding, in many cases clients may end treatment with significant residual symptoms. This has stimulated clinical research towards the development of treatments focused on different variables: a) helping clients understand how delusional perceptions are connected to their sense of self, and b) promoting a richer sense of personal identity as embedded in their unique self-narratives.*

Metacognitive Interpersonal Therapy (MIT) adapted for psychosis is one such therapy. In the last few years MIT has been subject to initial empirical validation with promising results. In this chapter, we describe the stages of treatment for a young man, at the onset of persecutory type of delusional disorder treated with MIT. According to MIT, PDs may be correlated with: 1) an experience of the self as ontologically vulnerable, a sense of being weak and inferior to others; 2) impaired metacognition, namely the ability – characterised by variable levels of complexity, to understand one's and others' mind(s).

We will show how MIT helped the client to improve their metacognitive abilities and access healthy parts of themself, in order to consider the persecutory ideas as an expression of his feeling of vulnerability, and to adopt a critical distance from that self-perception and from the perception of others' intentions as malevolent.

Introduction

People who hold a persecutory delusion may think that others are focusing their attention on them with malevolent intentions and plots. Such beliefs may result in significant suffering and disruption of their social life. Persecutory delusions (PDs) are common in psychosis (APA, 2013), and many people who experience

PDs do not respond well to either pharmacological or psychological treatments (Freeman et al., 2016; Salvatore, Buonocore, Ottavi, Popolo, & Dimaggio, 2018). Therefore, more effective forms of psychological treatment need to be developed. The most well-known intervention for PDs is cognitive behavioural therapy (CBT) (Freeman, Freeman, & Garety, 2008). In CBT the main therapeutic goals are to reduce stigma and to help clients to question delusional attributions. Third-wave CBT focuses on other PD sustaining factors, such as repetitive thinking, or intolerance of uncertainty (Startup et al., 2016) and cognitive biases (for example, "jumping to conclusions" Chadwick, 2008).

The merit of these approaches notwithstanding, many people with psychosis do not respond positively and end treatment with significant residual symptoms; interventions that focus on causal factors of delusions are considered a promising approach to improving therapeutic interventions (Mehl, Werner, & Lincoln, 2015). There is therefore room to improve the effectiveness of psychotherapy for PDs by helping clients understand the causal factors underlying their delusional ideas; namely, how these are connected to their sense of self. Moreover, psychotherapy might actually promote recovery by helping people with psychosis develop a richer sense of personal identity represented in their unique personal narratives (France & Uhlin, 2006; Dimaggio & Lysaker, 2010).

This perspective is grounded in two core ideas: first, delusions have meaning to the individual experiencing them. We have previously proposed (Salvatore et al., 2012a) that the onset of PDs may be correlated with an experience of the self as *ontologically vulnerable*. With *ontologically*, we refer to a pervasive experience of self – not concerning contingent experiences or contexts. This experience of self as vulnerable involves a sense of being weak and inferior to others. Individuals are not necessarily aware of their underlying vulnerability, which might be experienced in the form of anxiety, physical weakness or a vague sense of threat.

Second, PD involves the presence of impaired metacognition (Semerari, Carcione, Dimaggio, Nicolò, & Procacci, 2007). This concept refers to a spectrum of mental activities ranging from discrete acts in which individuals recognise specific thoughts and feelings to more sophisticated acts in which an array of intentions, thoughts, feelings and links between events are combined into larger and more complex representations. Metacognition includes "mastery", namely the ability to use metacognitive knowledge to solve the psychologically or emotionally challenging events and social problems occurring in daily life (Semerari et al., 2003, 2007; Dimaggio & Lysaker, 2010). In the case of PDs, clients may not understand that, for example, in certain situations, or interpersonal exchanges, they automatically perceive themselves as being vulnerable or inadequate, and others as intending to subjugate them. They often are not able to understand that their negative and crystallised attributions and perceptions do not necessarily correspond to reality. That is, they may lack the metacognitive capacity named "differentiation". Finally, they display low mastery; for example, they do not know how to respond to their PD, or they tend to respond dysfunctionally, for example resorting to fight/flight behaviours (Salvatore et al., 2018).

Therapy needs therefore to help clients to improve their metacognitive abilities, in order to understand persecutory ideas as an expression of feelings of vulnerability, and to adopt a critical distance from that self-perception. This is the aim of Metacognitive Interpersonal Therapy (MIT). MIT was first developed to offer support for a wide range of personality disorders, including borderline personality disorder (Dimaggio, Semerari, Carcione, Nicolò, & Procacci, 2007). It was subsequently manualised for personality disorders with aspects of emotional inhibition (e.g, avoidant personality; Dimaggio, Montano, Popolo, & Salvatore, 2015). In the last few years, MIT has been subject to initial empirical validation with promising results. It has demonstrated effectiveness in a single case series of clients with personality disorders (Dimaggio et al., 2017) and results have been replicated in a multiple-baseline single case series (see Gordon-King, Schweitzer, & Dimaggio, 2018). Moreover, Group Metacognitive Interpersonal Therapy (MIT-G) (Popolo & Dimaggio, 2016), devised in order to increase the applicability of the intervention for public mental health facilities as well as its cost-effectiveness, has demonstrated effectiveness through a pilot randomised clinical trial aimed to address its feasibility, acceptability and clinical significance (Popolo et al., 2018a). Another study replicated significant effectiveness in reducing symptoms and psychological suffering, and in improving metacognition and social functioning in 17 young adult outpatient clients with personality disorders (Popolo et al., 2018b) and in clients with borderline personality disorder and emotion dysregulation (Inchausti et al., 2020).

In this chapter, we describe the stages of treatment of John, a young man at the onset of a persecutory type of delusional disorder, treated with MIT adapted for psychosis (Salvatore et al., 2009; Salvatore et al., 2012b; Salvatore et al., 2018). The client described is a single person, and he has agreed by free and provided informed consent regarding the inclusion of his experience in this chapter. John is a pseudonym. No literal translation from Italian has occurred in the illustrative quotes offered later, pursuing the goal to keep the true affective meaning of John's frequent idiomatic expressions.

MIT adapted for psychosis aims to progressively foster metacognition, until clients are able to understand what kind of interpersonal events, or ideas about interpersonal interactions, trigger their PDs and what such delusions mean in their personal experience. After describing MIT's basic principles, we will present this man's experience in more detail, and then show how the treatment was conducted.

MIT basic principles

The main goal of MIT is to progressively promote metacognition. In particular MIT aims to foster the client's awareness of causes of emotional suffering and of how maladaptive interpersonal schemas – stereotyped ways of constructing the meaning of social relationship – drive dysfunctional social behaviour. MIT has its roots in cognitive behavioural therapy (CBT; Beck, 1976; Ellis, 1962), in which it maintains a focus on automatic thoughts and maladaptive schemas. MIT expands the concept of the schema, through incorporating a representation of others, and one's own unmet desires. Moreover, MIT uses CBT techniques for treating symptoms such as panic. Likewise, MIT incorporates techniques from Metacognitive Therapy (MT; Wells, 2011), in order to divert attention from perseverative thinking, for example rumination and worry. Unlike MT, MIT does not consider sustained attention to specific ideas as the sole or principal maintaining factor of symptom disorders.

In line with other theories (Hasson-Ohayon, 2012; Hasson-Ohayon, Kravetz, & Lysaker, 2017; Lysaker & Gumley, 2010), MIT sees the intersubjective process taking form in the therapeutic relationship as the central causal factor in the improvement of metacognition. Intersubjectivity involves what is occurring within the minds of two persons, and a mutual understanding of each's subjective experience (Stern, 2004). MIT therapists often explicitly hypothesized on patients' supposed mental states in order to foster patients' ability to understand his/her own mind, for example in order to make clients more aware of subjective experience: "It seems to me that you are talking about a sensation we all feel sometimes of being vulnerable"; "Your expression makes me think that you may be angry". This enables the client to discover that the therapist offers a human subjective experience, and this helps to increase the sense of their own subjectivity. Thus, it seems that intersubjectivity of the therapy conversations is a precondition for the development of self-reflection and the emergence of a narrative description of internal experience (Wachtel, 1993; Hasson-Ohayon, 2012).

Moreover, MIT practitioners help clients question their rigid and dysfunctional ideas about the self and others, and find new meanings in order to be in touch with personal wishes that they thought were beyond their reach. With people suffering from both personality disorders and psychosis, MIT adopts a step-by-step procedure in order to promote metacognition. MIT treatment of PD is schematically based on the following steps:

1) At the very beginning of treatment, when metacognitive capacity is too low, the therapist regulates the therapeutic relationship to avoid any potential ruptures and promotes a sense of safety in the session; they also work through the therapeutic relationship for the sake of emotion regulation.
2) From the very first therapy moments, the therapist works to bring to light any residual healthy self aspects, no matter how severely distressed the client is; the therapist tries to put clients in contact with what is human, universal, vital and creative that lies inside of them, elements that may have been obscured by PD. This increases hope and treatment motivation.
3) The therapist elicits specific narrative episodes during which expression of PD emerges. A narrative episode is a detailed account of a personally relevant event – where it is possible to explore the client's subjective experience, problematic emotions, meaning-making style and biased interpretations of the

self's and others' ideas and intentions. Such episodes bear information about what a client thinks and feels while engaging in social transactions and also about what self-image the client holds.

4) Exploring the narrative episodes: the therapist stimulates the client's understanding of the link, in a specific interpersonal interaction, between activating events, problematic thoughts, disturbing feelings connected to a perception of one's self as vulnerable and the onset of the PD.

Later, in more advanced stages of treatment, the therapist:

5) Helps the client use their awareness to achieve higher level mastery over PD.
6) Helps the client to construct a more complex sense of self, which includes a) more awareness and access to healthy aspects, namely their preferences, attitudes and personal goals and tries to let them act consistently, and b) capacities to understand that PD is connected to maladaptive schemas about self and others which are grounded in personal history.
7) Fosters daily life practices in order to form new capacities to relate with others grounded on a larger understanding of their minds.

All through therapy, MIT works to prevent and repair ruptures of the therapeutic relationship, because any intervention, no matter how technically correct, risks failing if carried out at a moment of disruption (Safran & Muran, 2000; Hasson-Ohayon, 2012; Hasson-Ohayon et al., 2017).

Case illustration: the story of John

John was a 32-year-old Caucasian male from a big town in southern Italy. He was an only child and at the time when he started therapy he lived with his parents, who were socially isolated, mistrustful and physically and verbally aggressive towards him. His maternal grandfather had experienced persecutory delusions at around the age of 40. Since his childhood, John had been hot-tempered and aggressive, he had also always felt different from others and experienced himself as an outcast. He had shown very little interest in school and had failed several years of study before achieving his high school degree. Then he had worked as a clerk in a supermarket. He had always been shy, and suspicious that colleagues might mock him. After work he spent his time in solitary activities, reading fantasy novels and writing short fiction. He had never had a romantic relationship with a woman. Some months before the beginning of therapy John had been berated at work by his boss for being too slow and some days later he had begun to experience ideas of reference. One day, John was in a bookshop and he started thinking that the owner and the customers were looking at him "strangely". Over the next few days, John became convinced that the book he was reading was about him and that the author wanted to warn him that he was in danger. The delusion became progressively richer and more complex. John thought that his favourite authors of fantasy novels and the bookseller were plotting in order to hamper his own creativity, preventing him from reading or writing. That was the cause of his anxiety and sleep deprivation. He did not show up to work, and wrote a letter to the authors of some novels he had read, scolding them and threatening to sue them.

One evening John was aggressive towards his father because the latter told him: "You are completely useless". John yelled at his father and threatened him, to the point that the neighbours called the police. John was admitted to hospital where he stayed for four weeks. He was discharged with pharmacotherapy (i.e. aripiprazole, sodium valproate and lorazepam) and then referred for psychotherapy with one of the chapter authors (GS). Pharmacotherapy improved John's sleep quality, diminished his hostility and aggressiveness, but only partially addressed his delusional experience. At times John remained convinced about the plot, and would become sad and ask his parents for help, becoming angry if they told him no plot existed.

John had never experienced other psychotic symptoms, meeting diagnostic criteria for a persecutory type of delusional disorder (APA, 2013). He had a certain level of insight about his illness, as witnessed by his ability to recognise that he experienced negative mental states as anxiety that troubled him. Even though minimal, this insight allowed him to accept oral pharmacotherapy. Overall, he had poor metacognitive skills. This difficulty in metacognitive capacity was assessed using the Metacognition Assessment Scale – Adapted (MAS-A) (Semerari et al., 2003; Lysaker et al., 2005). The MAS-A (for details see Chapter 1) contains four scales that reflect various forms of metacognitive activity: self-reflectivity, the comprehension of one's own mental states; understanding the mind of the other, the ability to comprehend other individuals' mental states; decentration, the ability to see a world in which others have independent motivations; and mastery, the ability to use knowledge of one's mental states to respond to social and psychological problems.

According to the MAS-A assessment, John was able to identify his anxiety and tendency to ruminate over negative thoughts about the people he thought persecuted him, and he was aware of his rage towards his father, by whom he felt humiliated. However, the assessment also showed that he was unable to recognise that these feelings of vulnerability triggered anxiety, rage and rumination. He also had a reduced ability to consider his perception and ideas as a reflection of reality and not as an actual reality; that is, metacognitive differentiation.

In regard to understanding the minds of others, John displayed a limited ability to grasp others' emotions and thoughts: he read others' intentions in a sophisticated delusional manner, without any decentration – that is, in social interactions, John was convinced that he was the centre, or cause, of others' behaviour. He interpreted a cordial expression by a neighbour, or a client of the library as dissimulating malicious intentions. Finally, John had poor mastery; in response to his PD and social situations that caused him emotional distress, his only solution was to avoid social interaction or in response to feeling insulted he could just worry about the offence taken.

John's psychotherapy, which we describe in detail next, was conducted in a private centre for psychotherapy, directed by a psychiatrist and psychotherapist (GS), and lasted for one year. Sessions were weekly and lasted about 45 minutes, for a period of about ten months. Therapy is currently ongoing, at the time of writing, with one session every two weeks. Therapy sessions were recorded with the patient's consent and the therapist transcribed verbatim the most significant dialogues of sessions. In the following paragraphs we describe a two-phase sequence for the sake of clarity, but in everyday clinical practice, therapy is more likely to move back and forth between the two phases until a problem is solved.

The first phase of therapy

Therapy at the outset was focused on: a) regulating the therapeutic relationship, providing containment and improving basic mastery skills; b) promoting the emergence of healthy self aspects, free from the influence of delusional ideas; c) understanding interpersonal schema related to PD and promoting advanced mastery strategies.

Regulating the therapeutic relationship, containment and improving basic mastery skills

In this very first phase, the therapist regulated the therapeutic relationship in order to prevent ruptures and promote a sense of safety in sessions. For this purpose, the therapist maintains a constantly validating attitude and keeps in mind that such a vulnerable and scared client tends to pay attention first and foremost to the non-verbal signals (intonation, prosody, posture, facial expressions and proxemics). Therefore therapists think particularly about their communication, in order to help the individual to regulate their emotions, and provide a sense of safety in the session (Porges, 2004).

In his first session, John appeared very anxious and withdrawn. He felt "stoned" by medications. The therapist did not interrupt John's complaints about how the author of his favourite book and the bookseller had plotted against him. Once John, all of sudden, asked him, embarrassedly: "Do you believe these things I have told you?"

Moments in which the client asks the therapist to "take sides" in regard to their delusional ideas are a point of high risk for relational ruptures. In MIT, the therapist maintains a non-judgemental position and tries to involve the client in shared therapeutic goals.

According to this position, the therapist calmly answered: "Listen John, I can imagine how important it can be for you to know that I believe you. [*John nodded*] But my role as a therapist is to understand your mental state and help you feel better, and not to decide whether your ideas about the world are right or wrong, in particular whether it is true that there is a plot against you. What interests and strikes me most is that thinking about the plot fully absorbs you and is an obstacle to your reading and writing and I fully understand this is frustrating and makes you sad and angry."

This intervention calmed John and was enough to let him focus on the emotional suffering triggered by the emergence of the delusional ideas as a problem that he had the power to act upon. The therapist's next step was the following:

T: "We can act upon our suffering and possibly soothe it. The first thing to do in this regard is change your attitude toward the ideas that make you suffer. What would happen if we were to consider these ideas just as a source of distress and to focus on trying to tone distress down?"

(John agreed with this goal, which gave the therapist room to negotiate relational and behavioural strategies for mastering the emotional suffering resulting from delusions.

At this stage, two strategies that are often useful are: resort to the therapist to seek reassurance and adopting behavioural strategies for the sake of shifting attention away from delusions.)

T: "Let's establish together how to tackle your worry about the plot. When it becomes overwhelming and makes you anxious, you might try calling me to discuss it, a bit as if we were in a session, just as we did today. If I am not available at that moment, you can send me a text or an email and wait for my answer. In the meantime, you could try distracting yourself by doing something you like. Let us think about what kind of activities may help you in these moments."

John agreed and, in this phase, called the therapist several times when he was prey to delusions, and felt helped. Gradually, after noticing that John relied on him at moments of emotional distress they both agreed that John increase his attempts to master suffering on his own, using a set of behavioural strategies, for example physical activity or listening to music.

Promoting the emergence of healthy self aspects

Promoting the healthy self aspects is a typical MIT operation (Dimaggio et al., 2015), and begins as early as the first session. By healthy self aspects we mean: a) ways of thinking and feeling and of representing oneself and others that are free from pathology; b) the trend to select behaviours focused on one's preferences and passions that they have overlooked in the past. Even clients with severe persecutory delusions display, in some moments of the therapy conversation, healthy self aspects, provided the therapist is able to note them. The therapist notes and brings to the client's attention to any moments in which he or she endorses a self-image different to the one tied to maladaptive schemas.

Helping clients stay in touch with the healthy self for as much time as possible is very important, as the more contact they have with it, the more they are able to maintain this positive self-concept in long-term memory and not let it fade away, or be wiped out by the negative self-images. Once the client has dwelt long enough on this self-image and has experienced positive states of mind, the therapist can use them as a point of leverage to help the client start to integrate positive self aspects with painful ones.

In the following example, taken from the second month of therapy, John was talking about his difficulty in writing creatively because of the plot against him. Negative arousal was low, so the therapist had room to share that he loved reading and was writing himself. He disclosed to John that he loved fiction and was a semi-professional novelist himself. John was pleasantly surprised. They talked about technical aspects of the writing process they used. John smiled and told the therapist that he was writing a medieval short novel, and that he loved describing the details of the scenes and of actions of characters. The therapist was very curious about this process, and realised that he was in touch with a really creative aspect of John, which he gave room to:

T: "John, it occurs to me I am witnessing something beautiful. Your tone of voice, your expression, your gaze, I see a totally different person from the one a few minutes ago who was talking about how he felt subjugated by the malicious intentions of others. This one is more self-confident, passionate, and loves sharing and expressing himself. Do you feel that?"

J (*smiling and nodding*): "Well . . . yes . . . when I read and write I feel comfortable. I know I'm good at it."

T: "Great. And, from this position of self-confidence and enthusiasm, what do you think about the vulnerable aspect of John?"

J (*thinks for a while*): "I'd love to write books and write as I did in the past. But I'm afraid those people will block me."

T: "I do understand your fear, but it is very important that we pay attention to these different ways see yourself. You pass from moments in which you feel a powerless victim of others you describe as threatening, to the point of being unable to do things you love, to other moments in which you experience energy, creativity and freedom of expression. This last part is alive and kicking and we need to stay within it as long as we can, so we give it room and power and it becomes a resource. It gains territory from the suffering part. So we have to give the desire to read and write more momentum, would you agree?"

J (*smiling*): "I do hope so! Thanks!"

Understanding interpersonal schema related to PD and promoting advanced mastery strategies

The key features in this moment of the therapy were as follows: eliciting a narrative episode in which delusions arise. Promoting a contextual awareness of the link between emotions related to appraisal of interpersonal relationships and insurgence of PD. This helped promote the awareness that a disturbed self-perception triggers delusions. When these steps are achieved, the next step is high-level mastery strategies to deal with delusions.

During the third month of therapy John was able to recognise a specific episode in which he started to have delusions:

J: "Either I look people straight in the eyes or I avoid their gaze because I know they are in contact with each other and with the bookseller. Or in any case they know everything and pretend they don't."

T: "Can you tell me a specific episode in which you were among people and you had these tendencies to look them in the eyes or avoid their gaze?"

J: "A couple of months ago, one of the last times I went to the bookshop. There was that tall man. I was looking through the shelves and when I passed by him a book slipped from his hands. People were around, I wanted to do something nice and take the book but I remained paralysed."

T: "You wanted to be nice?"

J: "I did, but fear stopped me."

T: "Was it fear?"

J: ". . . awe . . . of that man"

T: "Let's try to zoom in. You focus on that moment, fear that the man could react like . . . what?"

J: "Dunno . . . aggressive maybe? I didn't know what to say, the tone of voice to adopt, how to approach him."

T: "Very clear. And when you feared his aggression, and you felt scared and paralysed, how did you see yourself?"

J: "Like I couldn't react. I was prey to the situation."

T: "Well, I note that when you are recalling that moment you are like closing (*the therapist imitates his posture*). Do you remember how your body was back then? Was it similar?"

J: "Like I shrank, tiny."

T: ". . . so tiny . . . when like we feel vulnerable?"

J: "Yes, vulnerable, with no defence. Not ready to react."

T: "How did that feel physically?"

J: "My heart pounded. Short of breath. Hmm . . . throat was dry. Fingers trembled. And . . . legs . . . kinda weak they were, I felt like I was falling down. Couldn't keep my eyes wide open, the world was spinning around so fast."

T: "Quite an impressive description. It looks like the activation of the defence system, the one our ancestors had that helped to protect them from dreadful menaces. They felt vulnerable and fearful faced with a predator, and their body prepared to fight or fly."

J: "Yeah! Adrenaline!"

T: "Exactly."

At this point, consistent with MIT procedures, the therapist asked for related memories where a similar sense of vulnerability had been present and possibly caused suffering. John recalled a series of episodes before his admission to hospital, where he had felt vulnerable at work, in front of the boss and of his colleagues, and he had become mistrustful and hostile.

The therapist noted, with a validating stance, how vulnerability is a basic human experience. He then added:

T: "I reckon there's something else very important we've learned together. When we feel vulnerable and consequently frightened, we feel like potential victims, as our ancestors did when faced with a predator. We are automatically guided to feel a bit threatened by others. We can also become wary. In reality, what's happening is merely the consequence of the sensation of vulnerability. In practice feeling vulnerable leads us automatically to think that the other is going to attack us."

John was surprised and recognised himself in the process. The therapist suggested to John to try to monitor and identify the situations in which the self-perception as vulnerable would get activated, and then report them in the next session.

The therapist now promotes the client's use of this high-level psychological knowledge, which is understanding the interpersonal roots of symptoms, to master PD in a more sophisticated way. To facilitate recalling what was jointly formulated in session, the therapist left John the following memo: "John, remember that when you feel threatened, it's most probably also because you are feeling very vulnerable, and that it may happen to all of us when we feel vulnerable."

The therapist and John agreed that when John's sensation of being threatened returned, he could choose which mastery strategy to use from among those already used (for example, trying to recall the work done together in the session or writing down a note about his feelings in the moment in in order to discuss them with the therapist in the following session).

Advanced treatment phases

In more advanced phases, therapy was focused on a) consolidating healthy parts of self, b) promoting the awareness of the meaning of symptoms in relation to personal history; c) promoting theory of mind, encouraging social interactions, building more adaptive social skills.

Consolidating healthy parts of self

Access to a healthy self may be difficult at the beginning of treatment, as they surface but suddenly leave room to the dominant negative parts. Once clients have contact with healthy self aspects and have access to a more positive self-image, the therapist suggests John do some homework aimed at sustaining this over the week.

The therapist and John focused in session on the wish to write and read and so they gave a great deal of room in the therapy conversation to these themes, rather than sticking to PD-related issues. After some months John came into a session with a piece of his own writing, and read it aloud. The therapist noted how this was a sign of freedom of expression and listened with care and curiosity, which made John feel understood and supported in his wish for autonomy and creativity.

Promoting the awareness of the meaning of symptoms in relation to personal history

During the sixth month of treatment, John started to believe that his perception of vulnerability had taken shape gradually on the basis of negative experiences in his life:

J: "I was at primary school. We had to bring pictures we took, so I thought there was no other work to do, so my bag had just a snack inside. The teacher got pissed off and showed my empty bag to everyone. It seemed I had committed a serious felony. I had never felt so humiliated in my life."

T: "I do believe you. It is terrible for a kid to be exposed in that way."

J: "Yes. Like I was some scumbag."

T (*giggles*): "Quite a bitch the teacher, hmm?!"

J (*smiles*): "Indeed. So I was about to enter the social world . . . and started feeling vulnerable!"

T: "Indeed. But, did you tell the story at home?"

J: "Long time past, memory fading. But I remember my mum's face."

T: "Can you picture her expression?"

J: "Angry. Disgusted. She's a teacher too. She said something like it was completely on me."

T: "So you weren't soothed or supported as well?"

J: "Not at all! And it happened many times in primary school. These teachers mocked me, I made small mistakes, applied the wrong verb . . . they blamed me. Maybe I never felt understood."

T: "Sure! You weren't."

J: "I had a talk with my mother recently: I told her I would meet that bitch again and tell her it's so unfair to treat a child that way."

T: "You bet I'd support you!" (*both laugh*)

J: "And my mother retorted: 'You're aggressive, violent. You're mean!'. Without understanding the pain that lay beneath . . ."

John realised that, in many other episodes, when he had asked for understanding and comfort, his parents had let him feel humiliated, judged him or were aggressive to the point he felt "annihilated". This allowed the therapist to explain from a validating standpoint how he was driven by a schema rooted in his personal history:

T: "We understand now that in moments when you feel vulnerable, without defence you have learnt, from many experiences, that others will not understand your vulnerabilities and fragility. They will not say: 'It's okay, this has happened to me to, nothing to worry about, it's human, it will fade away.' No. Instead you learnt that others will judge you, blame you for your vulnerabilities: 'It's on you, your bad, wrong!' The expectation that things will repeat this way over and over again triggers suffering. But thanks to our work, we have seen that there is still a part of you that is alive and kicking, healthy, creative, one where reading and writing are not just shelters, but a part of you that nothing can take away from you. Is that true?"

J (*nodding, moved*): "Right this way . . . I realise it more and more . . . they always made me feel weaker, dumber than the others, inept. As a boy I tried to conceal it but without being aware, so that ideas grew stronger."

Promoting theory of mind, encouraging social interactions

We have seen how promoting the healthy self begins with promoting activities the client likes, possibly without exposing him to distressing social relationships. We can recall that John, in social situations, was easily prey to the vulnerability schema, so he felt negatively aroused and isolated himself. Isolation then served as a fertile soil for delusions to grow. Now that he was aware of the schema leading to PD, and more in touch with a sense of worthiness and creativity, the therapist suggested he perform a more difficult step, which was gradual exposure to social interactions. In these interactions, the client's ability to understand the mind of others in a more articulated way, regulating the tendency to ascribe malicious intentions to them, will be activated.

In MIT (Dimaggio et al., 2015) the understanding of others' mental states should be stimulated only after promoting a client's understanding of their own mind and of the relationship between negative emotions and symptom activation. This holds especially true for clients with paranoia. They need to understand that in interpersonal contexts in which they feel vulnerable they suffer because they feel defenceless. Then, they are more prone to ascribe malicious intentions to others as an instinctive protective mechanism. Suggesting in the first phases of therapy that others' intentions may be interpreted in different and possibly more benevolent ways would mean telling them: "Hey, be off-guard, no danger around". This would very likely increase their fear and likely deteriorate the quality of the therapeutic relationship. When instead the client is aware that sense of vulnerability is a subjective experience, has experienced healthy and efficient aspects of themselves, and experiences the therapeutic relationship as a source of safety and collaboration, the therapist can, tactfully, suggest that others are not necessarily malevolent.

Graded exposure to social situations can now also be a source of well-being for the client and offer a space for giving room to personal skills, abilities and interests. In this step, the therapist agreed with John that he sometimes got out from his home for a short walk. Once he felt ready, the next step was going to the bookshop he used to spend his time in. The therapist underscored that he just had to try. If he had not gone to the bookshop, it would not have been a problem, they would have worked in the next session on the disturbing feelings and ideas that had prevented him from completing the exposure, so as to better understand them.

John, albeit with some anxiety, accepted. In the following weeks, he reported many instances in which he had walked and discovered anew the pleasure of being in the open air. In one session, during the ninth month of therapy, he told how he could step into the bookshop and that the bookseller greeted him in a friendly way; the same bookseller who was the previous object of his delusions. He felt anxious and somewhat threatened, but only fearing that the bookseller would mock him. He remembered the therapist's suggestion about how important for his therapy it would be to satisfy his desire to feel free to get out and attend libraries, then he forced himself to browse some fantasy books. After some minutes, his anxiety progressively increased, so he left.

His therapist offered reinforcement for this exposure and aid which helped John to understand how his anxiety was too intense to bear after so much time without social contact. He told John that he had done very well in the exercise. He asked him to recall the scene and to try and guess what was passing through the bookseller's mind while he smiled at him:

T: "Now you are not anxious anymore, try to figure out different explanations for that smile . . . try to put yourself in his shoes."

J (*smiling*): "Uhm . . . Maybe he wanted to be kind . . . he hadn't seen me for a while."

T: "So maybe he had no bad intentions against you."

J: "Guess not . . . can't be sure."

T: "Absolutely John. I'm not asking you to be sure. No one can ever be sure about someone else's thoughts. What really matters is that you are less anxious and no longer feeling vulnerable. You also become able to form positive guesses about others' intentions, you can think they like you. So we discover that your ideas about what others think of you are not necessary true. Most importantly, we are now aware that the way you feel in the moment influences the thoughts you think are in the mind of the others. What do you think?"

P (*reflecting*): "I do think so."

Outcome

After 13 months of psychotherapy, John has a good outcome in regards to PD. He has only episodic delusions, mostly in interpersonal situations in which he meets new people. In these situations, he tends to get upset, but is able to use his improved meta-cognitive ability in order to regulate emotions by calling the therapist or remembering his words. This helps him to recognise that his feelings of vulnerability trigger emotional suffering and lead him to attribute malevolent intentions to others. On this basis, recalling what was discussed with the therapist, he tells himself that he can accept his vulnerability as a part of self, that others also have, without feeling menaced. He is now more able to differentiate his perception from reality and to understand the mind of others as not focused on him. His social withdrawal is much less present, and he is now a member of a reading club. He works as a clerk in a store. He continues to work together with the therapist, whom he now sees every two weeks, and he plans to live on his own. He still takes medication at a maintenance dosage (aririprazole: discontinued; lorazepam: only acutely anxious; sodium valproate: 600 mg).

Conclusions

We have described the treatment of a young man with PD, through MIT. We have shown that MIT does not try to directly challenge delusional beliefs. Instead, in the first treatment moments, when the PD was very pervasive, arousal very high, and metacognitive skills very low, the therapist adopted a validating and soothing attitude to help the client to regulate suffering related to the idea of being persecuted. On this basis, the therapist helped the client to consider the persecutory ideas as an expression of his emotional reactions, generated by activating interpersonal situations in which he felt vulnerable. This created the conditions for achieving an awareness that the contents of PD were rooted in maladaptive interpersonal schemas, formed during his personal development. In this schema, when the client felt vulnerable he expected to be severely judged and humiliated. The therapy helped the client to understand that this schema drove him to interpret the intentions of others towards him as only malevolent, and to avoid social contacts despite him desiring them. After therapy helped him to adopt a critical distance from that schema, the client was able to face social situations where negative emotions arose but he could regulate them. This way he regained social contacts, and gradually formed alternative ideas about what was passing through the minds of the others in order to prevent further withdrawal and live a richer social life.

From the very first phase, and throughout the therapy, the therapist promoted and then sustained access to healthy self aspects. In advanced therapy phases, the therapist helped the client to integrate in a more complex sense of self these new self aspects, driven by core life goals and passions he was driven by.

Here, we have described a two-phase sequence for the sake of clarity, but in everyday clinical practice, therapy is more likely to move back and forth between the two phases until a problem is solved.

Some important limitations need to be pointed out. Some variables uniquely related to the interests shared by client and therapist may have influenced both adherence and good outcome above and beyond the specific approach. The client had good cognitive functioning so results cannot be generalised to persons with PD and impaired cognition. Moreover, the illness was at its onset, so we cannot predict outcomes in more chronic conditions. Further research is needed on larger samples of persons with PD in order to test the MIT effectiveness. Nevertheless, MIT seems to be capable of both improving metacognition and reducing PD. It also appears able to sustain a recovered sense of self, through the integration of healthy self aspects. This makes the client capable of regaining social contacts, becoming creative and reaching well-being and a sense of a life worth living.

The client described has given his informed consent to the publication of this chapter. The name is fictitious, and sufficient changes were made to ensure his identity remains confidential.

References

American Psychiatric Association. (2013). *Diagnostic and statistical manual of mental disorders (DSM-5)* (5th ed.). Washington, DC: American Psychiatric Association.

Beck, A. T. (1976). *Cognitive therapy and the emotional disorders.* New York: International Universities Press.

Chadwick, P. (2008). *Person-based cognitive therapy for distressing psychosis.* New York: Wiley.

Dimaggio, G., & Lysaker, P. H. (2010). *Metacognition and severe adult mental disorders: From basic research to treatment.* London: Routledge.

Dimaggio, G., Montano, A., Popolo, R., & Salvatore, G. (2015). *Metacognitive interpersonal therapy for personality disorders: A treatment manual.* Hove, UK: Routledge.

Dimaggio, G., Salvatore, G., MacBeth, A., Ottavi, P., Buonocore, L., & Popolo, R. (2017). Metacognitive interpersonal therapy for personality disorders: A case study series. *Journal of Contemporary Psychotherapy, 47*(1), 11–21.

Dimaggio, G., Semerari, A., Carcione, A., Nicolò, G., & Procacci, M. (2007). *Psychotherapy of personality disorders: Metacognition, states of mind and interpersonal cycles.* London: Routledge.

Ellis, A. (1962). *Reason and emotion in psychotherapy.* New York: Lyle Stuart.

France, C. M., & Uhlin, B. D. (2006). Narrative as an outcome domain in psychosis. *Psychology and Psychotherapy, 79*(1), 53–67.

Freeman, D., Bradley, J., Waite, F., Sheaves, B., DeWeever, N., Bourke, E., . . . & Dunn, G. (2016). Targeting recovery in persistent persecutory delusions: A proof of principle study of a new translational psychological treatment (The Feeling Safe Programme). *Behavioural and Cognitive Psychotherapy, 44*(5), 539–552.

Freeman, D., Freeman, J., & Garety, P. (2008). *Overcoming paranoid and suspicious thoughts.* New York: Basic Books.

Gordon-King, K., Schweitzer, R. D., & Dimaggio, G. (2018). Metacognitive interpersonal therapy for personality disorders featuring emotional inhibition: A multiple baseline case series. *Journal of Nervous and Mental Disease, 206*(4), 263–269.

Hasson-Ohayon, I. (2012). Integrating cognitive behavioral-based therapy with an intersubjective approach: Addressing metacognitive deficits among people with schizophrenia. *Journal of Psychotherapy Integration, 22*(4), 356–374. http://doi.org/10.1037/a0029576.

Hasson-Ohayon, I., Kravetz, S., & Lysaker, P. H. (2017). The special challenges of psychotherapy with personas with psychosis: Intersubjective metacognitive model of agreement and shared meaning. *Clinical Psychology and Psychotherapy, 24*(2), 428–440. https://doi.org/10.1002/cpp.2012.

Inchausti, F., Moreno-Campos, L., Prado-Abril, J., Sánchez-Reales, S., Fonseca-Pedrero, E., MacBeth, A., . . . & Dimaggio, G. (2020). Metacognitive interpersonal therapy in group for personality disorders: Preliminary results from a pilot study in a public mental health setting. *Journal of Contemporary Psychotherapy*, *50*(3), 197–203. https://doi.org/10.1007/s10879-020-09453-9.

Lysaker, P. H., Carcione, A., Dimaggio, G., Johannesen, J. K., Nicolo, G., Procacci, M., & Semerari, A. (2005). Metacognition amidst narratives of self and illness in schizophrenia: Associations with insight, neurocognition, symptom and function. *Acta Psychiatrica Scandinavica*, *112*, 64–71.

Lysaker, P. H., & Gumley, A. (2010). Psychotherapeutic and relational processes and the development of metacognitive capacity following five years of individual psychotherapy: A case study of a person with psychotic symptoms. *Psychosis*, *2*(1), 70–78.

Mehl, S., Werner, D., & Lincoln, T. M. (2015). Does Cognitive Behavior Therapy for psychosis (CBTp) show a sustainable effect on delusions? A meta-analysis. *Frontiers in Psychology*, *6*, 1450.

Popolo, R., & Dimaggio, G. (2016). *Terapia Metacognitiva Interpersonale in Gruppo (TMI-G). Manuale per l'applicazione.* Centro di Terapia Metacognitiva Interpersonale, Roma, non pubblicato.

Popolo, R., MacBeth, A., Brunello, S., Canfora, F., Ozdemir, E., Rebecchi, D., . . . & Dimaggio, G. (2018b). Metacognitive Interpersonal Therapy in Group (MIT-G): A pilot noncontrolled effectiveness study. *Research in Psychotherapy: Psychopathology, Process and Outcome*, *21*, 155–163. https://doi.org/10.4081/ripppo.2018.338.

Popolo, R., MacBeth, A., Canfora, F., Rebecchi, D., Toselli, C., Salvatore, G., & Dimaggio, G. (2018a). Metacognitive Interpersonal Therapy in group (MIT-G) for young adults personality disorders. A pilot randomized controlled trial. *Psychology and Psychotherapy: Theory, Research & Practice*, *92*(3), 342–358. https://doi.org/10.1111/papt.12182.

Porges, S. W. (2004). Neuroception: A subconscious system for detecting threat and safety. *Zero to Three: Bulletin of the National Center for Clinical Infant Programs*, *24*(5), 19–24.

Safran, J. D., & Muran, C. (2000). *Negotiating the therapeutic alliance: A relational treatment guide.* New York: Guilford.

Salvatore, G., Buonocore, L., Ottavi, P., Popolo, R., & Dimaggio, G. (2018). Metacognitive interpersonal therapy for treating persecutory delusions in schizophrenia. *American Journal of Psychotherapy*, *71*(4), 164–174. https://doi.org/10.1176/appi.psychotherapy.20180039.

Salvatore, G., Dimaggio, G., Popolo, R., Procacci, M., Nicolò, G., & Carcione, A. (2009). Adapted Metacognitive Interpersonal Therapy for improving adherence to intersubjective contexts in a person with schizophrenia. *Clinical Case Studies*, *8*, 473–488.

Salvatore, G., Lysaker, P. H., Gumley, A., Popolo, R., Mari, J., & Dimaggio, G. (2012b). Out of illness experience: Metacognition-oriented therapy for promoting self-awareness in individuals with psychosis. *American Journal of Psychotherapy*, *66*, 85–106.

Salvatore, G., Lysaker, P. H., Popolo, R., Procacci, M., Carcione, A., & Dimaggio, G. (2012a). Vulnerable self, poor understanding of others' minds, threat anticipation and cognitive biases as triggers for delusional experience in schizophrenia: A theoretical model. *Clinical Psychology & Psychotherapy*, *19*(3), 247–259.

Semerari, A., Carcione, A., Dimaggio, G., Falcone, M., Nicolò, G., Procacci, M., & Alleva, G. (2003). How to evaluate metacognitive function in psychotherapy? The metacognition assessment scale its applications. *Clinical Psychology and Psychotherapy*, *10*, 238–261.

Semerari, A., Carcione, A., Dimaggio, G., Nicolò, G., & Procacci, M. (2007). Understanding minds: Different functions and different disorders? The contribution of psychotherapy research. *Psychotherapy Research*, *17*, 106–119.

Startup, H., Pugh, K., Dunn, G., Cordwell, J., Mander, H., Černis, E., . . . & Freeman, D. (2016). Worry processes in clients with persecutory delusions. *The British Journal of Clinical Psychology, 55*(4), 387–400.

Stern, D. N. (2004). *The present moment in psychotherapy and everyday life.* New York: Norton.

Wachtel, P. (1993). *Therapeutic communication: Knowing what to say when.* New York: Guilford Press.

Wells, A. (2011). *Metacognitive therapy for anxiety and depression.* New York: Guilford Press.

5

THE RECOVERY OF THE SELF IN ADULTS WITH DELUSIONS

A mentalization-based psychotherapy

Jeremy M. Ridenour

Abstract: *Therapists confront unique challenges when working with individuals who are experiencing psychosis, given their mistrust and tendency to misread the intentions of others. A Mentalization-Based Therapy for psychosis (MBT-p) approach to the treatment of delusions attends specifically to the affective and interpersonal factors undergirding the delusion. MBT focuses on how individuals form ideas about self and other and explores how these ideas can negatively impact their social interactions with others. A case example will be provided to illustrate specific mentalization-based interventions relevant to working with individuals with delusions.*

Garety and Freeman (2013) note that the treatment of delusions, among persons with diagnoses of psychotic disorders, has plateaued in the past decade and that various medications and psychological and social treatment interventions (e.g. CBT for psychosis and family interventions) have only yielded small to medium effects. Although antipsychotic medications might attenuate delusional intensity, they do not address the underlying mechanisms that give rise to the delusional framework (Kumar, Menon, Moritz, & Woodward, 2015). In particular, fixed delusions have proven resistant to both psychosocial treatment and medication (Turkington, Spencer, Jassal, & Cummings, 2015) and new psychotherapeutic models are needed to meet the needs of people who experience fixed delusions. In psychotherapy, some clinicians are hesitant to engage people who report delusions, often harboring worries that they might inadvertently reinforce the person's delusional certainty or defensiveness by exploring it in treatment (Arnold & Vakhrusheva, 2016). However, many individuals who are experiencing delusions desperately need to speak about them and understand the meaning of their experiences to aid them in their path of recovery and self-reclamation (Staring, van der Gaag, & Mulder, 2011). In fact, individuals experiencing psychosis have described their complex sense of agency in the onset and maintenance of psychotic symptoms and their efforts to actively frame and make sense of these confusing experiences (Jones et al., 2016). Given this reality, therapists can respond by trying to be co-investigators and work to help persons with psychosis develop deeper understandings of their experiences and ways of managing their distress.

Currently, the majority of therapeutic approaches available to treat delusions, such as cognitive behavioural therapy for psychosis (CBT-p) (Tai & Turkington, 2009) and Metacognitive Training/Therapy (MCT) (Kumar et al., 2015) primarily focus on the underlying information processing biases inherent to delusional ideation. For instance, CBT-p examines the evidence for the person's delusional beliefs and helps them to form alternative perspectives on their beliefs (Tai & Turkington, 2009). In contrast, MCT is a "back door approach" (Kumar et al., 2015) that does not directly challenge the person's delusion but instead attempts to restructure the framework that gives rise to the delusion. In MCT, the individual is exposed to various training modules that offer psychoeducation about the cognitive biases (e.g. jumping to conclusion bias and bias against disconfirmatory evidence) and social cognitive difficulties underlying delusion formation (Kumar et al., 2015). While these treatments have made some headway, I will argue in this chapter that they fail to attend to other aspects of delusions (e.g. personal meaning embedded in delusions, affective triggers for delusional ideation, and interpersonal relationships that provide a context for delusion formation). Although various therapies, outside of the cognitive tradition, approach delusions from a more holistic perspective (e.g. Metacognitive Reflection and Insight Therapy (MERIT – see Lysaker & Klion, 2017)), I will argue for the relevance of Mentalization-based Therapy for psychosis (MBT-p), which specifically targets the understanding of self and other that is often disrupted for individuals experiencing delusions.

I will first address the definition of delusions and controversies in the field with regard to how to conceptualize delusions. Next, I will introduce MBT-p as an emerging approach (Knauss, Ridenour, & Hamm, 2018) that aims to address some of the key interpersonal and affective dimensions that undergird delusional processes. Finally, I will describe a case study in which I worked with a young man, Taylor, who was experiencing a fixed delusion. Taylor is a pseudonym and he provided consent to have the case written about professionally.

Conceptualizing delusions

According to the DSM-5, delusions are fixed beliefs not amenable to change in light of conflicting evidence (American Psychiatric Association, 2013). The DSM-5 lists various types of delusions (e.g. grandiose, persecutory, referential) that are defined as bizarre if they are clearly implausible and unintelligible to same-culture peers. Research on delusions has largely proceeded from a cognitive paradigm. Beck and Rector (2002) have described the characteristics of delusional thinking: pervasiveness, intensity, conviction, significance, and inflexibility. They describe cognitive biases in delusional processes. First, the individual exhibits an egocentric bias in which events are interpreted as having direct personal relevance. He or she often imagines the world malevolently revolving around them. Second, persons experiencing delusions often demonstrate an externalizing bias in which mental events are understood as being caused by external agents. Third, individuals with delusions are prone to make hasty inferences and neglect alternative explanations, which has been termed the "jumping to conclusions" (JTC) bias (Garety & Freeman, 2013).

Although this cognitive approach has been the standard research paradigm, many have challenged the way it conceptualizes delusions. Phenomenological theorists have critiqued the DSM-5's definition of psychosis, with its focus on discrete symptoms and its neglect of first-person experience (Parnas, 2011). Instead, they have drawn on ideas from the history of phenomenological psychiatry to deepen understandings of psychosis. Sass and Parnas (2003) have advocated for an understanding of psychosis as fundamentally a "self-disorder", that is, it is driven by basic changes in self-experience (Nelson, Parnas, & Sass, 2014). Regarding delusions, Bleuler (1911) argued that individuals with delusions often live in a private, solipsistic universe that is relatively untouched by an external, social reality. Rather than conceiving of delusions as driven by cognitive distortions, they argue that individuals with psychosis have an altered ontological framework, in which experiences of self, world, reality, time, and space are changed (Sass & Byrom, 2015). From this perspective, a delusion might represent an effort to stabilize an inexplicable, chaotic world, as it offers a consistent cognitive structure through which to filter and organize experiences. For instance, an individual who feels chronically uncertain, fearful, and mistrustful of others might begin to explain this uncertainty by developing the idea that they are being spied on by a government agency. While this persecutory belief system might generate fear, it also provides structure to an individual's confusing, variable self-experience.

While these phenomenological theories attend to lived experience, they fail to account for the interpersonal and affective context of delusions. For instance, Ratcliffe (2015) contends that both the content and formation of ideas arise out of relationships and so social context should be considered when treating individuals with delusions. Fuchs (2015) suggests that delusions are characterized by a refusal to consider the other person's perspective and thus they represent a disruption of communication in which the individual no longer compares or contrasts their perspectives with those of others. Fuchs argues that individuals with delusions do not fully participate in the shared sense making that allows individuals to co-construct reality. In other words, individuals with delusional beliefs manifest difficulties in social cognition, which can be defined as the mental operations underlying social interactions (especially interpretation of, and responses to, the thoughts, feelings, and intentions of others). Of note, many terms have been used to describe the mental processes relevant to social interactions (e.g. mentalization, metacognition, theory of mind, social cognition, empathy) whose definitions overlap (Ridenour, Knauss, & Hamm, 2018). While the differences between terms are important, I will be using the term mentalization, given my background as a psychoanalyst and its grounding in developmental/attachment framework (Fonagy & Allison, 2014).

From this summary, we can conceptualize delusions in a twofold manner: 1) delusions represent a particular alteration in the basic world-orientation that contributes to changes in the individual's sense of self and 2) other people lose their status as epistemic agents (i.e. important resources of social information) for the individual experiencing the delusion. Fonagy and Allison (2014) have argued for the importance of restoring epistemic trust, that is, an individual's willingness to consider information from others as trustworthy and relevant to the self, for individuals with severe psychiatric disorders. From this perspective, psychotherapeutic treatment could target the relevant mentalization disturbances that are impaired by delusional processes.

Mentalization-based Therapy for Psychosis (MBT-p)

A mentalization-based framework is particularly appropriate to the treatment of individuals experiencing delusions because it attends to the interpersonal and emotional factors that undergird disruptions in one's reflective capacity. MBT (Bateman & Fonagy, 2001) views mentalization as the ability to think about people as intentional agents whose behavior is driven by internal states (e.g. thoughts, feelings, wishes, and desires). The capacity to mentalize emerges out of a child's secure attachment to a responsive caregiver who processes and regulates the child's emotions (see presentation and review of MBT in Chapter 1). Bateman and Fonagy (2016) have outlined three modes of thinking that antedate the development of mentalization in development: teleological mode (a focus on observable outcomes as opposed to mental states), psychic equivalence (concrete thought), and pretend mode (imaginative play). Psychic equivalence is characterized by a mind-world isomorphism in which the person assumes that their thoughts and feelings are direct representations of reality (Ridenour et al., 2018). This rigid certainty is common in individuals experiencing delusions who might claim to be omniscient and certain of other people's intentions (Kumazaki, 2015). Thus, MBT-p targets these difficulties in representations of self with the hope of promoting an individual's capacity to reflect upon their mental states of self and others in complex ways.

An MBT-p approach is characterized by epistemic humility, a focus on affective/bodily experience, attention to relationships (especially the therapy relationship), and a pragmatic intervention strategy (Debbané et al., 2016). First, the therapist adopts an empathic and curious "not-knowing stance" that is driven by the therapist's belief in the opacity of the mind, that is, the recognition that the knowledge of mental states is provisional and never fully known. Debbané et al. (2016) have argued that this position can counteract the rigid certainty with which some individuals with psychosis interpret the mental states of others. Second, the therapist and client recognize that the capacity for mentalization is dependent upon context and affected by emotional arousal (Bateman & Fonagy, 2013). Our ability to mentalize is variable and related to the amount of safety and security we feel in a given moment. For instance, if you feel unfairly attacked by your boss in the middle of a meeting, it can be very difficult to maintain an open, curious attitude about your boss's intentions. When our self-esteem is threatened, it is easy to default to simpler, less sophisticated modes of thought. Given this emotional focus, the therapist strives to help the client label their bodily and affective states (Debbané et al., 2016) to develop a greater capacity to contain and recognize the impact that emotions have on their interpretations of others. Third, Brent and Fonagy (2014) suggest that the therapy relationship can be a social laboratory, in which both the therapist and client's interpretations of the relationship can be explored, unpacked, and reflected upon. In addition to the therapy relationship, the therapist also invites the client to share narratives of interpersonal interactions to learn more about mentalization in everyday life. This affords both therapist and client the opportunity to analyze the client's default ways of understanding the mental states of self and other. Finally, the therapist's intervention strategy is pragmatic. Although mentalization emerges from the psychodynamic tradition, the therapist keeps their interventions short and simple with a focus on the present. The therapist largely avoids interpretations of the transference, or other unconscious content, and instead attends to the client's conscious experiences. Additionally, the therapist offers their own mental processes as a model. It is important that, when the therapist models their mental process, they recognize that their interpretations are fallible and thus prone to error. Finally, the therapist often stops and "rewinds" the therapeutic process when they notice that mentalization processes have broken down and pre-mentalization modes of thought emerge (Brent & Fonagy, 2014).

In its application to delusions, an MBT-p approach would focus on three issues: 1) the therapist would monitor the stance they assume relative to the client. The therapist would want to honour the opacity of mind to emphasize that they are not omniscient and cannot fully know reality. This could serve to counteract the mistrust or fear the client might experience when speaking with a therapist, and 2) the therapist and client would work together to establish the affective and interpersonal context under which delusional thinking emerges. For instance, Leonhardt and colleagues (2016) conducted a qualitative psychotherapy study that found psychotic content was most likely to emerge when the client felt inadequate or vulnerable, and 3) the therapist would strive to attend to the therapeutic relationship, which serves as a platform to understand the client's mentalization processes in real time. These various emphases should be facilitated by the MBT's pragmatic, grounded approach.

Case study

I will now introduce my work with a young man, Taylor. Taylor is a Hispanic man who grew up in a southeastern part of the United States, and he was 22 at the time of treatment. I served as his therapist for nine months in residential treatment. Taylor's early life was marked by severe chaos. His parents met via a religious cult, but his mother was excommunicated following her breaking of a central rule. In response, his mother gave Taylor to his father who took him to Mexico and Taylor stayed with his father between the ages of two and five. At the age of five, Taylor's mother hired a private investigator and eventually located him. With the aid of her friend, she "kidnapped" him and brought him back to the United States. This sequence of events was likely traumatizing for Taylor who lost not only his father, but also his paternal grandparents. In addition, he did not speak English and was with his mother who did not speak Spanish. Taylor had no recollection of these events other than vague, fragmented memories of living with his grandparents. He tended not to think about his early history.

His mother eventually remarried and Taylor's stepfather moved into the home during Taylor's adolescence. Taylor attended a predominantly white public school and was exposed to racism and discrimination from his peers. Prior to high school (and continuing into college), he had multiple romantic relationships that ended abruptly, though he could not recall the context of these breakups. In high school, he appeared to be an independent and freethinking person. He enjoyed exploring intellectual ideas and travelling to different parts of the world. As an adolescent, he avoided his home and his parents, who made him sad. During this period, his mother was diagnosed with cancer, which he largely ignored through avoiding her. He reported having a complicated relationship with his mother. His mother's banishment from the cult seemed traumatic for her and she never fully recovered. Although she felt hurt, she continued to believe in the cult leader and internalize the sense that she was evil for breaking the rules. He described his mother as either sick and depressed in bed, or cheerful, anxious, sentimental, naïve, and hysterical. Early on, he learned that his mother was not available, given her constant physical and psychological struggles. He adapted by using marijuana and trying to take up as little space as possible and minimize his needs, for fear of overwhelming her. In regard to his father, Taylor rarely saw him. He had difficulty relating to his stepfather, who Taylor felt wanted him to be more athletic.

At the age of 18, Taylor enrolled in college, where he adjusted well and excelled in his freshman year. He aspired to become a writer and was intellectually gifted. Although he had dated casually throughout high school and college, he began an important relationship at the age of 20. He dated his girlfriend for a couple of months and fell in love with her, but she eventually broke up with him for reasons that were unclear to him. Following the breakup, Taylor became suicidal and was hospitalized for the first time, and diagnosed with depression. Over the next couple of years, his thinking grew more bizarre and he was unable to finish college. For instance, he would agonize for hours over whether or not he should eat certain foods and found himself paralyzed by doubts and worries that something catastrophic would happen if he made the wrong decision.

Treatment context

During his senior year of college, Taylor had trouble completing his academic work and was plagued by suicidal ideation and confusion. In this context, he was referred to residential treatment. I worked as Taylor's individual therapist in a residential setting that treats complex psychiatric clients, through the use of intensive psychodynamic psychotherapy, medication management, social work, family therapy, substance use counselling, and groups in an open therapeutic community programme. I saw Taylor four times weekly in individual therapy that lasted for nine months. Taylor was a bright young man. During the beginning of his treatment he underwent psychological testing and his verbal IQ was in the 96th percentile. His treatment was funded by his stepfather's friend who was a wealthy philanthropist. For the purpose of this chapter, I will present some of our initial therapy sessions over the first two months. Next, I will describe the middle phase of the work in which we discussed his delusion. Finally, I will include some reflections at the end of the work and how I used an MBT-p framework to understand and work with him.

Initial phase

In our first session, Taylor's chief complaint was that he had lost contact with himself. He situated the problem as having begun three years prior, when his girlfriend had broken up with him in college. I will include some dialogue taken from the process notes I recorded after our session.

THERAPIST: "It sounds like you no longer recognize yourself."
TAYLOR: "I just don't really connect with who I am. I can't feel myself."
THERAPIST: "Did you lose a part of yourself or do you just feel your sense of self has diminished?"
TAYLOR: "I haven't lost anything in particular. I just feel like there's a shadow casting a shadow over who I used to be."

After our initial meeting, I met with Taylor and his mother to hear her perspective on his struggles. I asked her to tell me about him and she spent 15 minutes telling me a fragmented story about the kidnapping as a child, the cult, her cancer diagnosis, her recent separation from her husband, and the fact that Taylor was a survivor. I noticed that she seemed so overwhelmed by the traumas of her own life that she had trouble speaking about Taylor as distinct from herself. In this initial session, he painfully described a basic diminished self-presence, which Sass, Borda, Madeira, Pienkos, and Nelson (2018) have described as a loss of vitality of one's subjective self-presence. Taylor seemed to be expressing a primal loss of his sense of aliveness, a contact with his core sense of self that would have enabled him to feel "alive and kicking".

In the second session, he told me more specifically about how his thoughts could break down. He reported that sometimes he felt like his mind "folded" in on itself. He compared this thought loop to a train that cannot get a wheel back on the track. In these moments, his vision would become blurry. If he looked in the mirror, his eyes appeared menacing. He worried he might be dying. I asked if he was aware of any specific context that might lead to this breakdown, but he could not provide one. He then asked for a piece of paper and drew a diagram of his sense of self through time and how he would get knocked off his life trajectory. He also drew a picture of his brain and identified a logical and creative side of the brain. He stated that because his biological father was not in his life, he had lost access to his creative mind, although his reasoning was difficult to understand. He appeared anxious and pressured as he tried to convey his self-experience. Then we had this exchange:

TAYLOR: "I don't want to be dramatic. I just worry about my brain and my thoughts."

THERAPIST: "You keep saying you don't want to be dramatic, are you worried you're exaggerating your suffering?"

TAYLOR: "Yes, I'm not even sure it's a big deal."

THERAPIST: "Are you worried I'm judging you?"

TAYLOR: "Yes. I feel guilty talking about my problems. In the past, some therapists have told me that these thoughts I have about my brain and identity are just ideas. They told me not to worry too much about them."

THERAPIST: "But these have to do with the core of your identity. How could you dismiss them?"

In this exchange, I tried to understand Taylor's communication and his interpersonal concerns that might impact his ability to reflect on his thoughts, feelings, and interpretations (i.e. using the therapy relationship as a laboratory for mentalization). I understood Taylor as laying out a potential maternal transference, a concern that I would also be burdened by his problems and trivialize them. I later learned that Taylor's mother had once put a National Geographic Magazine picture of children starving in his bedroom, as if to suggest that other children had it worse off (though this seemed largely to be driven by her guilt and not his complaints). Taylor believed that his mother felt terrible about being unable to provide more financially and she seemed to vacillate between apologizing for her felt sense of inadequacy and trying to convince him that others were suffering more than them. In response to her fragility, Taylor struggled in expressing any distress for fear of overwhelming her, causing her to become more depressed, or being dismissed. However, I chose not to interpret the transference, but instead tried to establish a working alliance with Taylor. Brent (2009) discourages transference interpretations for individuals experiencing psychosis, as the feelings activated in the therapy relationship can be experienced as "real". Instead, I encouraged Taylor to share his thoughts, feelings, and insecurities that might emerge within the relationship to emphasize that I welcomed learning more about his experience of me and other people. I also heard his concern about being dramatic as being driven by a counter-identification with his mother whom he experienced as hysterical and self-involved.

In the next session, he spoke more about his confusion in making meaning of his thoughts. He told me that he was very anxious about the ideas that came into his mind. He told me he had developed a theory that the way we think about our parents psychologically impacts our sense of identity. Once, while working at a café, he had become worried that other people might be able to spontaneously replace his memories of his parents. For example, he saw a man in the café who looked like his father. He worried that he would make a connection with him and then this man would become his dad and replace his memories of his father. He seemed aware that this might be impossible but simultaneously worried that it might come true. I became aware of how porous his sense of self was and the omnipotent power he attributed to his thought (that is, as if thoughts could control reality). In a later session, I provided him with psychoeducation about thought-action fusion (i.e. a cognitive bias that refers to irrational causal relationships between thought and action), and its relevance to people experiencing OCD and schizotypy (Lee, Cougle, & Telch, 2005). This type of concrete mentalizing relates to the notion of psychic equivalence, in which the person believes their thoughts can control reality (Ridenour et al., 2018). In response, I said: "You know I have this image that your 'self' is like a tiny Velcro ball that anything can stick to you, making you feel vulnerable. It seems like you don't know how to check your own ideas. I think most people have enough of a sense of who they are that they can reflect upon themselves and their memories to determine whether an idea fits their self-concept. Without a strong sense of self, it seems like you can be colonized at any moment." He responded by affirming that he felt fearful all the time of his thoughts and often felt the need to dismiss new ideas, due to his concerns about suddenly transforming into a new person.

The following week, Taylor discussed a stressful experience he had had over the weekend. His friend recommended he watch a new TV show. In the episode, there was an image of a parasite coming out of an eyeball. This troubled Taylor who had always been scared of parasites. He became worried and tried to figure out why he was scared of parasites. He then decided that he must be scared of parasites because he is, in fact, a social parasite. As he arrived at this idea, he became confused and his thinking became abstract and difficult to follow. In this session, I worked to slow down the process (i.e. stopping and rewinding, Brent & Fonagy, 2014) to understand the logic of his associations. First, we worked to understand the potential emotional and social meaning of his thoughts, even the irrational ones. In therapy with people with experiences of psychosis, it is important to consider the personal and interpersonal themes that might imbed in all thoughts, even those that might be regarded as psychotic. After unpacking the process, we explored the possibility that he was desperately trying to attach meaning to his thoughts to minimize his emotional distress. It became clear that he was rushing ahead of himself and jumping to a conclusion (van der Leer, Hartig, Goldmanis, & McKay, 2015), trying to control his fear by knowing exactly why he was scared of parasites. We explored how panic and fear could drive him to reach for an explanation that did not actually correspond with his lived experience.

As treatment progressed, Taylor spoke about his anxiety around expressing his needs to others. We connected this to his sense that he had to protect his mother because she was fragile and depressed, which made it difficult for him to express any feelings of anger or criticism towards her. Near the end of the session, I asked him if he had ever thought what it would have been like for him as an infant to be given away by his mother to his father who took him to Mexico. In the process of our exchange and in an effort to punctuate his grief and anger, I used the phrase "she sold you down the river", at which point Taylor froze, seemingly upset but unable to articulate his feelings. I felt a sense of sadness and fear grip him, and I also felt despair. After the session, I became curious about the origin of the phrase "sold down the river". I looked it up and discovered it was a phrase that originated in the Southern United States when slave owners sold slaves down the Mississippi River. Not only did it mean that the slave would be permanently separated from their family, but it was essentially a death sentence. As I was reflecting on this session, I listened to the old African-American spiritual "Sometimes I Feel Like a Motherless Child" sung by Paul Robeson. I became filled with a tremendous grief and sense of loneliness, which Fromm-Reichmann (1959) has reflected upon as being a painful aspect in the lives of individuals with psychosis. I understood my associations and loneliness as my way of viscerally connecting with the experience of abduction and kidnapping given my background as a white southerner. I did not share this experience with him but tried to register the grief and terror of being separated from his family. I wondered about the dissociated affect he might be carrying around in connection to these traumatic separations and how it could impact his psychosis (Lysaker & Hamm, 2015). Some theorists have noted the experiential overlap between dissociation and psychosis (e.g. depersonalization, derealization see Sass et al., 2018), and the potential influence of trauma on both dissociation and psychosis (Ross & Keyes, 2009).

Middle phase and emergence of delusion

As we moved into the third month of Taylor's treatment, we explored some odd experiences that began to emerge. He spoke about trying to physically remove a "root" from his brain that he believed was blocking him from being in contact with his former self and possibly responsible for his breakdown. He told me that he thought he could physically alter his brain through the use of his thoughts. He said that he could sense his brain and was able to envision a topographic brain map in which he could scan the inner workings of his brain structure. Initially, I had difficulty understanding whether he was using a metaphor to describe his relationship to his mind or if he was being literal. As we explored his experience, he stated that he knew it was odd, but he thought that he could control his brain. He told me that he had descended into the "deepest layer of his being" and had stumbled into the "central command station", able to manipulate and control his experience and perception directly through altering his brain. When Taylor introduced the idea, I chose not to reality test this delusional idea, but instead tried to understand his first-person experience. Furthermore, I wanted to establish the emotional context when this type of thinking arose to better understand its function. Later, I would confront these ideas more directly.

In a later session, Taylor came in very panicked. He reported that he had destroyed his "memories" because he had undone the "knot" in his brain that bound the energy that allowed him to resist his apathy. I tried to understand his experiences and how he was relating it to his brain. He let me know that the day before he had been feeling very distraught. He had decided that it might be useful to try and enter into his brain and "push out" any alien objects that might account for his bad feelings. As he had attempted this, he had apparently untied a "knot", which made him extremely worried that he had destroyed his memories. In response to this painful and puzzling experience, I worked to contain his affect and also challenged his dogmatic certainty that he had actually permanently destroyed his memories. When I thought about Taylor's brain map, I also considered the developmental aspects. His concerns about alien roots in his brain made me think of how his parents were essentially *brain*washed by a cult who put destructive ideas into their mind. Furthermore, Taylor's early attachments were disrupted by his father taking him to a foreign country separate from his and his mother then "kidnapping" him, which was likely a traumatic, disorganizing loss. At times, I would draw connections between his mother's experience, of joining a cult in her 20s and dramatically shifting her worldview, and his brain map (at a similar age), though he had trouble seeing the links between their shared history. We focused more on his mother's traumatic experience because he knew so little about his father and had limited interactions with him after his mother took him back to the United States.

Taylor's delusion of the brain map brings to mind Jaspers' (1963) ideas on the delusional atmosphere and the formation of delusional systems. The delusional atmosphere refers to the elusive atmosphere that precedes the formation of the delusion. In this context, the individual has an experience of the uncanny in which the self is experienced differently, the world is imbued with new meaning, and there is change in the ontological fabric of the universe that is both subtle and ineffable (Ratcliffe, 2013). As a result, the individual's experience of the world is unstable and it seems both mysterious and disturbing. In the face of this warped reality, the individual strives to make sense of these alterations. Simultaneously, the individual also starts to become dislocated from social reality and loses their sense of existing in a shared, public world. Within this context, the individual experiences the delusion as a profound discovery that accounts for their altered sense of reality (Ratcliffe, 2013). In Taylor's case, he had been struggling for the past three years with a diminished sense of self-presence, disorganized thinking, and isolation. He longed both to understand and reverse these painful changes that made him feel unstable and confused. I held this concept in mind as he began to speak more directly about the brain map, which seemed to be a creative metaphor he had generated to explain these self-alterations. Of course, Taylor did not view it as a metaphor, especially in this phase of treatment. Taylor described his experience in physical terms, often stating that he could alter the physical shape of his brain through thinking, similar to the ways others experiencing psychosis described alterations in their sense of embodiment (Jones et al., 2016).

In the following month, I continued working to help Taylor learn about and develop insight into his struggles. I started to notice that he began to attribute all of his distress (e.g. negative feelings, social insecurity, and anxiety) to the brain map. In repeated sessions, he would describe feeling insecure and then would be unable to resist the urge to change his "brain" by concentrating on the map and shifting the structures around. Initially, I started to point out how the brain map was becoming expansive, attributing all of his experiences through this structure. I asked him what he thought I thought about the brain map. Taylor recognized that I might think he was psychotic, but he knew it was real because he felt physical sensations in his brain. I continued to link his delusional ideation with his efforts to control negative affect.

Near the end of the treatment, I decided to take a more confrontational stance towards the brain map. I challenged Taylor to not resort to "using" the brain map when he became anxious or insecure. He noticed that when he tried to resist altering the brain map he became disoriented. He thought this was evidence that the strategy did not work. I told him that I thought it made sense that he would feel more confusion without it, given that he relied on it like the North Star. I stated that I thought the brain map represented his efforts to provide stability to his highly unstable representations of reality. In the evening, he would often speak with the psychiatric nurses about his concerns that I did not know what I was doing. In the countertransference, there were moments when I felt powerless to help him manage without his delusional structure. I felt like the brain map was spreading like a virus, and I could see the way it provided him a much-needed sense of security. I was also feeling the pressure of his upcoming discharge and need to return home to outpatient treatment and college. Although I believed the brain map was a delusion, I also wanted to respect the opacity of mind, marking that both he and I were limited in our ability to grasp psychic reality.

Taylor soon disclosed that he was unsure whether he actually had a "mental illness" because he did not have the common symptoms of psychosis (e.g. hearing voices). He wondered if his problems were due to some unknown physical cause. He entertained the idea that his problems would simply go away if he stopped thinking about them. I continued to challenge his ideas about the brain map and his sense that he could control the inner workings of his brain via thought. I emphasized that thoughts have a limited influence on reality. I also told him I was skeptical about the brain map's existence, in part, because he had never been able to successfully manipulate it. As mentioned above, he would repeatedly try to alter his brain when feeling upset. I pointed out that his statement that he could control his brain would be equivalent to me claiming "I can read other people's minds just not in this treatment centre". I told him that I thought he was claiming to have a special ability, while also admitting that he had little capacity to wield it. I shared that I thought his belief that he could not control the brain map might be his way of justifying having no real influence. In fact, it made me wonder if it merely represented his wish to be in control of his confusing self-experience. I tried to intervene with humility, acknowledging that I was not omniscient. He initially responded with skepticism, given his physical experience of his brain. We continued to have this conversation over the next month, and he struggled to tolerate the idea that his brain map was delusional and was disoriented by this possibility. Taylor started to gain more insight into his troubles and noticed the ways he turned to his brain map in moments of insecurity. When he believed in the map, he felt in control. However, when he stopped thinking about his experiences though this prism, he became disoriented and anxious.

I empathized with emotional fear and uncertainty. We spoke about the way that his brain map served as a mechanism to explain his loss of self-presence, his altered thought processes, distorted perceptions, and emotional distress. Although it simplified his experience, it was starting to become all-pervasive. He noticed that he was withdrawing from others because he did not think anyone could understand his experience. I highlighted that this was another danger of settling on the brain map. We had repeated conversations about the brain map, his wavering belief, and how it was impacted by changing moods. At some point, he returned to the image that he had descended into the deepest "layer of his being". He described an image of seeing various TV screens that depicted the aspects of his brain. We spoke about how he did not have the "remote" to change the channel and that it was important to let go of his wish to control it.

Termination phase

In the final month of treatment, Taylor consolidated some of his learning in psychotherapy. While he had initially presented as confused and depressed, by the end of treatment he had developed a better perspective on his problems and had better ability to express and modulate his feelings. Throughout the work, he had become more open and would sometimes cry and think about the losses he had experienced over the course of his life. He could speak about how fear distorted his thinking. He also could appreciate how certain boundaries had become confused in his mind (e.g. reality vs. fantasy). This was evident when Taylor could notice that his thoughts could not spontaneously alter his identity. He appreciated the limits of his ideas and realized that thoughts do not unilaterally control reality. When he was starting to have a breakdown back in college, he had adopted the idea that perception shapes reality. We talked about how this was true, but only within certain parameters. I also created a document in which I outlined Taylor's learning in therapy, including his reasoning processes, his relationship to the brain map, the impact of his emotions on his thoughts, and alterations in his sense of self. Taylor had requested something written because he sometimes had trouble remembering what we talked about. I continued to encourage Taylor to think more about how context influences his reality perspective. He reported finding it helpful that I encouraged him to reflect upon the meaning of his thoughts. I sometimes normalized his odd thoughts by offering some of my own loose associations in sessions. I would use my mind as a model (Brent, 2009) to illustrate how I made meaning of my experiences and his experiences. I would point out ways that I might dismiss random thoughts and not grant them significance in an effort to teach that our thoughts do not have to control our sense of identity.

When reviewing his treatment, Taylor said that he thought it took many months in therapy to entertain the idea that his delusional experiences might not be "real". We spoke about how this could be complicated because our self-experiences feel "real" even when we know that all of us are prone to cognitive biases. Taylor spoke about how previously he had felt invalidated when clinicians or family members questioned his perception of reality. However, he learned over the course of therapy that he needs to be skeptical sometimes of his experiences in an effort not to get lost in thought, or overwhelmed with anxiety. It took many months of my carefully listening to his experience of his emotions before Taylor developed epistemic trust (Fonagy & Allison, 2014) in me and allowed me to be a real conversation partner regarding his delusional ideas. This was a very fragile process and required patience, humility, carefulness, and tolerance of ambiguity. Taylor would often speak about bizarre experiences that were hard to understand. I did not feel that I had the right to challenge his delusional ideas until it became evident that he was turning to this cognitive structure in the face of negative affect, insecurity, and social anxiety. With this information in mind, I treated the delusion as a defence, and a breakdown in mentalization, and worked to help him recognize how negative affect disrupted his reflective capacity. Unlike CBT and more traditional cognitive approaches which merely challenge the person's attributions to their ideas, I worked diligently to understand the meaning of his delusion, the emotional and interpersonal context in which it emerged, and the function it served psychologically (i.e. reducing confusion and disorientation).

Conclusions

Fixed delusions are difficult to treat and often not responsive to medications or psychosocial treatment (Turkington et al., 2015). In this chapter, I have argued that delusions can be understood in their interpersonal and affective context, and that MBT-p offers a helpful way of understanding and intervening therapeutically. In the case of Taylor, I worked to emphasize the significance of the therapeutic stance (opacity of mind), the relevance of mentalization difficulties for psychosis (e.g. psychic equivalence and omnipotence of thought), and the value of stopping and rewinding the process when negative emotions and insecurity trigger delusional thinking (Leonhardt et al., 2016). In addition, I also offered ideas about how to confront both the thought process and content of delusions. Within this space, I strove to recognize how delusional ideation represented a breakdown in mentalization and Taylor's effort to feel secure when he felt tremendous anxiety and distress. He began to explain all of his experiences through the brain map, which reduced both his curiosity and provided him with unquestionable authority. After months of exploring the development of these ideas and understanding his first-person experience, I confronted him in an empathic manner, recognizing how it was hard for him to sacrifice this sense of certainty, as it exposed him to fear. He was gradually able to tolerate different perspectives of his experience while not feeling invalidated by my challenges. MBT-p provides an important, pragmatic framework that allows the therapist to understand the experiences of clients grappling with psychosis and intervene in an experience-near, sensitive manner.

Limitations and future directions

There are several limitations to this case study. First, Taylor was exceptionally verbally gifted and it is questionable whether this approach would have been possible for individuals who evidence less insight and verbal facility. Second, I saw Taylor in intensive psychotherapy (four times weekly) for nine months. This process was long and painstaking and it is unclear how much time is needed before individuals can start to gain distance from their delusions and think about the meaning of their experience. Third, MBT-p is an emerging psychotherapy that is currently being researched (Weijers et al., 2016) and its efficacy has yet to be established. Fourth, I focused less on attachment and its relevance to mentalization and psychosis (Brent, 2009) during the discussion of the case study. Finally, MBT-p is in its early stages and less has been written about how it can be applied to the various symptom presentations of psychosis (e.g. disorganized thinking, negative symptoms, hallucinations, etc.).

MBT-p is a promising approach that aims to empower people to develop their capacities to reflect upon the mental states of self and other. Future studies could research how MBT-p could be applied to individuals struggling with dissociation and psychosis, given the overlap for individuals who have experienced trauma (Ross & Keyes, 2009). In addition, more case studies are needed to illustrate how therapists are applying MBT-p to individuals presenting with different symptoms such as disorganized thinking or negative symptoms. Finally, future efforts could explore MBT-p and similar therapies such as MERIT (Lysaker & Klion, 2017) overlap and what are the distinct factors that differentiate these approaches (see discussion Chapter 1).

References

American Psychiatric Association. (2013). *Diagnostic and statistical manual of mental disorders* (*DSM-5*). Washington, DC: American Psychiatric Association.

Arnold, K., & Vakhrusheva, J. (2016). Resist the negation reflex: Minimizing reactance in psychotherapy of delusions. *Psychosis, 8*(2), 166–175.

Bateman, A., & Fonagy, P. (2001). Treatment of borderline personality disorder with psychoanalytically oriented partial hospitalization: An 18-month follow-up. *American Journal of Psychiatry, 158*(1), 36–42.

Bateman, A., & Fonagy, P. (2013). Mentalization-based treatment. *Psychoanalytic Inquiry, 33*, 595–613.

Bateman, A., & Fonagy, P. (2016). *Mentalization-based treatment for personality disorders*. Oxford: Oxford University Press.

Beck, A. T., & Rector, N. A. (2002). Delusions: A cognitive perspective. *Journal of Cognitive Psychotherapy*, *16*(4), 455–468.

Bleuler, E. (1911). *Dementia praecox: oder Gruppe der Schizophrenien*. Leipzig: F. Deuticke.

Brent, B. K. (2009). Mentalization-based psychodynamic psychotherapy for psychosis. *Journal of Clinical Psychology*, *65*(8), 803–814.

Brent, B. K., & Fonagy, P. (2014). A mentalization-based treatment approach to disturbances of social understanding in schizophrenia. In P. H. Lysaker, G. Dimaggio, & M. Brune (Eds.), *Social cognition and metacognition in schizophrenia: Psychopathology and treatment approaches* (pp. 245–259). Gurgaon: Elsevier Science and Technology.

Debbané, M., Benmiloud, J., Salaminios, G., Solida-Tozzi, A., Armando, M., Fonagy, P., & Bateman, A. (2016). Mentalization-based treatment in clinical high-risk for psychosis: A rationale and clinical illustration. *Journal of Contemporary Psychotherapy*, *6*(4), 217–225.

Fonagy, P., & Allison, E. (2014). The role of mentalizing and epistemic trust in the therapeutic relationship. *Psychotherapy*, *51*(3), 372–380.

Fromm-Reichmann, F. (1959). Loneliness. *Psychiatry*, *22*(1), 1–15.

Fuchs, T. (2015). The intersubjectivity of delusions. *World Psychiatry*, *14*(2), 178–179.

Garety, P. A., & Freeman, D. (2013). The past and future of delusions research: From the inexplicable to the treatable. *The British Journal of Psychiatry*, *203*(5), 327–333.

Jaspers, K. (1963). *General psychopathology* (7th ed., J. Hoenig & M. W. Hamilton, trans.). Manchester: Manchester University Press.

Jones, N., Shattell, M., Kelly, T., Brown, R., Robinson, L., Renfro, R., . . . & Luhrmann, T. M. (2016). "Did I push myself over the edge?": Complications of agency in psychosis onset and development. *Psychosis*, *8*(4), 324–335.

Knauss, D., Ridenour, J., & Hamm, J. A. (2018). Emerging psychotherapies for psychosis. *Journal of Psychiatric Practice*, *24*(5), 348–353.

Kumar, D., Menon, M., Moritz, S., & Woodward, T. S. (2015). Using the back door: Metacognitive training for psychosis. *Psychosis*, *7*(2), 166–178.

Kumazaki, T. (2015). Persecutory delusions and first-person authority. *Theory & Psychology*, *25*(1), 80–95.

Lee, H. J., Cougle, J. R., & Telch, M. J. (2005). Thought–action fusion and its relationship to schizotypy and OCD symptoms. *Behaviour Research and Therapy*, *43*(1), 29–41.

Leonhardt, B. L., Kukla, M., Belanger, E., Chaudoin-Patzoldt, K. A., Buck, K. D., Minor, K. S., . . . & Lysaker, P. H. (2016). Emergence of psychotic content in psychotherapy: An exploratory qualitative analysis of content, process, and therapist variables in a single case study. *Psychotherapy Research*, *28*(2), 1–17.

Lysaker, P. H., & Hamm, J. A. (2015). Phenomenological models of delusions: Concerns regarding the neglect of the role of emotional pain and intersubjectivity. *World Psychiatry*, *14*(2), 175–176.

Lysaker, P. H., & Klion, R. E. (2017). *Recovery, meaning-making, and severe mental illness: A comprehensive guide to metacognitive reflection and insight therapy*. London: Routledge.

Nelson, B., Parnas, J., & Sass, L. A. (2014). Disturbance of minimal self (ipseity) in schizophrenia: Clarification and current status. *Schizophrenia Bulletin*, *40*(3), 479–482.

Parnas, J. (2011). A disappearing heritage: The clinical core of schizophrenia. *Schizophrenia Bulletin*, *37*(6), 1121–1130.

Ratcliffe, M. (2013). Delusional atmosphere and the sense of unreality. In *One century of Karl Jaspers' general psychopathology* (pp. 229–244). Oxford: Oxford University Press.

Ratcliffe, M. (2015). The interpersonal world of psychosis. *World Psychiatry, 14*(2), 176–178.

Ridenour, J., Knauss, D., & Hamm, J. A. (2018). Comparing metacognition and mentalization and their implications for psychotherapy for individuals with psychosis. *Journal of Contemporary Psychotherapy, 49*(8), 1–7.

Ross, C. A., & Keyes, B. B. (2009). Clinical features of dissociative schizophrenia in China. *Psychosis, 1*(1), 51–60.

Sass, L. A., Borda, J. P., Madeira, L., Pienkos, E., & Nelson, B. (2018). Varieties of self disorder: A bio-pheno-social model of schizophrenia. *Schizophrenia Bulletin, 44*(4), 720–727.

Sass, L. A., & Byrom, G. (2015). Phenomenological and neurocognitive perspectives on delusions: A critical overview. *World Psychiatry, 14*(2), 164–173.

Sass, L. A., & Parnas, J. (2003). Schizophrenia, consciousness, and the self. *Schizophrenia Bulletin, 29*(3), 427–444.

Staring, A. B., van der Gaag, M., & Mulder, C. L. (2011). Recovery style predicts remission at one-year follow-up in outpatients with schizophrenia spectrum disorders. *The Journal of Nervous and Mental Disease, 199*(5), 295–300.

Tai, S., & Turkington, D. (2009). The evolution of cognitive behavior therapy for schizophrenia: Current practice and recent developments. *Schizophrenia Bulletin, 35*(5), 865–873.

Turkington, D., Spencer, H., Jassal, I., & Cummings, A. (2015). Cognitive behavioural therapy for the treatment of delusional systems. *Psychosis, 7*(1), 48–59.

van der Leer, L., Hartig, B., Goldmanis, M., & McKay, R. (2015). Delusion proneness and 'jumping to conclusions': Relative and absolute effects. *Psychological Medicine, 45*(6), 1253–1262.

Weijers, J., ten Kate, C., Eurelings-Bontekoe, E., Viechtbauer, W., Rampaart, R., Bateman, A., & Selten, J. P. (2016). Mentalization-based treatment for psychotic disorder: Protocol of a randomized controlled trial. *BMC Psychiatry, 16*(1), 1.

6

TRANSFERENCE AND COUNTERTRANSFERENCE IN THE RECOVERY OF SELF IN METACOGNITIVELY-ORIENTED THERAPIES FOR PSYCHOSIS

Rebecca Bargenquast, Robert D. Schweitzer and Kate O'Connor

Abstract: *Metacognitive-oriented psychotherapy models have emerged as an effective means of supporting people with a history of psychosis to lead richer and more meaningful lives. The therapeutic dynamic, which relies on an intersubjective process between therapist and client, has the potential to enhance or to hinder therapy. However, this intersubjective process, including the role of transference and countertransference involved in metacognitive therapies, has not been well understood or articulated. Accordingly, this chapter will draw on a psychodynamic framework to explore the intersubjective nature of the relationship, by focusing on transference and countertransference within a metacognitive-oriented psychotherapy. We refer to a composite case study to highlight potential interpersonal complexities and challenges faced by therapists working with people who experience psychosis within a recovery-oriented, psychotherapeutic framework. We propose sensitive and curiosity-driven explorations of the therapeutic relationship itself as part of the therapeutic agenda. The approach is cognisant of the emergence of transference issues within the therapy and suggests how exploration and articulation of such issues may add to the client's self-structure and renewed sense of self across multiple domains in their life.*

We are witnessing a renewed interest in the psychotherapeutic treatment of people with psychotic spectrum disorders which is both exciting and challenging (Hamm, Hasson-Ohayon, Kukla, & Lysaker, 2013). This interest in psychological approaches is occurring against a background of increasing knowledge of neurobiology and, at the same time, the psychological and relational factors underpinning a diminished sense of self, which lie at the core of mental distress. Translating knowledge of this sense of self into clinical practice, Metacognitive Reflection and Insight Therapy (MERIT, see Chapter 1; Chapter 11) addresses core components of human functioning including "freedom from symptoms, developing a sense of hopefulness, the attainment of work and love, and restoration of a sense of wholeness of one's sense of being" (Lysaker & Klion, 2017, p. 4). The model, drawing on dialogical theory (Hermans, 1996), in which story and storytelling are considered to be at the core of identity, informs a theory of change. It aims to facilitate change at a deep and subjective level and recognises an integrated sense of self as being at the core of emotional and psychological well-being. However, previously only limited attention has been paid to the relational, or unconscious, aspects of the therapeutic relationship and the ways in which these aspects are expressed in the treatment paradigm (Hasson-Ohayon, Kravetz, & Lysaker, 2017).

This chapter seeks to extend our understanding of the intersubjective elements of the model by examining the role of countertransference and transference, as potentially critical elements in the process of recovery. That is, we wish to acknowledge unconscious dimensions of the relationship between the person seeking assistance and therapist and argue for the inclusion of these dimensions within the context of a metacognitive-oriented approach. In this contribution, we will draw on the potential learnings from a composite case, whom we refer to as Mr L, involving a long-term therapeutic encounter, complicated by erotic transference issues. The composite case is drawn from a trial of a metacognitive-oriented therapy with people diagnosed with psychotic spectrum disorders (Bargenquast & Schweitzer, 2014a). The therapy was guided by a set of principles, referred to as metacognitive narrative therapy, that are consistent with an integrative therapy, later formalised as MERIT (Lysaker & Klion, 2017). This contribution builds on intersubjective metacognitive models (Hasson-Ohayon et al., 2017) by extending understanding of the therapeutic alliance as a relational and intersubjective process towards recognition of the unconscious components of the relationship. The learning points, presented at the end of the chapter, have the potential to contribute to an understanding of the relational dynamics involved in metacognitive-oriented therapies for psychosis and potential outcomes when complicated by transference reactions. The chapter contributes to a broader understanding of relational dynamics in the psychotherapeutic treatment of people with a history of psychosis.

Transference and countertransference

Relational dynamics in psychotherapy have been addressed extensively since psychology was established as a discipline. Since Freud's (1913) original theory of transference, which focused on unconscious dynamics in the therapeutic relationship, a number of theorists have pointed to the central nature of the relationship between therapist and client. This chapter proposes that the therapeutic alliance is a starting point in the development of a relationship which, in turn, lies at the core of therapeutic change. The fact that the therapeutic relationship involves two people and, as such, is evocative of other relationships is understood as a relational perspective of therapy. In addition to the reality-based aspects of the relationship (i.e. the working alliance), non-rational and unconscious aspects, such as transference and countertransference, emerge within this dyad and warrant exploration.

Transference and countertransference are active in every significant relationship. Transference refers, in part, to the feelings experienced by a client towards their therapist, which are derived from earlier significant relationships. These feelings are usually associated with one or more figures from the past, which are repeated with the therapist in the present situation. As such, transference provides a glimpse of significant relationships from the client's past. By definition, thus, the transferential component of the relationship is a repetition. Similarly, counter-transference involves the therapist's feelings within the therapeutic relationship. More precisely, countertransference can be understood as the aspect of the thera-pist's experience that is evoked in response to the client's transference. Within the broader context of the therapist's experiences of the client, countertransference is present alongside responses which have origins in the therapist's own history and relational blueprint, as well as separate manifestations of the therapist's "real", non-transferential relationship to the client (King & O'Brien, 2011). Through their relational experiences in the therapy, the therapist is said to become a recep-tive instrument in their understanding of the complexes and resistances which may distort their understanding of the client (Freud, 1913). Winnicott (1947) observed that "If we are to become able to be the analysts of psychotic patients we must have reached down to very primitive things in ourselves" (p. 61), allud-ing to the fact that primitive impulses and affectively-laden responses are not only part of the client's domain, but are also part of the experience of the therapist. That is, both people in the therapeutic dyad possess and are subject to non-rational, unconscious parts of self, which are played out during the therapeutic encounter.

Awareness of these processes arguably lies at the core of all psychotherapy. Despite this, the recognition and expression of transference and countertransfer-ence have been somewhat neglected in the emerging literature on metacognitive and mentalization-based treatments for psychosis. To enhance awareness of these constructs within metacognitive-oriented therapies for psychosis, Horowitz's (2002) observation has salience: "Countertransference becomes window or wall, either widening the therapist's own experience of self and in turn deepening the connection to the client's reality or erecting a barrier that prevents access to the internal experience of both client and clinician" (p. 240). That is, through the thera-pist's interrogation of their own experience they are better able to understand the lived experience of their client.

Intersubjectivity and the therapeutic relationship

The loss of sense of self experienced by people with psychosis not only leads to impaired first-person awareness, but also impaired second-person awareness. This means connections with others are often experienced from outside of the relation-ship, that is, in the third person, resulting in the person's social world becoming problematic. Disturbances in intersubjectivity in psychosis may be conceived in terms of the experience of the person in relation to their therapist (Hasson-Ohayon et al., 2017).

The difficulties experienced by people with psychosis are well illustrated in the writings of Lysaker and colleagues, who describe the fundamental dysfunction as a "collapse of the dialogical self", which results in a profound disturbance in the construction and development of personal narratives (Lysaker & Lysaker, 2001). The narratives of people suffering with symptoms associated with a diagnosis of schizophrenia often lack coherence and as such are conceptually and temporally disorganised. The person's self-narrative may fail to portray the person as the story's protagonist, lack a sense of their being meaningfully connected to others, and these are often difficult to understand, thus appearing meaningless to listeners (Lysaker & Klion, 2017).

Characteristic difficulties in psychosis have also been described by McGlashan (1983) in terms of: (1) A basic mistrust and expectation of harm from others; (2) a marked ambivalence in relationships, which may be expressed in terms of a need or longing for merger based on intolerance of loneliness, and withdrawal along with a tendency towards isolation due to terror associated with closeness; and (3) weak or absent ego boundaries resulting in difficulty differentiating one's own thoughts and impulses from those of others. This may lead to a sense of self-impoverishment and loss of agency and narrative complexity (Lysaker, Roe, & Buck, 2010).

The ways in which therapists may address the needs of people seeking help will vary, based on an array of factors including therapists' theoretical assumptions and agreement between the therapist and client on the essential meaning of the psychotherapy (Hasson-Ohayon et al., 2017). However, at the core of all approaches is the need to establish a relationship with the person, which in essence involves an intersubjective process occasioned by the meeting of two minds. Within this context, intersubjectivity provides both a basis for relatedness and also acts as a precondition for the development of self-reflection, the capacity to share meaningful narratives (Hasson-Ohayon et al., 2017), and the emergence of mind within the confines of a relationship "with another" (Ferro & Nicoli, 2018). Therapist attributes, which may determine their capacity to form a relationship with the person, may include an interest in, and capacity to tolerate, intense affect, dependency, and ambiguous communication (Fenton, 2000). The psychotherapist is thus required to be flexible, creative, and willing to admit when they are wrong, and recognise that aloofness, critical pomposity, and rigidity are potentially undermining for a therapeutic encounter.

These considerations have been similarly expressed in MERIT, along with other factors, such as the degree to which the therapist is encouraged to enter into a relationship with the person and allow their own thinking to be a part of the therapy (Hasson-Ohayon et al., 2017). If the initial encounters are traversed successfully, a background feeling of security and predictability will increasingly characterise the therapy.

The process of metacognitive-oriented therapy has been described variously by different writers (see review in Chapter 1). Salvatore, Russo, Russo, Popolo, and Dimaggio (2012), in a case study referring to a person presenting with a delusional disorder, have described the process as promoting an awareness of painful emotions. The articulation of awareness may be associated with greater understanding of the social circumstances eliciting feelings of vulnerability; understanding how the influence of disrupting affects leads to description of the intentions of others, which may or may not be reality based; and promoting feelings of strength and self-efficacy in relation to self. Part of the process of meaning making may thus relate to the meaning of the therapeutic relationship itself, and the dynamics which both person and therapist bring to the interaction. In responding to people who experience psychotic states, cognisance needs to be taken of the degree to which the person may experience social interaction as threatening – a threat to the self through either engulfment or annihilation (Lysaker, Johannesen, & Lysaker, 2005).

The role of transference in metacognitive therapy

Metacognitive therapy, at its core, facilitates the stimulation of self-states, and promotes capacity for decentration. This act of stimulation, and the connection between this process and internal working models, may also have the effect of stimulating "transference" in the relationship between the person seeking assistance and therapist. The phenomenon is further complicated by the psychodynamics associated with psychotic experiences and the thesis that psychosis may well represent a response to unbearable aspects of reality and, in psychodynamic language, represent a defence in maintaining a sense of self. Consequently, the clinician needs to remain alert to mental states, and to be continuously curious and reflective in relation to what transpires interpersonally over the course of the therapy. It is noteworthy that therapy does not follow a linear path, hence the therapist needs to remain aware of expressions of such distortions. The challenge for the therapist is to work with the person to form more complex and integrated ideas around the emergence of feelings in relation to the therapist without resorting to simplistic explanations.

Relational distortions, which lie at the heart of transferential relationships, may well emerge in the relationship reflecting both conscious and unconscious aspects of both the therapist and the person seeking assistance. These may involve a rational part of the person, who maintains a reality-derived understanding of self and other, including recognising the personal qualities of the other; a "neurotic" transference, where the understanding is characterised by distortions which have an "as if" quality. Or the relationship may be characterised by a psychotic transference, as evident in erotic transference, in which distortions are often intense and refer to more primitive (in the sense of psychosocial development) feelings emerging within the therapy.

The role of countertransference in metacognitive therapy

The role of countertransference has not been well articulated in metacognitive therapies, despite metacognitive therapies recognising intersubjective elements within the therapeutic process. To better appreciate the significance and intensity of countertransference reactions in the treatment of people suffering from a range of deficits associated with a diagnosis of schizophrenia, it is valuable to revisit the psychoanalytic literature on the treatment of people with a diagnosis of schizophrenia.

Both Rosenfeld (1987) and Jung (1963) spoke of the risk of psychological encounters inducing lasting psychic disturbances in the therapist, if they themselves do not possess a strong character and capacity for containing the person's, at times overwhelming, responses. Given the person's aforementioned challenges differentiating themselves and others, as well as the intensity and severity of psychotic symptoms, the therapeutic space can evoke a sense of unreality, confusion, or dissociation in the therapist. The strength of projections from persons suffering with symptoms associated with psychosis can also mean that the therapist may start to feel that the projections have a realistic element (Rosenfeld, 1987). Therapists are described as commonly experiencing strong feelings of anger, despair, boredom, hopelessness, and frustration that may mirror the inner experiences of their client (Bargenquast, 2012). Fromm-Reichmann (1954) emphasised the importance of therapists addressing their countertransference responses in working with people who may have received a diagnosis of schizophrenia, stating that the successful reparation of ruptures in treatment is contingent on the therapist not becoming too frightened, discouraged, or narcissistically hurt by their occurrence.

Therapists working from a metacognitive perspective have described their responses to people in terms ranging from engagement to boredom. More significantly, themes revealed in interviews with therapists have alluded to the therapists' difficulties in separating their own thoughts and feelings at times from those of the person seeking assistance. Therapists have referred to both a sense of being-with-another and also to a contrasting lived experience of nothingness (Hutton, 2012). We have little knowledge of therapist responses to erotic transference which is likely to be complex given the nature of the transference.

The therapeutic approach

Metacognitive narrative therapy formed the foundation of a clinical trial involving eight patients, all of whom had received a diagnosis of schizophrenia. Following ethical approval for the study, participants were provided with weekly therapy for a period of one to two years. The study provided evidence of gains in recovery and metacognition, which were maintained at two years follow-up. Metacognitive narrative therapy, as conceived at the time of the study (Bargenquast & Schweitzer, 2014a), was an integrative recovery-oriented treatment, which acknowledges that recovery may involve restructuring of more subjective aspects of human experience, including personal narrative and the sense of self as meaningful agent in the world (Lysaker, Glynn, Wilkniss, & Silverstein, 2010; Lysaker & Lysaker, 2010; Lysaker & Roe, 2012; Lysaker, Roe, & Kukla, 2012; Silverstein & Bellack, 2008). More recently, the therapeutic model has been formalised into a structured approach, MERIT (Lysaker & Klion, 2017). Rather than being focused on symptom reduction, the therapy aims to enhance the client's capacity to live a rich and meaningful life by supporting the development of their capacity to think about themselves and others, and to form coherent and complex stories about their life (Bargenquast & Schweitzer, 2014b). The person is encouraged to think about themselves, think about others, and think about themselves in relation to others, within sessions. This process of reflection, based upon mutuality, rather than a therapist as expert, facilitates the development of increasingly complex metacognitive tasks (e.g. discussion of different thoughts, feelings, or wishes that emerged as the session unfolds) (Lysaker, Gagen, Moritz, & Schweitzer, 2018). In alignment with the recovery model (Lysaker, Roe et al., 2010), the therapy aims to create an intersubjective space within the therapeutic relationship where the client is able to develop a greater sense of themselves as a protagonist in their own life.

The case of Mr L

Mr L is a composite case, which draws on a number of people's experiences within a psychotherapy trial (Schweitzer, Greben, & Bargenquast, 2017). While parts of the case are fictional, to protect client confidentiality, presented excerpts are adapted from real therapy sessions. The presented treatment outcomes reflect an amalgamation of commonalities found across a number of cases in the trial.

Mr L was in his early 50s when he presented to the clinic. He had a history of psychotic symptoms, with several hospital admissions over the previous 30 years. After moving to Australia with his family from Africa as a young child, he reported being primarily raised by his mother and maternal grandparents, as his father continued to maintain properties in Africa. He reported a close relationship with his mother and strong feelings of a loss of closeness with her following the birth of his siblings. Mr L reported a history of sexual abuse during his early years, but did not disclose further details of these experiences. He came from a family where achievement was highly regarded, but where he himself had not been academically successful. He reported some academic and social difficulties throughout his schooling, during which time he reportedly felt ostracised. Mr L's work history was mixed with long periods of unemployment. He was divorced, and had no children. He reported some contact with family and also occasionally with his extended family.

Mr L had had his first psychotic experience in his early 20s, during which he had heard voices saying both that he was useless and incompetent, while others were reassuring. He had a meaningful relationship during his early 20s, which led to marriage, followed by divorce. He appeared pained by this experience, with seemingly little understanding of the reasons leading to his separation. He did, however, refer to his sexual relationship with his ex-wife, and expressed feelings of guilt in this regard, which he associated with an experience during which he believed that he had raped his wife. Mr L reported being diagnosed with schizophrenia following his first hospitalisation in his early 20s. Prior to engaging in therapy, he had been hospitalised numerous times in response to psychotic symptoms, including a number of long-term admissions. He reported having been treated with electroconvulsive therapy during his early 20s.

Mr L engaged in 52 sessions of metacognitive narrative therapy as part of a pilot study within a university training psychology clinic (Bargenquast & Schweitzer, 2014a). His therapist was a graduate trainee, in her final year of training. She was trained in metacognitive narrative therapy and attended fortnightly group supervision for the duration of the treatment.

Mr L presented to therapy with grandiose delusional belief, incongruent and inappropriate affect, and tangential, disorganised speech. He reported a history of delusional beliefs and expressed overvalued ideas. For example, he believed he was a decorated veteran, who had played an integral part in the Vietnam War. Mr L shared that he had difficulties connecting with others and forming meaningful relationships. He reported an intense desire for relationships with others and, at the same time, a deep fear of intimacy which he associated with feeling overwhelmed, or being unable to meet the expectations of others. Mr L reported a desire to engage in therapy but found it extraordinarily difficult to "own" the idea of personal wishes, desires, or hopes, preferring instead to justify his engagement in therapy in terms of a wish to contribute to the research trial. The closest he came to expressing some sense of personal desire related to a wish to be better able to form relationships and hoped to one day remarry.

Mr L presented with, what may be termed, a monological narrative (Lysaker & Lysaker, 2006), in which his stories and broader ideas about himself and the world were rigidly governed by a limited number of inflexible self-positions, such as self-as-man (a dominant, masculine, aggressive, and demanding husband figure) or self-as-innocent (naïve, cooperative, passive, victimised, and childlike). Due to the nature of his narratives, he struggled to engage in a meaningful interpersonal process of co-creating narratives with his therapist. Instead, he engaged in detailed and tangential stories with limited awareness of others' experiences, knowledge, and presence in the conversation. He appeared to experience confusion and uncertainty in social interactions, and would attempt to reduce his confusion by creating elaborate and implausible stories of what may have been happening for the other person. Mr L evidenced a limited capacity to think about the experiences of others as separate from himself, often exaggerating his own importance in the minds of others (i.e. limited capacity for decentration).

He evidenced some capacity for self-reflection and ability to observe that his thoughts and feelings were fallible. He intellectualised, and often appeared to use clichéd phrases rather than more meaningful exchanges. When challenged by the therapist, he would often respond with confusion, anger, or disappointment:

MR L: "The universe is a vast and empty space, full of disappointment."
THERAPIST: "*You* feel disappointed."
MR L: "I don't understand what you mean."

The therapeutic relationship

In the early stages of the therapy, the therapist focused on developing a strong therapeutic relationship with the client by maintaining a curious and "not knowing" stance. During the initial stages, the therapy was characterised by both therapist and client being invested in the treatment process. Reviewing videos of the therapy, as part of the group supervision process, suggested that Mr L quickly developed an intense positive transference towards the therapist, while the therapist reported on her own countertransference experiences in terms of experiencing him as "endearing", "harmless", and "childlike". We may infer that the therapist was responding to a very vulnerable part of Mr L, and begin to think about the meanings of the person's experience in terms of relationships outside of the therapy.

Mr L's experience of the therapist, from a relatively early stage in the treatment, appeared to be complicated by an erotic transference. Mr L made increasingly overt comments, revealing his romantic feelings towards her, over the course of the treatment. Despite the level of rapport which appeared to develop early in the therapy, the therapist's endeavours to think about Mr L's motivations for engaging in treatment, and her encouragement for him to think about his responses, difficulties resulted at times in avoidance of Mr L's feelings by both Mr L and his therapist. These responses were particularly evident as she worked towards establishing an agenda, sharing her mind, and stimulating Mr L's reflective capacity. He would, at times, change the topic, and focus instead on the role he saw himself playing in assisting in a research project and contributing to the learning of the student therapist. He would express his desire to contribute his wisdom and experience to solve problems related to mental illness in the broader community. He found it difficult to talk about himself. At times he would ask the therapist for assurance that he was helping her and the researchers. However, he would then fall back to his experience of desire towards the therapist:

MR L: "It's just a physical thing . . . But it means so much more, it means, it means that, as a man, I'm ready to make you my wife. To make you heaven. To ask you, to leave the option open to you to have a relationship with me. That's what it means."

THERAPIST: "Okay. So I recall a few weeks ago you were upset by a lady friend of yours who thought that you and I were boyfriend and girlfriend. And I—"

MR L: "I found that hard . . . I found that annoying most of all and I thought well, you know, perhaps I've said some things or indicated some things . . . that you and I were more than therapist and patient."

(Session 19)

During a follow-up session, Mr L reported that he found his feelings for the therapist difficult to manage, stating:

MR L: "Life is such that we're attracted to the other sex and the thing was, probably, probably I went to places I shouldn't have gone to, in my experience with the therapist. And there were parts that just scared the living daylights out of me. It took me up to three weeks one time just to pull myself together emotionally enough to go back again."

A consistent narrative throughout Mr L's therapy centred on his struggle with an intense need for closeness and dependency within relationships and, conversely, feelings of great aggression and hostility towards those on whom he felt dependent. This theme mapped onto Mr L's self-positions, whether these related to areas of competence, loneliness, or self as desirous. He generally presented, and described himself, as gentle, passive, tolerant, and unquestioningly compliant, but then at times would describe his own aggressive impulses during which he experienced himself as aggressive and powerful, as evidenced in this excerpt:

MR L: "I've never learnt how to do it [kill] and I never want to know, but I have no conscience, I'd just kill and kill and kill more and it wouldn't have any domain over me . . . It's a terrible thing to say, but I'd be killing anyone that brushed me up the other. I could wipe them out, wouldn't worry me. I'd probably be in jail but at least, I tell you what, there would be some scum that wouldn't be around you know . . . I would enjoy it."

(Session 13)

The expression of such feelings revealed parts of Mr L's self-experience but the context in which they were revealed, that is, within the therapeutic relationship, also warrants attention. On some level, he may have also been referring to the anger he felt towards the therapist, who was unresponsive to his invitations for a closer relationship. While the expression of powerful emotions within therapy can be difficult for many, if not most, therapists, it is worth speculating on optimum responses. For instance, the therapist could have acknowledged Mr L's aggressive feelings and the context within which they were expressed, as such: "*You* want *me* to know about this dangerous part of you".

From observations of Mr L's reports across the course of the therapy, he struggled with integrating feelings of dependency and aggression in relationships over the course of his life, particularly with significant female figures, including both his mother and ex-wife. A similar dynamic was observed in Mr L's relationship with the therapist. He was consistently seen to engage with her in a complimentary and agreeable manner; however, he later expressed anger towards the therapist for her perceived "rejection" of his romantic feelings towards her.

The therapist provided a retrospective account of her experience in working with Mr L, during which she reported experiencing feelings of fear and emotional unsafety in response to Mr L's expressions of sexual desire towards her, and his anger at her perceived rejection of him. She also reported experiencing similar feelings during Mr L's disclosure of past violence directed towards his wife. In these instances, the therapist would adopt a relatively inactive stance within the therapy.

It would be attractive to place our own values onto the dynamics elicited within this therapeutic relationship, or retreat to the comfort of "therapeutic distance".

However, on reflection, the interactions may also be seen as evidence of Mr L's aliveness, which contrasted with a history of withdrawal and psychosis in response to unbearable affect. In fact, within the therapy and the presence of the erotic elements described, he appeared to become more fully alive, during which he expressed more primitive drives. These events became still more salient, in the context of his personal history which included childhood abuse, as he became increasingly attached to the therapist. It could be argued that some aspects of his mental life reveal a potency, or vitality, which had previously been absent from his life.

Mr L and his therapist's difficulties negotiating his romantic feelings towards her persisted over the course of treatment, as demonstrated by Mr L's request in his final therapy session to have an ongoing relationship with her. Despite this, Mr L appeared to be more able to tolerate some separateness from the therapist over time, as demonstrated by an increased tolerance of their having separate minds, that is, different thoughts, feelings, and perceptions. For example, Mr L evidenced an increased willingness to correct his therapist's reflections if they did not fit with his experience, rather than passively agreeing in a bid to maintain a sense of oneness. In a follow-up interview, Mr L reported valuing the opportunity he had had to be truthful with his therapist about his feelings toward her, and stated that the process had helped him to develop more enduring and positive relationships with women in his life, including a new important female friend.

The therapist worked toward increasing Mr L's awareness of self, which stimulated his awareness of losses, particularly those associated with a previously important relationship. This process was associated with a number of positive changes observed in Mr L over the course of therapy: his narratives became more reality based and easier to follow; he and his therapist were also observed to have some more experiences of separateness; and Mr L demonstrated an increased tolerance for difficult feelings that he had previously split off from, such as loss and grief relating to his mental state, sadness and regret about aspects of his past, and frustration and anger towards others he perceived as having let him down. The manifestation of the transference provided an opportunity to better understand Mr L's relationships, his experience of one or more people who featured significantly in his earlier life, and his experience of the therapy. The process is consistent with a process referred to in the early literature as ego-differentiation and ego-integration (Searles, 1963), or in more contemporary literature, as a process of formulating that which was unformulated (Stern, 1987). This process may also be described in terms of an increasing capacity for flexible and coherent movement among self-positions, with the exchange of information and stories between these aspects of self resulting in a more complex, narratively structured self (Hermans, 2001)

In the weeks leading up to the termination of therapy, Mr L and his therapist engaged in some discussions concerning how difficult the ending would be for him, and explored some of the practicalities of this, such as alternative ways for Mr L to fill his time and alternative referral options. On reflection, we recognise that the therapist may have avoided exploring Mr L's understanding of their relationship, and the meanings of the relationship for him. With hindsight, the process of termination could have been undertaken with more discussion of his feelings in relation to the ending of relationships. Generally, the use of traditional transference interpretations is not recommended in the treatment of psychosis as people who experience difficulties with metacognition can struggle to link feelings in the therapy relationship to experiences from past relationships (Brent, 2009). Despite this, relationship issues need to be attended to within the therapist's mind and also within the therapeutic relationship, especially when such factors impede the progress of the therapy. As noted by Gabbard (1994), the longings for love and for sexual gratification have the potential to elicit enactments within the therapeutic setting. Within this context, the therapist needs to be attentive to the person's affective states, and be willing to assist the person to recognise and name these states (Lysaker & Klion, 2017). Attending to transference and countertransference does not necessarily require traditional interpretation, in which present feelings are explicitly linked to past relationships, but rather requires the therapist's capacity to think about what is occurring within the therapy relationship and assist the person to put words to their affective experience of the therapy process.

The therapy process provides a here-and-now relational experience to be reflected upon, and as such a powerful opportunity to develop a person's capacity to think about self, other, and self-in-relation to others. This can be a particularly challenging task in the context of erotic transference, as the feelings associated with love and lust may well be dissociated from one another, and interfere with the therapist's ability to maintain a dual state of awareness in which they are both a participant in the therapy, but also an observer of the therapy process. That is, the therapist is required to be both an observer of their own mental states and an observer of the person seeking assistance and their mental states, as well as of the emergent experience of the relationship itself. The experience of curiosity and reflective practice evolved into an iterative process which lies at the heart of metacognitive practice, as the therapist and person seek to form more complex and integrated constellations of self as part of the recovery process.

The process of termination was challenging for Mr L, given his unresolved romantic feelings towards his therapist and his difficulty making meaning of their relationship. This stage was also not easy for the therapist, as she engaged with Mr L, recognising that her own intuitions, tensions, wishes, and emotions were not always easy to share. Following termination, the unresolved difficulties may have been evident in the fact that Mr L would return to the clinic at his scheduled appointment time for several weeks. He would speak with administrative staff and sit in the clinic waiting room. It is also worth noting that the length of treatment, and the nature of the termination (i.e. forced termination due to the research trial coming to an end), were additional complicating factors. For many with enduring difficulties in relation to metacognitive capacity and psychotic symptoms, 12 months of treatment is not sufficient to achieve optimum outcomes (Karon, 2008).

Unlike traditional psychoanalytic practice, within which transference issues may be "interpreted", working with people who have a history of psychosis, and against a background of early abuse, the therapist is encouraged to focus on identifying and labelling the person's mental states (emotions, thoughts, fantasy). The person is encouraged to draw upon their own relationships to consider alternative perspectives on their experience. Ideally, the therapist would focus on the person's affective experiences, which may have involved love, distress, anger, disappointment, regret, and hurt. The intervention would require the therapist to use their own mind as they seek to understand the process of termination, and through sharing their mind, encourage the person to become increasingly aware of his own mental states as well as the therapist's state of mind (Brent, 2009). This requires the therapist to be aware of their own mental states and capacity to reflect in the face of intense affect. The presented case study demonstrates the significant challenges faced by therapists in the process of dealing with transferential issues. The relational aspect of the interaction may well be characterised by the therapist feeling overwhelmed by emotion and both parties struggling to facilitate a reflective process, in which the therapeutic relationship can be thought about.

Treatment implications

Mr L reported finding therapy helpful, and had improved on measures of narrative coherence and grandiosity at the end of treatment, as well as showing a minor improvement in self-perceived recovery at two-year follow-up. Despite this, he evidenced some deterioration in metacognitive functioning and showed a lack of improvement in overall symptoms at the end of therapy. This raises the important question of transference and countertransference and whether the emergence of transferential responses requires particular skills in addressing the mental states associated with such experiences.

The client factors present in this case – being the severity of Mr L's psychotic symptoms, early history of abuse, history of aggression, and expressions of sexual and romantic desire towards the therapist – resulted in profound countertransference responses for the therapist, that persisted over the course of treatment. She reported a range of feelings such as derealisation, fear, emotional unsafety, being lost, dissociation, distress, and confusion, and at the same time, she also reported feelings of nurture and care in response to her identification with the suffering which he described. Such responses are highlighted by Bargenquast and Schweitzer (2014b) as not uncommon for therapists engaging in psychotherapy with people with a history of psychosis.

In the midst of such an intense emotional atmosphere, the therapist's overly passive stance within therapy sessions reflected her struggle to find a balance between allowing the client to create and explore his own narratives, versus providing a stabilising and cohesive framework in which the therapy could take place. In retrospect, it may have been useful for the therapist to more actively elicit narrative episodes, in which Mr L was better able to identify other times during which he experienced romantic feelings, the complex states involved, and assist him to recognise the commonalities and distinctions between those experiences and his experience within the therapy. The task is not easy, regardless of the experience of the therapist, as they need to deal with complex feelings which are often deeply personal, and reveal the emotional demands of engaging in relationships complicated by personal and often traumatic histories. We previously referred to Winnicott (1947) and his reference that working with people who are dealing with psychosis requires that therapists are also able to reach "down to very primitive things in ourselves", highlighting the role of self-awareness.

Mr L's experience illustrates that the meaning-making process which underpins MERIT is complex, and therapy may be more effective if the therapist not only has an understanding of aspects of their own mind, but also takes an active and engaged role in treatment and avoids any unintended perpetuation of the client's feelings of confusion and disempowerment, while targeting interventions to the client's current level of functioning.

The dynamics around transference and countertransference explored in this chapter also highlight the contagious nature of the sense of "confusion" that comes with psychotic presentations. Just like the person seeking assistance, therapists can also struggle to hold onto their capacity to think, reflect, and make meaning. The challenge is to engage empathically with the person, and identify the relationship between aspects of self and self-in-relationship, with a view to promoting differentiation and integration of the self.

Managing erotic transference within the therapeutic relationship is inevitably difficult, and even more challenging for relatively inexperienced therapists (Rockett, 2000; Rodgers, 2011). Addressing erotic transference can be particularly difficult when complicated by the client's difficulties with reality testing, as clients with psychosis can misunderstand interpretations related to sexual material or experience the therapeutic relationship as seductive (Rosenfeld, 1987). In the treatment described above, this dynamic may have impaired the therapist's ability to support the client to make meaning of how therapy and the therapist fit into his world, inadvertently perpetuating his experience of confusion and uncertainty about the therapeutic relationship. The outcome was mixed with improvements in some areas, and a lack of change in others, which may have been tied to a level of ongoing distress and unresolved feelings about the therapeutic relationship at termination. It is thus imperative to recognise both transference and countertransference dynamics, and the potential impact of unacknowledged erotic transference on treatment outcomes, when working with people who present with psychotic disorders.

While metacognitive therapy does not specifically address transference, it recognises that the therapy process is intersubjective, involving the sharing of minds. Within this context, transference is likely to form an important ingredient in psychotherapy with people with psychosis, as it provides essential information about aspects of the person's relational world. This is evidenced in the case of Mr L, where his feelings towards the therapist could be traced to similar dynamics with other important female figures. Mr L's unresolved feelings towards the therapist at the end of treatment also reflected similarly unresolved patterns in relationships throughout his life. This case highlights the importance of "dealing with" both overt and implicit issues in the therapeutic relationship. In our experience, avoiding such dynamics may well contribute to the person's sense of confusion and impede progress.

The issue of transference is particularly significant in MERIT, as the therapeutic approach has a specific requirement that the therapist work with, and attend to, the person's agenda within an empathically engaged relationship (Hasson-Ohayon et al., 2017). The agenda refers to the person's wishes, hopes, desires, plans, and purposes which they bring to the therapeutic encounter. The goal is to develop greater awareness of wishes and intentions which may be overt or more subtle. In the example provided, being attuned to the needs of the person seeking assistance was challenging for the therapist, given the life stage of each of the participants, the tensions around the person's history, and the primitive nature of his impulses which emerged over the course of the treatment. The dynamics revealed in the case highlight the importance of surfacing and addressing dynamics which may be experienced as threatening for both the person and the therapist. Avoidance of such dynamics may impede the establishment of a joint agenda for therapy. Being open to unconscious elements which manifest within the relationship has the potential to contribute to a more sensitive exploration of the full range of components of the person's self-structure.

References

Bargenquast, R. (2012). *Metacognitive narrative psychotherapy: A recovery-oriented intervention for enhancing self-experience in people with schizophrenia*. Unpuplished thesis. Queensland University of Technology, Brisbane.

Bargenquast, R., & Schweitzer, R. D. (2014a). Enhancing sense of recovery and self-reflectivity in people with schizophrenia: A pilot study of metacognitive narrative psychotherapy. *Psychology and Psychotherapy: Theory, Research and Practice, 87*(3), 338–356. https://doi.org/10.1111/papt.12019.

Bargenquast, R., & Schweitzer, R. D. (2014b). Metacognitive narrative psychotherapy for people diagnosed with schizophrenia: An outline of a principle-based treatment manual. *Psychosis, 6*(2), 155–165.

Brent, B. (2009). Mentalization-based psychodynamic psychotherapy for psychosis. *Journal of Clinical Psychology, 65*(8), 803–814.

Fenton, W. S. (2000). Evolving perspectives on individual psychotherapy for schizophrenia. *Schizophrenia Bulletin, 26*(1), 47–72. https://doi.org/10.1093/oxfordjournals.schbul.a033445.

Ferro, A., & Nicoli, L. (2018). The new analyst's guide to the galaxy: Questions about contemporary psychoanalysis. *Psychoanalytic Psychology, 36*(1), 93–98. http://doi.org/10.1037/pap0000224.

Freud, S. (1913). On the beginning of treatment: further recommendations on the technique of psychoanalysis. In J. Strachey (Trans.), *The standard edition of the complete psychological works of Sigmund Freud* (pp. 122–144). London: Hogarth Press.

Fromm-Reichmann, F. (1954). Psychotherapy of schizophrenia. *American Journal of Psychiatry, 111*, 410–419.

Gabbard, G. O. (1994). On love and lust in erotic transference. *Journal of the American Psychoanalytic Association*, *42*(2), 385–403. https://doi.org/10.1177/000306519404200203.

Hamm, J. A., Hasson-Ohayon, I., Kukla, M., & Lysaker, P. H. (2013). Individual psychotherapy for schizophrenia: Trends and developments in the wake of the recovery movement. *Psychology Research and Behavior Management*, *6*, 45–54. https://doi.org/10.2147/PRBM.S47891.

Hasson-Ohayon, I., Kravetz, S., & Lysaker, P. H. (2017). The special challenges of psychotherapy with persons with psychosis: Intersubjective metacognitive model of agreement and shared meaning. *Clinical Psychology & Psychotherapy*, *24*(2), 428–440. http://doi.org/10.1002/cpp.2012.

Hermans, H. J. M. (1996). Voicing the self: From information processing to dialogical interchange. *Psychological Bulletin*, *119*(I), 31–50.

Hermans, H. J. M. (2001). The dialogical self: Toward a theory of personal and cultural positioning. *Culture & Psychology*, *7*(3), 243–281. https://doi.org/10.1177/1354067X0173001.

Horowitz, R. (2002). Psychotherapy and schizophrenia: The mirror of countertransference. *Clinical Social Work Journal*, *30*, 235–244.

Hutton, L. (2012). *Engaging with patients suffering from schizophrenia: An interpretative phenomenological analysis of therapists' experience.* Unpublished thesis. Queensland University of Technology, Brisbane.

Jung, C. G. (1963). *Memories, dreams, recollections.* London: Random House, Inc.

Karon, B. P. (2008). An "incurable" schizophrenic: The case of Mr. X. *Pragmatic Case Studies in Psychotherapy*, *4*(1), 1–24. https://doi.org/10.14713/pcsp.v4i1.923.

King, R., & O'Brien, T. (2011). Transference and countertransference: Opportunities and risks as two technical constructs migrate beyond their psychoanalytic homeland. *Psychotherapy in Australia*, *17*(4), 12–17.

Lysaker, J. T., & Lysaker, J. T. (2001). Schizophrenia and the collapse of the dialogical self: Recovery, narrative and psychotherapy. *Psychotherapy: Theory, Research, Practice, Training*, *38*(3), 252–261. http://doi.org/10.1037/0033-3204.38.3.252.

Lysaker, P. H., Gagen, E., Moritz, S., & Schweitzer, R. D. (2018). Metacognitive approaches to the treatment of psychosis: A comparison of four approaches. *Psychology Research and Behavior Management*, *11*, 341–351. https://doi.org/10.2147/PRBM.S146446.

Lysaker, P. H., Glynn, S. M., Wilkniss, S. M., & Silverstein, S. M. (2010). Psychotherapy and recovery from schizophrenia: A review of potential applications and need for future study. *Psychological Services*, *7*(2), 75–91. https://doi.org/10.1037/a0019115.

Lysaker, P. H., Johannesen, J., & Lysaker, J. (2005). Schizophrenia and the experience of intersubjectivity as threat. *Phenomenology and the Cognitive Sciences*, *4*, 335–352.

Lysaker, P. H., & Klion, R. E. (2017). *Recovery, meaning-making, and severe mental illness: A comprehensive guide to metacognitive reflection and insight therapy* (1st ed.). New York, NY: Routledge. https://doi.org/10.4324/9781315447001.

Lysaker, P. H., & Lysaker, J. T. (2006). A typology of narrative impoverishment in schizophrenia: Implications for understanding the processes of establishing and sustaining dialogue in individual psychotherapy. *Counselling Psychology Quarterly*, *19*, 57–68. https://doi.org/10.1080/09515070600673703.

Lysaker, P. H., & Lysaker, J. T. (2010). Schizophrenia and alterations in first person experience: A comparison of six perspectives. *Schizophrenia Bulletin*, *36*, 331–340.

Lysaker, P. H., & Roe, D. (2012). The processes of recovery from schizophrenia: The emergent role of integrative psychotherapy, recent developments, and new directions. *Journal of Psychotherapy Integration*, *22*(4), 287–297. https://doi.org/10.1037/a0029581.

Lysaker, P. H., Roe, D., & Buck, K. D. (2010). Recovery and wellness amidst schizophrenia: Definitions, evidence, and the implications for clinical practice. *Journal of the American Psychiatric Nurses Association, 16*(1), 36–42. https://doi.org/10.1177/1078390309353943.

Lysaker, P. H., Roe, D., & Kukla, M. (2012). Psychotherapy and rehabilitation for schizophrenia: Thoughts about their parallel development and potential integration. *Journal of Psychotherapy Integration, 22*(4), 344–355. https://doi.org/10.1037/a0029580.

McGlashan, T. H. (1983). Intensive individual psychotherapy of schizophrenia: A review of techniques. *Archives of General Psychiatry, 40*, 909–920.

Rockett, R. (2000). The conceptualization and utilization of erotic transference and countertransference by inexperienced female psychotherapists. *Dissertation Abstracts International, 61*(3B), 1651.

Rodgers, N. M. (2011). Intimate boundaries: Therapists' perception and experience of erotic transference within the therapeutic relationship. *Counselling & Psychotherapy Research, 11*(4), 266–274.

Rosenfeld, H. A. (1987). *Impasse and interpretation: Therapeutic and anti-therapeutic factors in the psychoanalytic treatment of psychotic, borderline and neurotic patients.* London: Routledge.

Salvatore, G., Russo, B., Russo, M., Popolo, R., & Dimaggio, G. (2012). Metacognition-oriented therapy for psychosis: The case of a woman with delusional disorder and paranoid personality disorder. *Journal of Psychotherapy Integration, 22*(4), 314–329. https://doi.org/10.1037/a0029577.

Schweitzer, R. D., Greben, M., & Bargenquast, R. (2017). Long-term outcomes of metacognitive narrative psychotherapy for people diagnosed with schizophrenia. *Psychology & Psychotherapy, 4*, 668–685. https://doi.org/10.1111/papt.12132.

Searles, H. F. (1963). Transference psychosis in the psychotherapy of chronic schizophrenia. *International Journal of Psychoanalysis, 44*, 249–281.

Silverstein, S. M., & Bellack, A. S. (2008). A scientific agenda for the concept of recovery as it applies to schizophrenia. *Clinical Psychology Review, 28*, 1108–1124.

Stern, D. B. (1987). Unformulated experience and transference. *Contemporary Psychoanalysis, 23*(3), 484–491. https://doi.org/10.1080/00107530.1987.10746199.

Winnicott, D. W. (1947). Hate in the counter-transference. *Journal of Psychotherapy and Research, 3*(4), 350–356.

7

THE POTENTIAL FOR REDUCTION OR DISCONTINUATION OF ANTIPSYCHOTIC MEDICATION WITH THE USE OF METACOGNITIVE REFLECTION AND INSIGHT THERAPY (MERIT)

Kelly D. Buck and Paul H. Lysaker

Abstract: *While antipsychotic medication has been the first-line of treatment for psychosis, this practice has been questioned for some people, and interest has grown in procedures which may help to reduce and potentially discontinue the use of these medications in the long term. Little is known though about what psychosocial interventions might support these processes. In this chapter, we discuss four aspects of how Metacognitive Insight and Reflection Therapy (MERIT) might support persons diagnosed with psychosis to reduce or discontinue use of antipsychotic medication. We suggest that four interrelated aspects of MERIT, specifically promoting meaning-making; achieving agency; developing a conjoint sense of one's personal challenges and abilities; and promoting the ability to use a growing sense of one's self and others to meet one's needs can support this process. MERIT warrants further study for its potential in aiding medication reduction or discontinuation.*

Introduction

Metacognitive Insight and Reflection Therapy (MERIT; Lysaker & Klion, 2017), which is also explained in the introduction of this book and additional chapters (Chapter 1; Chapter 11; Chapter 3), is an integrative form of psychotherapy whose core purpose includes helping adults diagnosed with serious mental illness, including psychosis, to form increasingly integrated ideas about themselves and others. These improvements in metacognitive capacity are then thought to promote recovery when they better enable individuals to evolve a more personally meaningful sense of the challenges they face. People, then, are subsequently better able to decide and act in ways that they think can most effectively respond to those challenges.

Considered as a whole, MERIT thus seeks to both support sense making and also promote action in the world; intuitively, this is consistent with core elements of the current understanding of personal recovery, including that recovery must be self-directed (Leonhardt et al., 2017). While a significant volume of work has been undertaken relating to the process of sense-making itself (Kean, 2009; Pérez-Álvarez, García-Montes, Vallina-Fernández, & Perona-Garcelán, 2016; Roe &

Lysaker, 2013; Stanghellini & Lysaker, 2007), there has been less exploration of the process of supporting people diagnosed with psychosis, as they come to make self-directed decisions in response the difficulties they face in the world. Hasson-Ohayon, Arnon-Ribenfeld, Hamm, and Lysaker (2017) discussed how the development of self-reflectivity allows for a greater sense of agency and others have made similar observations across other case reports (Hamm & Lysaker, 2018; James, Leonhardt, & Buck, 2018; Leonhardt et al., 2016; Buck & George, 2016; Lysaker et al., 2015). In these and other works, reflection and action are posited to have a recursive relationship, in which sense making and action inform and build upon one another. As a deeper sense of self enables more complex action, more aspects of self are revealed which can then be integrated into a person's sense of themselves in the world. But what does this look like at a more concrete level when confronting real-life dilemmas and challenges as well as the pursuit of differing paths to recovery?

An answer to this question seems especially important for understanding how to support the actions of persons diagnosed with psychosis when they choose a course of recovery which defies long-standing, traditional medical, and social practices. Are there unique aspects of MERIT that can support people making and enacting these particular kinds of choices? Certainly, supporting persons who follow treatment plans offered by a dominant paradigm is likely to be less complex than helping persons navigate a path which challenges more widely held beliefs about recovery in serious mental illness. To explore this issue, the current chapter examines how several core activities of MERIT can support the actions of persons who have chosen a course of recovery which may involve reducing and/or discontinuing antipsychotic medication.

One common perspective of the core of the traditional medical model has been the idea that the path from psychosis to wellness uniformly begins with the acceptance of a mental health diagnosis that demands prolonged, if not continuous, somatic treatments, including antipsychotic medication (Kane, 2013). For over half a century, treatment with antipsychotic medication has been the most commonly accepted first-line response for those diagnosed with psychosis (Leucht et al., 2012, 2013). In the United States, antipsychotic medication has been proposed as directly treating the phenomena which causes psychotic experience and, in many cases, it is presented as a treatment that should go on for a lifetime (Goff et al., 2017; Karson, Duffy, Eramo, Nylander, & Offord, 2016). In fact, it has been asserted that to discontinue, or significantly reduce, antipsychotic medication is irresponsible and likely to provoke relapse, leading to a further decline in psychosocial function among persons diagnosed with psychosis (Correll, Rubio, & Kane, 2018).

Yet, as psychosis has been increasingly revealed to be a poorly understood group of psychological, social, political, and medical phenomena – with complex causes, courses, and associated forms of suffering (Guloksuz & van Os, 2018) – a narrow path from insight, to medication adherence, to recovery has been begun to be challenged. As psychosis is increasingly understood as more than one single entity, it becomes apparent that there may be other valid paths to wellness or recovery. Specifically, with emphasis on the long-term effects of antipsychotic medication, and with consideration of ethical and human rights related issues, there is support that there could other paths to recovery that may include the reduction or discontinuation of antipsychotic medication after its initiation, as opposed to an indeterminate course of treatment (Moncrieff, 2015; Moncrieff & Middleton, 2015).

Assuming then that antipsychotic medication reduction and/or discontinuation is a meaningful potential path to recovery, it seems important to identify how to support people who choose this path (Ostrow, Jessel, Hurd, Darrow, & Cohen, 2017). In response to this need, this chapter will explore whether MERIT can be of any assistance, and if so, how. In response to these questions, this chapter will explore how the reflective practices of MERIT can be uniquely helpful by promoting the availability of an integrated and diverse sense of self needed to navigate through, and respond to, the challenges which may emerge from the process of antipsychotic medication reduction or discontinuation. To do so, we will first discuss the reasons why persons diagnosed with psychosis might choose to discontinue medication and then explore several of the challenges the process of going through antipsychotic medication reduction and/or discontinuation may pose for a developing identity. We will next discuss four specific, though inter-related, ways in which MERIT might support persons as they pursue antipsychotic medication reduction. These include promoting meaning-making, attaining agency, developing a conjoint sense of one's personal challenges and abilities, and developing the ability to use a growing sense of self and others in a way to act and effectively reduce distress and allow for the meeting of emotional, psychological, and social needs. Finally, we will touch on the implications for thinking about how to promote recovery in general though psychological therapies as well as highlight potential limitations and directions for future study.

As a point of clarification before beginning, the purpose of this chapter is not to suggest any course of treatment for any one person. We also are not suggesting antipsychotic medication reduction or discontinuation is the best course for everyone. With respect to the current literature, this course may make great sense for some, just as long-term medication treatment makes sense for others. Some who decide to try to reduce or discontinue antipsychotic medication may not be successful and may find that medications or an alternative approach may be more appropriate. In this chapter, we merely intend to explore how the reflective practice of MERIT can support persons who make a choice to pursue this course. Last, we will not discuss the decision many face in first episode psychosis of whether to take antipsychotic medication in the first place. Instead, in this chapter we will focus only on persons already prescribed antipsychotic medication who choose to reduce or discontinue it.

The argument for considering the reduction and discontinuation of long-term use of antipsychotic medication for persons diagnosed with psychosis

Before addressing how to support the discontinuation or reduction of antipsychotic medication, it seems important to first consider some reasons why persons

diagnosed with psychosis might choose to do so. First, and perhaps most immediately concerning, long-term antipsychotic use has been associated with the
development of other forms of non-psychiatric medical comorbidities, including diabetes, obesity, hyperlipidemia, and cardiovascular disorders. (Alvarez-
Jimenez et al., 2008; Daumit et al., 2008; De Hert, Detraux, Van Winkel, Yu, &
Correll, 2012; Dorph-Petersen et al., 2005; Foley & Morley, 2011). These medical conditions, while adding to the burden of disability and reducing quality of
life, can also shorten a person's life span. Second, it has also been found that over
time these medications may adversely affect brain function. Research, for example, has linked level of antipsychotic usage with smaller gray matter volumes,
progressive decrement in white matter volume, and greater cerebrospinal fluid
volumes regardless of illness severity or drug and alcohol use (Ho, Andreasen,
Ziebell, Pierson, & Magnotta, 2011; Moncrieff, 2007). A third set of reasons
persons may seek to reduce or discontinue long-term antipsychotic medication
is that it can affect one's subjective sense of functioning including experiencing
impairments in attention and concentration, akathisia, insomnia, weight gain,
and sleepiness (Dibonaventura, Gabriel, Dupclay, Gupta, & Kim, 2012). Given
the deleterious effects any of these factors might have on functioning, it is not
surprising that research also suggests that better psychosocial outcomes in some
long-term studies are associated with medication discontinuation among adults
diagnosed with schizophrenia (Harrow, Jobe, & Faull, 2012; Harrow, Jobe, Faull, &
Yang, 2017).

From a broader perspective, many may seek antipsychotic medication reduction
or discontinuation because the claimed effects of long-term antipsychotic use may
not be as robust as they have been previously suggested. In other words, for some
the benefits of long-term use may not outweigh the risks noted above. While antipsychotic medication has been found to be effective for positive symptoms (such
as hallucinations), it does not appear to affect other equally concerning symptoms.
Multiple studies have found that negative symptoms, which include avolition,
apathy, blunted affect, and anhedonia, are not affected by antipsychotic treatment
(Fusar-Poli et al., 2014) and may lead to range of poorer outcomes such as lower
quality of life (Ho, Nopoulos, Flaum, Arndt, & Andreasen, 1998), reduced social
functioning (Hunter & Barry, 2012), and reduced attainment of recovery (Milev,
Ho, Arndt, & Andreasen, 2005). Additionally, discontinuing antipsychotic medication also does not appear to always result in the loss of any initial gains. In a
long-term follow-up study, Harrow et al. (2012) reported there was no evidence
that antipsychotic discontinuation led to increased frequency of relapse. Wunderink, Nieboer, Wiersma, Sytema, and Nienhuis (2013) reported that service users
with first episode psychosis who discontinued medication experienced twice the
rate of recovery of those who continued a maintenance dose. A meta-analysis
conducted by Kishi et al. (2019), in comparing first episode service users (FEP)
who discontinued antipsychotic treatment versus a group who received maintenance treatment, found 45.7% of the sample who had stopped medication at the
12-month follow-up did not experience a relapse, and of those who were found to

have discontinued at the 18–24-month follow-up, 39.4% experienced no relapse. Likewise, Wils et al. (2017) identified that 30% of a group diagnosed with FEP had obtained remission after not being on antipsychotic medication at a 10-year follow-up. In a survey in the US by Ostrow et al. (2017), of 250 adults who were taking a variety of medications, including antipsychotic medication, involved in discontinuing at least one or more medications, 82% reported satisfaction with their decision to discontinue.

Finally, antipsychotic medication reduction or discontinuation may make sense when a person's goals are unrelated to the potential benefits of medication. Research on the personal definitions of wellness in the face of psychosis suggest that recovery reflects far more than symptom remission. A qualitative study recently suggested that for persons diagnosed with psychosis health more often means finding enduring connections with others and a sense of personal agency and self-worth (Leonhardt et al., 2017). In other words, key aspects of health are unrelated to medication and may involve respect for the treatment preferences of adults diagnosed with psychosis, preferences which are documented by a wealth of evidence to involve a desire for antipsychotic medication reduction and discontinuation. For example, it has been suggested that approximately 50% of service users who are prescribed an antipsychotic medication take 70% or less than what is prescribed to them (Goff, Hill, & Freudenreich, 2010). Respect for service user preference and also the need for the exploration of non-pharmacological treatments is furthermore a matter of human rights as recently indicated by a special report by the United Nations (2017). It is also consistent with findings that many diagnosed with serious mental illness do not desire treatments that relieve symptoms but instead are respectful of how they think about and respond to the world (Moritz et al., 2012).

Challenges to the process of antipsychotic medication reduction and discontinuation for persons diagnosed with psychosis

While it may be straightforward for some, we would suggest that for others, the decision to discontinue or reduce antipsychotic medication for psychosis may be quite complex and have to do with a person's own basic sense of self or developing identity. As previously discussed, the decision to reduce or discontinue medication may reflect a wish to take charge of one's own life and to feel that one's identity is more than what might be called a "psychiatric patient". Thus, at stake is not just a response to an illness, but to an evolving participation and management of one's own life.

With this in mind, we can see at least three hurdles which may occur at the points where medicine and identity intersect during the process of medication reduction and/or discontinuation. The first of these may be the negative reactions of others who had been previously supportive to the person reducing or discontinuing medication. For example, often guided by stigmatizing beliefs, some previous members of a social network might fear that the person trying to reduce or discontinue medication cannot manage their own life or even responsibly make this decision. Previously hidden stigma, held by persons who had been supportive, may come into the open when persons diagnosed with psychosis take charge of their lives and contradict the stereotype that mental illness is synonymous with a total inability for self-control. As this underlying stigma arises, these others may withdraw support and appear critical, leading persons trying to reduce or discontinue antipsychotic medication to doubt their decisions or become demoralized, hindering their progress (van Zelst, 2009).

A second challenge may occur in the face of symptom exacerbation. Some symptoms, previously affected by medication, including anomalous experience or aberrant salience, may become more prominent and persons may also fear that their emergence signals failure. Supportive others may also fear the return of symptoms. Setbacks may be mistaken for failure and may be as invalidating as the stigmatizing reactions of others. Even if there is no symptom exacerbation, anxiety and anticipation about the return of psychosis may emerge, resulting in a hypersensitivity to distress and guarding against emotional pain which can also be limiting and result in false signals of failure.

Beyond this, a major challenge to successful antipsychotic reduction and/or discontinuation may occur as persons begin to try to enact a new identity, which is not defined by the diagnosis or the use of medication to manage a diagnosed illness (Buck et al., 2013). For many, it may not be as simple as anticipated; new social demands and roles may emerge which were not expected. Some of these may indeed be new but some may be related to the loss of social roles that were once comfortable. When we return to activities from our past, it may become apparent that these activities are more complex and difficult than we remembered, leading us to doubt whether we can do them any longer. Suffice to say, finding the world more complex and taxing than expected, along with symptom exacerbations and stigma, can be a monumental challenge to antipsychotic reduction and/or discontinuation in addition to activities that are integral to a developing identity. These challenges could ultimately work against a person's basic stance of self-directed recovery, calling its foundations into question and culminating in a negative outcome by any recovery informed definition.

MERIT and the promotion of a personally meaningful sense of challenges and responses to a diagnosis of psychosis

As referred to in many other chapters of this book (Chapter 11; Chapter 3; Chapter 9) a key foundation of MERIT is the assumption that an impediment to wellness for persons diagnosed with serious mental illness is difficulty integrating information within the flow of life in a way that allows persons to have available to themselves a sense of who they are, who others are, and what things are confronting them (Lysaker, Hamm, Hasson-Ohayon, Pattison, & Leonhardt, 2018; Lysaker et al., 2019). In the view of MERIT, persons diagnosed with serious mental illness have particular difficulties with integration of self-reflection, awareness of the thinking of others, and the use of that understanding to confront challenges in the world. They may experience many different things in their minds and bodies, including bodily sensations, thoughts, wishes, and emotions, but be unable to fully integrate and understand those experiences. For example, sitting in a classroom a person may be aware that her foot is tapping, there is warmth in her face, and that she is having thoughts about a grocery list. However, these experiences may not be integrated into a larger, more complex sense of self and others. As a result, it may not be possible to detect larger patterns and decide what to do in response to those patterns or to determine what they mean. In this state, the self, others, and the world can appear to a person as fragments which do not fit together as part of a larger picture. In such a fragmented world, the person may not have the awareness she was feeling angry about something happening in the classroom, and that she could then choose to respond or not.

MERIT uses the term metacognition to describe the processes which allow persons to fit the pieces of experience together in an evolving way and to respond to dilemmas based on knowledge of self and others. Metacognitive processes are envisioned as having both automatic and effortful elements and as requiring the synthesis of perceptual and reflective actions along with embodied and cognitive activities. Metacognitive deficits, within this model, refer to difficulties integrating information which result in fragmented experiences and are conceptualized as multi-determined, possibly the result of any number of medical, social, or psychological phenomena. MERIT seeks to help persons become better able to develop metacognitive capacity or overcome metacognitive deficits by thinking with them about the fragments they experience and working with them to jointly sort out or make meaning of those fragments.

The intent though is not to just better assemble those fragments but to help the person become better able to cohere fragments into a larger sense of themselves and others that is personally meaningful to them. Applied to a psychiatric diagnosis and decisions about treatment, MERIT often involves thinking about potentially anomalous self-experiences including traumatic experiences that preceded, or proceeded from, psychosis. It can also involve thinking about the self as more than a person with an illness, and challenging the view that persons diagnosed with psychosis are not capable of directing their own life or managing routine daily stressors. MERIT practitioners are further interested in the whole person, who is engaged in sense making in relation to their own unique personal and cultural history. Therapeutically, this process is understood as taking place between people and not as the clinician deciding what is true or motivating the other person to endorse a belief. Meaning is made dialogically (Buck et al., 2013), in a way that is consistent with the values espoused by the United Nations General Assembly report (2017) including the need to restore dignity, be sensitive to stigma, and to promote agency while being particularly attentive to power differentials which position persons diagnosed with mental illness as less able or their ideas as less valid than those of others.

MERIT seeks to promote the development of metacognitive capacity through eight interrelated elements which have been described elsewhere (Lysaker & Klion, 2017). Examinations of MERIT case reports have suggested that in its application to unique persons and their unique challenges, it generally facilitates effective responses to challenges by assisting persons in developing a more coherent sense of self which leads to a greater sense of agency and action (Hamm & Lysaker, 2018). Personal experience, memories, and perceptions of others may be pieced together into a larger cohesive picture, leading to a sense of being able to take and follow a course of action. Metaphorically, this can involve persons moving from a place in which they feel like a leaf in a windstorm to a position in which they have a richer and nuanced sense of what they want in life and how to pursue it.

MERIT and antipsychotic medication reduction and/or discontinuation

Addressing the issue of supporting persons during the process of antipsychotic medication reduction and/or discontinuation, we suggest that there are four interrelated reflective practices characteristic of MERIT which may be of use. The first of these is continuous reflection about experiences in the world and integration of those experiences into an evolving, subjective sense of self. In MERIT, growth in metacognitive capacity allows for more than the development of just an abstract sense of oneself. MERIT does not enable persons to see their "real" or "true" self; enhanced metacognitive capacity is not believed to engender a sense of self that can be known, in the manner of an objective fact or even necessarily as something that is more transparent or even less contradictory. Instead, a series of complex relationships among different experiences may emerge and as each of these sets of relationships are themselves seen as related to other sets of relationships, particular aspects of experience can take on unique meanings they could never hold if understood in isolation. As what were once relatively unrelated fragments of experience become related to one another in temporal sequences, different things naturally begin to be imbued with differing degrees of meaning, allowing for there to be more facets of the self available as experiences unfold (Lysaker & Buck, 2006). For example, a person who previously saw themselves as either "schizophrenic" or "president of Egypt" might come to see themselves also as loving animals, as regretting past drug use, as enjoying stamp collecting, and as missing a deceased cherished figure from their youth.

MERIT thus seems well positioned to help persons going through the process of antipsychotic medication reduction and/or discontinuation to make sense of the stigma of others that emerges as well as symptom exacerbations or unexpected social demands by seeing those as pieces of experience which could be understood in multiple different ways. MERIT allows for another's belief in their incompetence, a paranoid thought, and certain fears to be named without these invalidating other non-illness related aspects of identity. For example, a person might be able to think of a paranoid belief as an experience best understood as feeling unsafe in social situations and not as a signal that they are not able to manage their own life. Another person might be able to see how part of them feels inadequate and unsure in new social situations but also to see that there is more to their identity than just that one aspect.

A second reflective aspect of MERIT, which may support antipsychotic reduction or discontinuation, is a continuous focus on a sense of agency. As alluded to above, a core element of MERIT is the rejection of any assertion that a person's behavior is not meaningful or motivated, no matter how disordered it may appear. MERIT thus continuously reinforces the idea that the person is never "unmotivated" but always has wishes and desires that they are seeking, albeit possibly not in optimal ways. For example, a withdrawn person might come to see their withdrawal as their attempt to avoid humiliation or another person may come to see their speech pattern as expressing rage over a history of trauma.

The promotion of agency, within the process of antipsychotic reduction and/or discontinuation, could enable persons to hold onto an enduring sense of why they chose this path and to alter it as the process unfolds. Utilizing a sense of agency, antipsychotic discontinuation and/or reduction could remain foremost the person's decision, but also a project which could have many variations including deciding to slow down the process without one losing ownership over that process. The events furthermore that unfold during the reduction and/or discontinuation could also be seen as something the service user could influence in an agentic manner, including, for example, dealing with others' stigmatizing doubts, troubling experiences, or psychosocial challenges for which they feel unprepared. MERIT might support a person to not only name the stigma of another who sees them as dangerous, or to recognize their terror when facing the challenge of working, but also to patiently see themselves as potentially able to come to grips with these even if they feel paralyzed in the moment.

The third potentially relevant general practice of MERIT is its focus on meaning as being constructed intersubjectively. As described by Hasson-Ohayon, Kravetz, and Lysaker (2017), psychotherapy that is intersubjectively focused can be a forum for discussing and thinking about the experience of medication in a nuanced manner and also in ways that empower decision making. Given its focus upon promoting a therapeutic alliance and the overall quality of interpersonal connections (Vohs et al., 2018; Lysaker et al., 2015), MERIT might also be expected to promote resilience as it helps persons to recognize the effects of interpersonal interactions and to be able to negotiate those as they occur, again seeing them as pieces of experience but not allowing them to define their identity. For example, with a better sense of how one responds to others it might be possible to manage the invalidating experiences of others when they doubt the chances of success of medication reduction and/or discontinuation. A better ability to connect to others might also emerge, enabling the person to form more connections with others, ultimately aiding the successful response to new psychosocial challenges.

The final general practice of MERIT we will mention concerns a focus on metacognitive mastery, as distinct from self-reflectivity and reflections about others. In MERIT, metacognitive mastery refers to the use of knowledge of the self and others to frame and respond to challenges. This ability is believed to vary between individuals with persons who experience the world in more fragmented ways tending to have less complex means available to them to respond to the world (e.g. withdrawing from situations rather than effortfully thinking differently about it). Applied to emergent struggles during the process of antipsychotic reduction and/or discontinuation, MERIT is likely to be able to help persons see themselves as coping as best as they can and not to interpret, for example, their withdrawal from the stigma of others as evidence of inadequacy but instead as a response to the world which reflects the best means they have as an agent for responding. As mastery is also promoted it may further be that persons will become even better able to respond to potential symptoms and learn to have a fulfilling life in spite of still having disturbing experiences. This aspect of mastery keeps the focus on action, allowing for a more balanced view of coping in the world such that an imperfect life, for example one where there is still stigma and symptoms to be confronted, could be experienced as fully satisfying.

As a final comment about these elements, while we have presented them here separately, it is expected that they should influence one another synergistically. Concretely, thoughts about the process of antipsychotic reduction and/or discontinuation would be discussed along with the person's wishes as an agent, their experience of the therapist during the encounter, and their overall capacities for mastery. These factors might assist during antipsychotic reduction and/or discontinuation as persons become better able to name their needs and make sense of their experience of themselves and others during antipsychotic reduction and/or discontinuation.

Discussion, limitations, and directions for future study

MERIT, as a form of psychotherapy, seeks to assist persons diagnosed with psychosis to make sense of the challenges they face and how they want to respond to them. In this chapter we have explored how this process may uniquely assist persons seeking to reduce and/or discontinue antipsychotic medication. Concretely, we have suggested that, particularly when antipsychotic reduction and/or discontinuation is a matter inextricably related to a person's sense of self, MERIT may offer assistance through its focus on meaning-making, agency, intersubjectivity, and metacognitive mastery. Specifically, these processes may help persons successfully navigate their course through antipsychotic reduction and/or discontinuation even in the face of emergent stigma and symptom exacerbation as well as unexpected psychosocial challenges.

However, these reflections also raise several interesting and important questions. For example, antipsychotic reduction and/or discontinuation poses some risks. Thus, it can be asked at what point do the risks become so great that the mental health professional should encourage stopping the process? Alternatively, should clinicians always support antipsychotic reduction and/or discontinuation? Do the processes we have described suggest a different model that goes beyond shared decision making? Certainly, meaning is made jointly in MERIT but beyond these decisions, there is also the assessment of risk. Are we looking at a practice which, as it evolves, might be better described as *shared risk taking*? Beyond this, at what point should we accept such a risk? Buck, Buck, Hamm, and Lysaker (2016) have suggested that to confirm someone's abilities may mean to challenge them. To what extent does this apply to antipsychotic reduction and/or discontinuation? We offer no answers here but instead pose these issues as requiring research which not only explores the viewpoints of persons diagnosed with psychosis and those seeking to provide treatment, but also explores transparently the ethical demands and conflicts these questions pose.

Finally, there are limitations. Using MERIT to support reduction or discontinuation is time consuming and intensive and requires close communication between therapist and prescriber, working in concert, and having a shared belief in the benefit of this type of treatment; some prescribers may have yet to embrace the idea. Recently it was reported that only 45% of prescribers were identified as "helpful" in a medication discontinuation survey in the US (Ostrow et al., 2017). While it may be unusual, the author of this chapter can both provide MERIT and prescribe medications, which is ideal for being able to assess the changes in the service user and concurrently change, reduce, or discontinue medications. Obviously, this role is uncommon and not always available or practical in mental health treatment centers. In some cases, those who seek to perform a dual role of prescribing and doing MERIT may feel pressures that could contradict the tenets of MERIT, for instance, feeling as though ethically they must take an expert or authoritarian stance. Persons who discontinue medications have often found the process to be difficult due to many side effects or even withdrawal, necessitating close support and monitoring throughout the process (Cerovecki et al., 2013; Ostrow et al., 2017). Last, our reflections in this chapter are based on experience and meant to serve as a start. There are no studies that have examined the potential for using MERIT to reduce and/or discontinue medications. However, this would seem to be an important area of research, heeding the United Nations General Assembly (2017), the side-effect profile of these medications, and the many documented cases of service users' ability to recover from serious mental illness without medications.

References

Alvarez-Jimenez, M., Gonzalez-Blanch, C., Crespo-Facorro, B., Hetrick, S., Rodriguez-Sanchez, J. M., Perez-Iglesias, R., & Luis, J. (2008). Antipsychotic-induced weight gain in chronic and first-episode psychotic disorders. *CNS Drugs, 22*(7), 547–562.

Buck, K. D., Buck, B. E., Hamm, J. A., & Lysaker, P. H. (2016). Martin Buber and evidence-based practice: Can the lion really lie down with the lamb? *Psychosis, 8*(2), 156–165.

Buck, K. D., & George, S. E. (2016). Metacognitive reflective and insight therapy for a person who gained maximal levels of metacognitive capacity and was able to terminate therapy. *Journal of Contemporary Psychotherapy, 46*(4), 187–195.

Buck, K. D., Roe, D., Yanos, P., Buck, B., Fogley, R. L., Grant, M., . . . & Lysaker, P. H. (2013). Challenges to assisting with the recovery of personal identity and wellness for persons with serious mental illness: Considerations for mental health professionals. *Psychosis, 5*(2), 134–143.

Cerovecki, A., Musil, R., Klimke, A., Seemüller, F., Haen, E., Schennach, R., . . . & Riedel, M. (2013). Withdrawal symptoms and rebound syndromes associated with switching and discontinuing atypical antipsychotics: Theoretical background and practical recommendations. *CNS Drugs, 27*(7), 545–572.

Correll, C. U., Rubio, J. M., & Kane, J. M. (2018). What is the risk-benefit ratio of long-term antipsychotic treatment in people with schizophrenia? *World Psychiatry, 17*(2), 149–160.

Daumit, G. L., Goff, D. C., Meyer, J. M., Davis, V. G., Nasrallah, H. A., McEvoy, J. P., . . . & Lieberman, J. A. (2008). Antipsychotic effects on estimated 10-year coronary heart disease risk in the CATIE schizophrenia study. *Schizophrenia Research, 105*(1–3), 175–187.

De Hert, M., Detraux, J., Van Winkel, R., Yu, W., & Correll, C. U. (2012). Metabolic and cardiovascular adverse effects associated with antipsychotic drugs. *Nature Reviews Endocrinology, 8*(2), 114.

Dibonaventura, M., Gabriel, S., Dupclay, L., Gupta, S., & Kim, E. (2012). A patient perspective of the impact of medication side effects on adherence: Results of a cross-sectional nationwide survey of patients with schizophrenia. *BMC Psychiatry, 12*(1), 20.

Dorph-Petersen, K. A., Pierri, J. N., Perel, J. M., Sun, Z., Sampson, A. R., & Lewis, D. A. (2005). The influence of chronic exposure to antipsychotic medications on brain size before and after tissue fixation: A comparison of haloperidol and olanzapine in macaque monkeys. *Neuropsychopharmacology, 30*(9), 1649.

Foley, D. L., & Morley, K. I. (2011). Systematic review of early cardiometabolic outcomes of the first treated episode of psychosis. *Archives of General Psychiatry, 68*(6), 609–616.

Fusar-Poli, P., Papanastasiou, E., Stahl, D., Rocchetti, M., Carpenter, W., Shergill, S., & McGuire, P. (2014). Treatments of negative symptoms in schizophrenia: Meta-analysis of 168 randomized placebo-controlled trials. *Schizophrenia Bulletin, 41*(4), 892–899.

Goff, D. C., Falkai, P., Fleischhacker, W. W., Girgis, R. R., Kahn, R. M., Uchida, H., . . . & Lieberman, J. A. (2017). The long-term effects of antipsychotic medication on clinical course in schizophrenia. *American Journal of Psychiatry, 174*(9), 840–849.

Goff, D. C., Hill, M., & Freudenreich, O. (2010). Strategies for improving treatment adherence in schizophrenia and schizoaffective disorder. *The Journal of Clinical Psychiatry, 71*, 20–26.

Guloksuz, S., & Van Os, J. (2018). The slow death of the concept of schizophrenia and the painful birth of the psychosis spectrum. *Psychological Medicine, 48*(2), 229.

Hamm, J. A., & Lysaker, P. H. (2018). Application of integrative metacognitive psychotherapy for serious mental illness. *American Journal of Psychotherapy, 71*(4), 122–127.

Harrow, M., Jobe, T. H., & Faull, R. N. (2012). Do all schizophrenia patients need antipsychotic treatment continuously throughout their lifetime? A 20-year longitudinal study. *Psychological Medicine, 42*(10), 2145–2155.

Harrow, M., Jobe, T. H., Faull, R. N., & Yang, J. (2017). A 20-year multi-followup longitudinal study assessing whether antipsychotic medications contribute to work functioning in schizophrenia. *Psychiatry Research, 256*, 267–274.

Hasson-Ohayon, I., Arnon-Ribenfeld, N., Hamm, J. A., & Lysaker, P. H. (2017). Agency before action: The application of behavioral activation in psychotherapy with persons with psychosis. *Psychotherapy*, *54*(3), 245.

Hasson-Ohayon, I., Kravetz, S., & Lysaker, P. H. (2017). The special challenges of psychotherapy with persons with psychosis: Intersubjective metacognitive model of agreement and shared meaning. *Clinical Psychology & Psychotherapy*, *24*(2), 428–440.

Ho, B. C., Andreasen, N. C., Ziebell, S., Pierson, R., & Magnotta, V. (2011). Long-term antipsychotic treatment and brain volumes: A longitudinal study of first-episode schizophrenia. *Archives of General Psychiatry*, *68*(2), 128–137.

Ho, B. C., Nopoulos, P., Flaum, M., Arndt, S., & Andreasen, N. C. (1998). Two-year outcome in first-episode schizophrenia: Predictive value of symptoms for quality of life. *American Journal of Psychiatry*, *155*(9), 1196–1201.

Hunter, R., & Barry, S. (2012). Negative symptoms and psychosocial functioning in schizophrenia: Neglected but important targets for treatment. *European Psychiatry*, *27*(6), 432–436.

James, A. V., Leonhardt, B. L., & Buck, K. D. (2018). Metacognitive reflection and insight therapy for schizophrenia: Case study of a patient with a co-occurring substance use disorder. *American Journal of Psychotherapy*, *71*(4), 155–163.

Kane, J. M. (2013). Improving patient outcomes in schizophrenia: Achieving remission, preventing relapse, and measuring success. *The Journal of Clinical Psychiatry*, *74*(9), e18–e18.

Karson, C., Duffy, R. A., Eramo, A., Nylander, A. G., & Offord, S. J. (2016). Long-term outcomes of antipsychotic treatment in patients with first-episode schizophrenia: A systematic review. *Neuropsychiatric Disease and Treatment*, *12*, 57.

Kean, C. (2009). Silencing the self: Schizophrenia as a self-disturbance. *Schizophrenia Bulletin*, *35*(6), 1034.

Kishi, T., Ikuta, T., Matsui, Y., Inada, K., Matsuda, Y., Mishima, K., & Iwata, N. (2019). Effect of discontinuation v. maintenance of antipsychotic medication on relapse rates in patients with remitted/stable first-episode psychosis: A meta-analysis. *Psychological Medicine*, *49*(5), 772–779.

Leonhardt, B. L., Benson, K., George, S., Buck, K. D., Shaieb, R., & Vohs, J. L. (2016). Targeting insight in first episode psychosis: A case study of metacognitive reflection insight therapy (MERIT). *Journal of Contemporary Psychotherapy*, *46*(4), 207–216.

Leonhardt, B. L., Huling, K., Hamm, J. A., Roe, D., Hasson-Ohayon, I., McLeod, H. J., & Lysaker, P. H. (2017). Recovery and serious mental illness: A review of current clinical and research paradigms and future directions. *Expert Review of Neurotherapeutics*, *17*(11), 1117–1130.

Leucht, S., Cipriani, A., Spineli, L., Mavridis, D., Örey, D., Richter, F., . . . & Kissling, W. (2013). Comparative efficacy and tolerability of 15 antipsychotic drugs in schizophrenia: A multiple-treatments meta-analysis. *The Lancet*, *382*(9896), 951–962.

Leucht, S., Tardy, M., Komossa, K., Heres, S., Kissling, W., & Davis, J. M. (2012). Maintenance treatment with antipsychotic drugs for schizophrenia. *Cochrane Database of Systematic Reviews*, *5*(5): CD008016.

Lysaker, P. H., & Buck, K. D. (2006). Moving toward recovery within clients personal narratives: Directions for a recovery-focused therapy. *Journal of Psychosocial Nursing and Mental Health Services*, *44*(1), 28–35.

Lysaker, P. H., Hamm, J. A., Hasson-Ohayon, I., Pattison, M. L., & Leonhardt, B. L. (2018). Promoting recovery from severe mental illness: Implications from research on metacognition and metacognitive reflection and insight therapy. *World Journal of Psychiatry, 8*(1), 1.

Lysaker, P. H., & Klion, R. E. (2017). *Recovery, meaning-making, and severe mental illness: A comprehensive guide to metacognitive reflection and insight therapy.* London: Routledge.

Lysaker, P. H., Kukla, M., Belanger, E., White, D. A., Buck, K. D., Luther, L., . . . & Leonhardt, B. (2015). Individual psychotherapy and changes in self-experience in schizophrenia: A qualitative comparison of patients in metacognitively focused and supportive psychotherapy. *Psychiatry, 78*(4), 305–316.

Lysaker, P. H., Kukla, M., Vohs, J. L., Schnakenberg Martin, A. M., Buck, K. D., & Hasson Ohayon, I. (2019). Metacognition and recovery in schizophrenia: From research to the development of Metacognitive Reflection and Insight Therapy. *Journal of Experimental Psychopathology, 10*(1), 2043808718814992.

Milev, P., Ho, B. C., Arndt, S., & Andreasen, N. C. (2005). Predictive values of neurocognition and negative symptoms on functional outcome in schizophrenia: A longitudinal first-episode study with 7-year follow-up. *American Journal of Psychiatry, 162*(3), 495–506.

Moncrieff, J. (2007). Understanding psychotropic drug action: The contribution of the brain disabling theory. *Ethical Human Psychology and Psychiatry, 9*(3), 177–187.

Moncrieff, J. (2015). Antipsychotic maintenance treatment: Time to rethink? *PLoS Medicine, 12*(8), e1001861.

Moncrieff, J., & Middleton, H. (2015). Schizophrenia: A critical psychiatry perspective. *Current Opinion in Psychiatry, 28*(3), 264–268.

Moritz, S., Favrod, J., Andreou, C., Morrison, A. P., Bohn, F., Veckenstedt, R., . . . & Karow, A. (2012). Beyond the usual suspects: Positive attitudes towards positive symptoms is associated with medication noncompliance in psychosis. *Schizophrenia Bulletin, 39*(4), 917–922.

Ostrow, L., Jessell, L., Hurd, M., Darrow, S. M., & Cohen, D. (2017). Discontinuing psychiatric medications: A survey of long-term users. *Psychiatric Services, 68*(12), 1232–1238.

Pérez-Álvarez, M., García-Montes, J. M., Vallina-Fernández, O., & Perona-Garcelán, S. (2016). Rethinking schizophrenia in the context of the person and their circumstances: Seven reasons. *Frontiers in Psychology, 7*, 1650.

Roe, D., & Lysaker, P. H. (2013). The importance of personal narratives in recovery from psychosis. In *Experiencing psychosis* (pp. 25–34). London: Routledge.

Stanghellini, G., & Lysaker, P. H. (2007). The psychotherapy of schizophrenia through the lens of phenomenology: Intersubjectivity and the search for the recovery of first-and second-person awareness. *American Journal of Psychotherapy, 61*(2), 163–179.

United Nations General Assembly. (2017). *Report of the special rapporteur on the right of everyone to the enjoyment of the highest attainable standard of physical and mental health.* Human Rights Council. Retrieved from www.ohchr.org/EN/HRBodies/HRC/RegularSessions/Session29/Documents/A_HRC_29_33_ENG.DOCX

van Zelst, C. (2009). Stigmatization as an environmental risk in schizophrenia: A user perspective. *Schizophrenia Bulletin, 35*(2), 293–296.

Vohs, J. L., Leonhardt, B. L., James, A. V., Francis, M. M., Breier, A., Mehdiyoun, N., . . . & Lysaker, P. H. (2018). Metacognitive reflection and insight therapy for early psychosis: A preliminary study of a novel integrative psychotherapy. *Schizophrenia Research, 195*, 428–433.

Wils, R. S., Gotfredsen, D. R., Hjorthøj, C., Austin, S. F., Albert, N., Secher, R. G., . . . &
Nordentoft, M. (2017). Antipsychotic medication and remission of psychotic symptoms
10 years after a first-episode psychosis. *Schizophrenia Research, 182,* 42–48.

Wunderink, L., Nieboer, R. M., Wiersma, D., Sytema, S., & Nienhuis, F. J. (2013). Recovery in remitted first-episode psychosis at 7 years of follow-up of an early dose reduction/
discontinuation or maintenance treatment strategy: Long-term follow-up of a 2-year randomized clinical trial. *JAMA Psychiatry, 70*(9), 913–920.

8

NARRATIVE ENHANCEMENT COGNITIVE THERAPY (NECT)

The recovery of the self from internalized stigma

David Roe, Amit Yamin, Ilanit Hasson-Ohayon, Paul H. Lysaker and Philip T. Yanos

Abstract: *Narrative Enhancement and Cognitive Therapy (NECT) is a manualized, group-based intervention that is directed towards helping people who have been labeled with a psychiatric diagnosis recover their sense of value and decrease internalized stigma. It relies heavily on psychoeducation, cognitive behavioural techniques, and personal story-telling, or "narrative enhancement" exercises. In this chapter we describe the rationale for NECT and its curriculum, followed by an illustration of a fictional group to demonstrate its application, before reviewing the current body of research supporting its effectiveness. Finally, we discuss how NECT relates to self-reflectivity, awareness of the other, decentration and mastery as core aspects of metacognition.*

Introduction: the challenge of recovery of self after internalizing public stigma

Many distinguished theorists, including Kraepelin, Mead, Bleuler, and Kohut have emphasized that the individual's experience of self is a central theoretical construct to understand wellbeing. The simple sense of who we are is a fundamental part of our most basic experience as humans (Mead, 1934). A familiar sense of self over time and across situations is a core foundation on which we rely in order to begin to communicate with others, interact effectively with our environment, and require reflective and narrative abilities(Roe & Davidson, 2005; Lysaker & Lysaker, 2010). There is piling evidence from a broad range of sources that many people labeled as having experienced psychosis have significant changes in self-experience (Lysaker & Lysaker, 2010; Lysaker et al., 2019) such as loss of agency and loss of the cohesiveness of one's personal identity (McCarthy-Jones, Marriott, Knowles, Rowse, & Thompson, 2013). Thus, in order to have a sense of who we are, we need to think about the way we perceive ourselves, the way others perceive us, and to be able to make a story out of this reflective knowledge. In addition to have a familiar and stable sense of who we are (or "identity"), also important is the prevailing way we evaluate and feel about our self – that is, the extent to which we feel positive about our self ("self-esteem") and see ourselves as having impact and control in relation to external events ("self-efficacy").

Anomalous experiences, such as delusional beliefs, hallucinations, disorganized thinking, and extreme affective states, can pose major challenges to our sense of self and identity. On the most basic and direct level, these sorts of experiences pose questions such as "how reliable are my thoughts if I became so strongly convinced about something that no one else agrees with?" Or, "who am I if I can't contain or cope with the intensity of my own emotions?" Beyond this, and perhaps even more importantly, however, is one's awareness or anticipation of how these experiences are perceived by others, and how they render one fundamentally "different". As the modified labeling theory perspective of stigma (Link, Cullen, Struening, Shrout, & Dohrenwend, 1989) proposes, an awareness of negative stereotypes about mental illness (such as that people with psychosis are doomed to a life in institutions and incapable of contributing to society) has been absorbed by many people over history. As though these experiences of psychosis are not confusing and overwhelming enough, an awareness of how one is likely to be perceived and interpreted by others can potentially have a powerful effect on one's sense of self and identity.

The more we feel estranged from our most intimate thoughts and feelings, the more we are prone to feel confused and threatened by them (Roe & Davidson, 2005). Consequently, we are more likely to be influenced by the way others see us, or the way we imagine they do (Thoits, 2011). Our intensified confusion as to who we are, and a growing reliance on the perceptions of others, can make us particularly vulnerable to the widespread stigma associated with psychosis. Research has found the stigma of psychosis to be common, painful, and harmful, robbing people of many life opportunities (see Yanos, 2018, for a summary).

Going further, our core identity and sense of self is known to be strongly influenced by the social categories that others use to describe us (Yanos, 2018). In the case of psychosis, when stigmatizing attitudes, strongly held by others (e.g. dangerousness, incompetence, inability to work), are perceived as legitimate, they impinge upon self-concept, making it more difficult to establish identities distinct from the stigmatizing label. As a result, people with psychosis often come to internalize these stigmatizing views held by others (Corrigan & Watson, 2002). This process, typically referred to as self-stigma, involves the loss of previously held, or hoped-for identities (e.g. self as student, self as worker, self as parent, etc.) and the adoption of identities based on stigmatizing views (e.g. self as dangerous, self as incompetent). Gradually, the internal and intimate way a person comes to understand, interpret and make sense of his or her own thinking and feelings can be taken hostage by the internalization of public stigma, posing a major challenge to core experiences of self and identity.

These are the processes which Sue Estroff (1981) described several decades ago in her landmark ethnographic study, *Being Mentally Ill*. In this, she summarized how "a part-time or periodically psychotic person can become a full-time crazy person in identity and being" (p. 223). Estroff (1989) hypothesized that the personal and social loss of self might be a key definition, or even cause, of chronicity. Thus, experiences labeled as delusions and hallucinations, which are more common than typically thought (Van Os, Linscott, Myin-Germeys, Delespual, &

Krabbendam, 2009), may have a rapid and dramatic impact on a person's identity mostly because of the meaning attributed to them and negative stereotypes attached to them and eventually internalized. Thus labels create a tidal wave which can forcefully shift a person from living a "normal" life to one in which he or she is labeled, discriminated against, and comes to adapt the identity of a "psychiatric patient".

The effect of taking on the identity of a "psychiatric patient" can exert an influence that can be more impactful than the psychotic symptoms themselves (see Yanos, 2018, for a review). Patricia Deegan described this in her recollection of her own disengagement from interest in life (sitting in a chair, smoking cigarette after cigarette) after a psychiatric hospitalization. As she described, "it is not so much mental illness that I am observing" but rather "the flame of a faltering human spirit" which resulted from "putting on those warped glasses" that lead to "viewing yourself as others see you" (Deegan, 1993, p. 8). How does one overcome the effects of internalized stigma and rekindle "the flame of a faltering human spirit"? Such a question about the recovery of sense of self and identity was robustly posed by Deegan (1993) when she asked: "How do we reclaim and recover our sense of value when we have been devalued and dehumanized?" (Deegan, 1993, p. 8).

Narrative Enhancement and Cognitive Therapy (NECT) was developed in an effort to take a step towards meeting the challenges highlighted by Deegan. NECT is a manualized, 20-session group-based intervention that addresses self-stigma through psychoeducation, application of cognitive behavioural techniques, and personal story-telling, or "narrative enhancement" exercises (Yanos, Roe, & Lysaker, 2011). Through these combined approaches, NECT aims to help people who have been labeled with a psychiatric diagnosis recover their sense of value and reclaim their personhood. In this chapter we will describe the rationale for NECT and its curriculum, before presenting a fictional group to demonstrate it and reviewing the current body of research supporting it.

Narrative Enhancement Cognitive Therapy (NECT): an intervention aimed at reducing self-stigma and contributing to the recovery of the self

Several research teams have developed interventions that aim to decrease self-stigma in order to facilitate recovery (see Yanos, Lucksted, Drapalski, Roe, & Lysaker, 2015, for a review). As noted earlier, NECT is one such intervention. NECT combines psychoeducation that addresses stigmatizing views about mental illness, cognitive restructuring that teaches skills needed to identify and challenge negative thoughts about the self, and elements of narrative psychotherapy focused on transforming one's life story in more empowering ways. NECT is group-based, as this format allows participants to receive feedback and support from peers and provides opportunities for interactions with an audience for story-telling. NECT employs a manual (Yanos, Roe, & Lysaker, 2013) designed to be "user-friendly" and easily implemented in routine. public-sector treatment settings (such as day treatment, outpatient treatment, supported housing, and assertive community treatment).

The manual features a guide for the practitioner aimed at helping to explain the rationale, tone, and technique of each section, as well as hand-outs that can be used to guide group discussions. In addition, the manual includes worksheets that can be used to help group members learn and practice skills for coping with internalized stigma by identifying cognitive distortions or dysfunctional attitudes related to having a mental illness, and ultimately by constructing more complex personal narratives in which the narrator and protagonist have identities which go far beyond the confines of what is prescribed by self-stigma.

The five stages of the intervention:

NECT begins with an introduction: The purpose of this is to begin the process of assessing where the person is with regard to his or her experience of self. In particular the goal is to begin to explore the impact of the experience of psychosis on one's sense of self and identity, and whether the person feels they had an impact on the symptoms and course of illness and recovery. Such exploration helps the person to reflect on the degree to which they experience their self as a separate entity from the diagnosis or as engulfed by the diagnosis (which would suggest a high degree of internalized stigma). In order to undertake this reflection, each participant engages in exercises designed to elicit a description of him/herself (conveying the focus and interest first and foremost in him or her as a person) and a description of the reason for which he or she is seeking help (implying that it is solely up to the person to define the reasons).

These self-conceptualizations are elicited through written group exercises (although participants have the opportunity to dictate responses in the event that they are unable to write). The goal at this stage is to convey a clear and strong message that we are interested in them and value their perceptions, and to emphasize a constructivism approach to encourage active exploration and honest dialogue, allowing a range of perceptions to be heard. The purpose is to gradually establish a shared understanding rather than a "psychoeducational" enforced understanding.

The 2nd stage focuses on psychoeducation: The purpose of this segment of the intervention is to provide participants with the current empirical knowledge, with the aim of challenging "myths" that reflect stigmatizing views. Psychoeducation is conducted in an interactive manner while stigmatizing myths – such as that people with mental illness are dangerous, cannot work, cannot have relationships, or recover – are discussed and challenged using existing scientific evidence. Didactic teaching is avoided. Instead, we emphasize the development of a dialogue between two different kinds of knowledge – the first is scientifically updated information on issues related to stigma and the second is the person's own lived experience. Emphasis is placed on the idea that self-stigma would not exist were it not for public stigma. We explicitly state that the ultimate solution for self-stigma is to erase public stigma, but rather than waiting passively for this to happen, we invite participants to take an active stand by learning to identify and combat the self-stigma they are struggling with in their everyday life.

The third stage of NECT relies on cognitive restructuring: This section starts by teaching the basic principles of cognitive restructuring, including the connection between thoughts and feelings, how thoughts and feelings influence behaviour, what an irrational belief is, types of irrational beliefs, how to monitor thoughts, and how to challenge irrational beliefs. Participants then engage in exercises in which they attempt to identify, challenge, and consider replacing inaccurate beliefs and/or dysfunctional cognitions about self, illness, and self in relation to illness. Information is provided on common misconceptions, related to stigmatizing views of psychosis, and thinking errors related to these misconceptions. For example, a person might hold the belief that they should avoid trying to form an intimate relationship because it could be stressful and lead to a relapse. NECT focuses on trying to help a person learn to "Be a scientist" (essentially traditional cognitive restructuring by examining evidence that supports or challenges such underlying generalized assumptions that "intimate relationships are stressful" and the direct link between stress and relapse). Additional cognitive techniques include learning and practising to "Take your own advice" (what one would say to someone else who presented the same issue), and using a "No judgment zone" (which focuses on the judgmental nature of the words that are used in the thought, for example "I woke up late and did not get to work on time. I am a complete loser and should have known I could never keep a job") and the use of "self-talk statements" ("this is challenging but I have faith that I can make it").

The fourth stage and "heart" of the intervention is the Narrative Enhancement section: After participants have completed the psychoeducation and cognitive restructuring sections and have had the opportunity to develop group cohesion, they are encouraged to write (or tell) and share stories within the group. Phenomenological observations suggest that psychosis often involves a profound diminishment in a person's ability to narrate the evolving story of his or her own life (Lysaker, Wickett, Wilke, & Lysaker, 2003; Roe & Davidson, 2005). Many may have stopped feeling entitled to narrate stories of their lives, due to the internalization of stigmatized views. In the process of narration, though, people can reconnect with important parts of their lives and come to experience themselves as more complete people with multiple identities (such as a friend, parent, employee, athlete, volunteer, etc.) and not only as someone reduced to a diagnostic label that he or she has been given. Given the opportunity to narrate and re-own various parts of one's story and identity, within an audience of outsider witnesses, people get the opportunity to activate what they have earlier learned in the cognitive restructuring section, challenge some of the stigmatic attitudes attached to their diagnosis, avoid internalizing it and instead differentiating themselves from their diagnostic label and give new meaning to life experiences.

Narrating a story, via metacognitive or mentalization ability, is highly important for meaning-making in the recovery process (see Chapter 13; Chapter 2; Chapter 11). Research suggests that narration (or story-telling) is a fundamental human practice that allows people to shape their understandings of the world and themselves (Bruner, 1987). It has been argued that narrative transformation is essential to the process of identity transformation, particularly among people who have experienced psychosis. Their sense of self has been threatened by the way they think and feel about these experiences, as well as by explicit and implicit messages they have been subject to from others.

NECT emphasizes that at the heart of the recovery process is the active process of trying to figure out, make sense of, and construct meaning from the range of one's mental health experiences, and to integrate them into a cohesive, flexible personal story which one can live with and communicate to others if one chooses (see Hasson-Ohayon & Lysaker's discussion of recovery, Chapter 1). Narrow stories often include "thin descriptions" such as: "I am a schizophrenic", "I have a brain disorder", "I was always the black sheep of the family" are all too often stories "fed" and reinforced by others. Research has shown (Roe, Hasson-Ohayon, Kravetz, Yanos, & Lysaker, 2008) how people diagnosed with psychosis may display high levels of "insight", based on standard assessment tools, when in fact they may be passively accepting the diagnostic label or actively trying to fit themselves in to a narrow story. Of note, overlap between standard measures of insight and self-stigma has been shown across a few samples (Hasson-Ohayon, 2018). Narrative enhancement, which entails story-telling and processing feedback, is central to the crucial activity of constructing a story in which the person identifies themselves as author and protagonist. The narrative enhancement section, thus, aims to help broaden these narrow stories so that they can be seen as falling along an understandable timeline which points to future hopes and the sense of the person as an active agent who can affect their destiny.

In order to facilitate this process, the group facilitators try to help participants bring together previously fragmented and isolated aspects of the self by being an audience to the story. The group leader encourages participants to explore the way (content and process) participants tell their stories and respond to their difficulties in thinking about themselves (and being center or/and an active agent). The group facilitators try to help participants recognize their right to have and create their own story, and reflect on the challenges, strengths, and hopes their story entails. A further focus during this section is to discuss how the types of stories may be influenced by cognitive distortions, which can in turn be inspired by popular (and erroneous) beliefs about mental illness. This module therefore attempts to integrate aspects of the previous two sections (psychoeducation and cognitive behavioral therapy (CBT)) to help participants go beyond learning to identify and challenge distorted cognitions ("I'll never be able to work because I was admitted to a psychiatric hospital"). Instead, it focuses on integrating new beliefs into a broader story about one's self over time, emphasizing the horizon and potential future when not constrained by self-defeating beliefs. Thus, the ultimate goal is to enable participants to learn and practice skills that offer opportunities to negotiate and rewrite their personal stories and experiences, and subsequently also their possible future while internalizing the empowering role of the narrator of these stories.

Finally, NECT ends as it begins, with the invitation to describe oneself and one's reason for seeking help. It is an opportunity to go back to these questions after the NECT journey, compare whether and how these descriptions may have changed and, if so, what has contributed to these changes and the meaning they hold for the person.

Recommended structure of the intervention

It is recommended that the group include approximately 20 sessions and be conducted by two leaders, in order to give more personal attention when needed, strengthen continuity, and provide the facilitators with the opportunity to discuss the group process together and provide mutual support. The ideal size of the group is five to eight members, not including facilitators. Each group meeting should last approximately one hour and begin with a five- to ten-minute structured section in which participants are welcomed and allowed to add to the day's agenda. This "check-in" time also allows participants to give a brief reflection on their experiences that week, report how they did with homework assignments, and raise any questions or concerns they may have. Following "check-in" is the main section which lasts for roughly 50 minutes. During this part of the session, group members together review and complete roughly two to three pages of worksheets, while discussing the content and expressing the thoughts and feelings these generate. Group members are encouraged, but not required, to read from worksheets in order to facilitate participation in the group. During the session participants have time to process what they have learned, make comments on the usefulness of the group, and offer one another support.

NECT – group illustration

The following description of an NECT group is provided to illustrate its structure and elements, as well as to demonstrate the processes participants often go through within the group. The described group is fictional, although based on the authors' experience in conducting and supervising NECT groups over the last decade.

People who were using supportive housing services, and who were eligible because they had psychiatric disability, were exposed to a brief presentation about

NECT and were invited to join a group that was about to begin. Eleven people signed up and the first two sessions were attended by seven to nine people, who evolved into a core group of eight participants after the third session. There were various levels of group attendance at each session, with six participants completing between 18–20 weekly sessions. Two of these participants, Ella, a 36-year-old woman, and Danny, a 27-year-old man, will be described in some detail.

The group was conducted by two therapists (one woman and one man), one of whom was a social worker and the other a psychiatric nurse, and who had both been working in recovery-oriented community mental health services for over five years. Both had completed a two-day NECT training course, after which they attended bi-monthly group supervision which included additional training focused on the therapeutic techniques used in NECT and practicing its curriculum.

The first two NECT sessions were dedicated to orientation, getting to know one another and agreeing on group expectations and norms. These were followed by the first three exercises which included an invitation for participants to describe themselves, the reason they were accessing the service, and the interaction between the two.

When asked to describe herself, Ella took some time before saying: "I am 36, still single. I'm a lonely person that no one wants to be in touch with, and I totally understand why". She then shared that she had had a few friends in high school, but since her first hospitalization, at age 22, she had often felt different and lonely and thought that people did not want to be around her. Danny described himself as "26-year-old, schizophrenic" and added that he wanted to develop a career in printing, just like his Dad. Danny mentioned he had a supportive family who wanted him to succeed in life, and then described their disappointment due to his ongoing struggle to find work, never managing to hold on to a job for more than a few months. Later on in the session, when invited to describe the reason for accessing the service, Ella stated that she attended because she had a mental illness that she would often dream would just disappear and allow her to go back to how she had felt in her late teens. Danny said he was accessing services because he had a "weakness" and stated it was not a big part of him, and that he sometimes wondered why he had even been given a diagnosis and why his psychiatrist recommended he take medication. He said he heard voices sometimes, which most of the time did not bother him very much, nor was he sure he wanted them to go away. Danny also shared the feeling that no one could ever really understand him. When confronted by another participant who stated: "Voices are bad and dangerous" and said Danny must take medication or else he would never find a job. The group facilitator pointed out that group members apparently had a range of different experiences and feelings about these issues and that none was necessarily "right or wrong". She encouraged the group to continue to explore and share these experiences. In response, the same group member still insisted that Danny should take his medication, and Danny commented: "Just as I said, no one could understand me".

After group members began to get to know one another, had established a group contract, and the active exploration of self-conceptions had begun, the group moved on to the psychoeducation module of the intervention. As stated before, to be able to reject stigmatizing attitudes, the psychoeducation module helps provide participants with knowledge ("facts") aimed at challenging incorrect and untrue attitudes ("myths") about mental illness. While reading together from the manual and discussing common myths such as "people with mental illness tend to be violent", "people with mental illness cannot work", and "people never recover from mental illness", and reading the facts challenging these myths, an authentic and lively discussion began in the group. Danny, as well as another group member, stated it was not a myth that people with serious mental illness can't work, but rather an absolute truth. He said that in his heart he really knew he could never get a real job in printing, and that employers were right for not giving him work, and added that by trying again and again he only fooled himself.

After reading a potential description of recovery, a lively debate began as to whether recovery was possible. Two participants claimed there was no such thing as recovery. One of them explained that the fact he had been taking medication for years proved that he had not recovered, while the other added, quite angrily, that anyone who states that people with serious mental illness can recover ignores how much he and his peers had suffered and how their lives had changed because of their illness. A few others said that they were doing better in some ways than they had in the past, but were not recovered, while two others said they were working on their recovery.

The group facilitators then helped make the distinction between "cure" and "personal recovery", referring to the ability to explore and choose personal goals and make progress towards them, despite occasional or persistent symptoms and even though seeking out support from mental health services. The discussion of these issues was quite lively, and occasionally heated, with participants sharing more of their thoughts and feelings about these loaded topics and how their own personal experiences contributed to the degree to which they tended to adopt negative stereotypes (for example "people with serious mental illness can't work"). Given the opportunity to share these experiences and the feelings associated with them, such as pain, shame, guilt, and anger, some were able to use the information presented to them to help challenge these stereotypes.

At this stage, the concept of stigma was presented and participants were invited to share their personal experiences. This led to the sharing of some painful stories. For example, Ella told the group how she had worked in a kindergarten for six months, until two parents, who apparently found out she had a "psychiatric history", insisted she stop working there and even threatened they would move their children to a different kindergarten. Ella shared, with tears, how much she had loved the children and how much they had loved her, and described how ashamed and defeated she felt when the management decided to fire her for reasons supposedly not related to the parents' pressure, instead of standing up for her. She described how she had felt deeply let down, particularly by parents of other kids with whom she felt she had a strong positive connection, but chose to remain silent and did not actively back her up or vocally disagree or argue with the other parents.

Ella got a lot of support from the group and was especially moved by a participant, who was a mother of two children, saying she wished her kids had had the opportunity to be nurtured and looked after by Ella. Another participant said it was the worst kind of discrimination and that he got so upset every time he was exposed to such injustice. Danny then shared that he had decided to stop even trying to get a date since the recent one who, just like those before, had politely slipped away when he shared the reasons he had left college, when he first developed psychosis during the second semester of his freshman year. He felt so humiliated, mumbling some sort of excuse, which made him feel like a "loser". Danny then added quietly, so that he was heard only by the people sitting next to him: "And I know she was right, I really am a loser".

The group was quiet and the facilitators and group members appeared to feel tense with some sense of sadness. One topic that came up was whether, when, with whom, and how much did people feel they wanted and could share with others. The dilemma and conflict between wanting to be open and honest and share things without feeling ashamed, and the common, painful experience of rejection which sometimes followed, evoked a lot of discussion and emotions. It was also possible at this point, in light of what Ella and Danny had shared, to begin to distinguish between stigma and self-stigma and demonstrate how negative stereotypes are often internalized and lead to painful feelings and sense of hopelessness. This process of distinguishing between stigma and self-stigma involved reflection about self and other as well as about the differences between them and the realization of the existence of different narratives.

At this point Danny commented that he was skeptical about the group's ability to change how society perceives people with mental illness, since stigma is so strong and persistent. Even his therapist, he felt, often acted in a patronizing manner and talked to him as if he was a kid. This led to a heated discussion about public stigma with a lot of frustration and anger, as well as some growing sparks of feeling a sense of power, which was partly produced by the awareness of the injustice and the righteous anger it evoked. This contributed to a sense of group cohesiveness, whereas participants shared the growing recognition that they were an oppressed group. Feelings ranged between despair in light of stigma being so widespread, and hope induced by the validation they were not alone and what they were experiencing was real, wrong, and oppressive.

The facilitators emphasized that self-stigma was not a sign of weakness, or an illness, but rather a direct consequence of the public stigma. Some participants felt relieved to discuss how they would never have felt self-stigma had they not been so brutally and frequently subject to public stigma. Sessions were intense, with emotional shifts between feeling like victims and active agents of social change. Some group members expressed the thought that stigma must first be erased, while others said it was time to start trying to gain control and change what they felt they could change. The facilitators were empathetic to the justified anger and pain which stigma generated, while at the same time they also conveyed their belief that they need not to wait until public stigma ends before they try to learn and apply ways to challenge and reject public stigma.

This led to the opportunity to begin moving to the cognitive restructuring section. After taking some time to learn to distinguish between thoughts and feelings, and teaching how they influence behaviour, basic principles of cognitive restructuring were taught and practiced. At this stage, the connection between self-stigmatizing views and cognitive thinking errors was made, inviting participants to learn ways to challenge misconceptions about themselves.

When inviting participants to share examples of when they had had negative thoughts about themselves, and which had led to negative feelings and behaviour, Ella hesitated but then decided to share a thought she had had the week before. She had really wanted to join a Facebook group of people interested in children's education, but she had immediately dismissed that thought because she was sure someone would find out about her "psychiatric history" and would then definitely "kick her out" of the virtual group. Anyway, she thought, she had nothing valuable to contribute to the discussion about education, since she had no children and was consuming psychiatric services, so she might as well give up this silly idea.

This was an opportunity for the facilitators to explain some common universal negative ways of thinking – cognitive biases, such as "All or Nothing Thinking" (seeing the world in extremes), catastrophizing (expecting the worst to happen), using a negative mental filter (seeing only the negative and ignoring the positive), and labeling (applying labels instead of focusing on the facts). While attempting to identify the negative ways of thinking in Ella's example, a group member suggested she used "catastrophizing", convincing herself that nothing good could come out of her actions and believing the worst would happen (being thrown out of the Facebook group). Another participant suggested that Ella used "labeling", thinking she had nothing meaningful to contribute to others. The facilitators pointed out that later on in sessions participants would have the chance to learn to use alternative ways of thinking, which could lead to less self-stigma. But before they got there, other members were invited to share experiences and identify the negative ways of thinking they used.

Danny then sighed and shared the thought that he could never find a job in printing and hold on to it, and said he was sure his family would eventually move away from him, because of the loser he is. "Why even bother trying?" Danny mumbled to himself, not sure if anyone heard him. After being empathetic to Danny's frustration and sense of hopelessness, the group was invited to explore with him the negative ways of thinking he displayed, such as "catastrophizing", using a negative Mental Filter and "labeling".

This was the time for introducing the group to alternative ways of thinking, which are cognitive strategies that participants can learn and practice, in order to challenge self-stigmatizing thoughts. Specific cognitive strategies, such as "being a scientist" (examining the evidence for the thought), "taking your own advice" (thinking how a close person would look at the situation), and trying to stay out of judgment, were taught and then practiced within the group and in everyday life between sessions.

By offering Ella an opportunity to challenge her former thought about joining the Facebook group, she was asked if participants could try to suggest alternative ways of thinking. Ella said she was curious to hear them, since she could not think of any other way to understand the situation. One member then asked Ella: "How can you say you have nothing to contribute to the topic of children's education, after telling us about the good work you have done in the kindergarten, and the great connections you established with the kids?" ("Being a scientist"). Another participant said she felt Ella always contributed something meaningful to group discussions and that she had learned a lot from her wisdom ("Being a scientist"). She added that Ella should not be so judgmental towards herself, especially when the parents and management were the ones who should have been ashamed of their behaviour ("No judgment zone"). Facilitators then asked Ella if some of these alternative thoughts were relevant to her, and she shared she had never thought of it in this way. She then smiled and said it made her feel less ashamed and a bit more hopeful, but that she was still not sure she could try to join the Facebook group.

When turning to Danny's example, participants suggested alternative thoughts such as: "You did the best you could", "You didn't give up after a few times, which shows you have a lot of determination" ("Being a scientist"), and "I wish I knew what I wanted to do with my life, as you do, don't be so tough on yourself" ("Take your own advice", "No judgment zone"). Asking Danny if any of these thoughts were relevant to him, he commented that it was nice to get support from the group, and yet he was not sure at all that it would have any effect on him. He shared that he was really tired of trying again and again to find the right job, to be a good boy to his parents and to find a girlfriend, and he hoped these strategies they had learned would help, but that he was still skeptical, and afraid to be disappointed again if they did not.

In the following sessions, participants were invited to practice these strategies in everyday situations, and report and share within group what it was like for them. While some group members shared that they were struggling with this, since it was hard to remember to use these strategies and it sometimes felt artificial and awkward, others, including Ella, reported having been able to apply them and had experienced some small positive change. Ella shared how after a long time longing to reach out to a friend she once had, she had finally found the courage to do so, thanks to her use of the "No judgment zone" strategy, reminding herself she was a positive person and that although she sometimes felt bad, she could be a good person to talk to and to hang out with.

Before moving ahead to the narrative module, the facilitators invited each participant to choose a positive self-statement they could use in everyday life, in times of need. Danny chose to write down on a note the sentence suggested by another participant: "I am doing the best I can". He put it in his wallet, so he could pull it out next time he felt frustrated or defeated.

After exploring how people experience themselves, focusing on myths about mental illness and the way they contribute to stigma and self-stigma, and after learning and practicing alternative ways of thinking, it was time to move on to the last section, and perhaps the "heart" of NECT, the narrative part. This section focused on story-telling, which is a powerful way to gain a sense of control over events, make sense of them and draw connections between them, help strengthen one's sense of self and identity and decrease self-stigma. Facilitators emphasized there was no "right" way to tell a story, and that listeners had a significant role as they became "outsider witnesses" who could reflect upon the story and give feedback to the story teller. Participants were asked to listen in an empathetic and non-judgmental manner, reflect upon what stood out for them and what they had learned about the person telling it, and about his or her strengths and hopes.

Each person had the opportunity to first write down his or her story and then read it out loud and get feedback on it. Participants were invited to share stories about themselves, about their experience coping with what they were struggling with (including the experience of mental illness or however they referred to it), and about their strengths, successes, and hopes in life.

Ella took some time to write and then said that she hesitated whether to share, since it was very personal, but decided she would, since the group felt at this stage like a secure place to be in and to share difficult experiences. Ella then started talking, and seemed to be shrinking in her chair, embarrassed and avoiding eye contact. She then said:

> Since as long as I can remember, I have been lonely. I used to wait for girls to invite me to play with them, but only rarely did they. I always felt different in a way I can't explain, always wanting to fit in, knowing it could not really happen. After being hospitalized at the age of 22 and being labeled with a psychiatric disorder, I truly thought my life had ended. If it hadn't been for my mother, I would probably be dead today. I was sure it would be better for everyone if I was dead. Thanks to her, after a few months in bed, I understood I had to begin trying to do something with my broken life, but I had no idea what to begin with. Going to therapy helped me connect again to the dream I always had, to work with children, and do my best so that no child would ever feel alone as I felt as a child. Although I couldn't concentrate in academic studies and get a degree in education, I found, with the help of my therapist, a kindergarten I could work in, as an assistant. As I shared with you before, I loved the kids and I think they loved me too. All of that vanished when I was fired. I was devastated, ashamed of my mental illness, and perhaps even worse, felt guilty for having tried to get a 'normal job' and be part of 'normal society'. I felt as though I deserved to have been discovered and that firing me was a justified punishment for having tried to trick them and pretend I was normal and could do ordinary things like work. I struggled to get up in the morning after that for months. I felt totally hopeless, ashamed and defeated. Thanks to the group, I recently renewed a connection with one

friend I had, and I now feel it is time for me to give myself another chance in life. I feel that I deserve it and understand that maybe I am not the one to blame, but rather the people who fired me just because of my psychiatric history. I feel that I am not alone anymore, realizing injustice will continue to exist, but also realizing that maybe I could choose not to surrender to it.

A silence overtook the room, while everyone took a moment to think about Ella's story. Only then could Ella raise her eyes from what she had written, coming across Danny's eyes, noticing a teardrop and feeling the impact her story had made. The facilitator then asked if anyone wanted to share what they felt and what they had learned about Ella, her challenges, strengths, and hopes, from her story. Danny volunteered to be the first and then said he felt as though Ella was telling his story. He added he was moved by her sincerity and by the way she talked about her family, especially her mum, as an anchor and such a solid source of support during times of despair. Another participant shared that she was inspired by Ella's ability to "get up on her feet" even after feeling there was nothing worth living for. She said she wished that she herself would find the motivation and strength to fight her depression and begin to live, and do something with her life. Another group member shared that he "knew from the inside" what it was like to want so much to belong, yet to experience so much rejection just as Ella described. He wished he could reach out to a friend he once had, learning from Ella that even when things sometimes felt impossible, you should not give up and that good things might yet come, since no one knows what lies ahead. Ella then had the chance to thank the group and said she was glad she overcame her fear to share, because it gave her a lot of hope to hear her friends resonate to her story, validating it and sharing what it meant to them. Facilitators then thanked Ella for sharing, inviting other participants to take a step forward and also do so, in the following sessions.

As the group proceeded in the narrative module, a growing sense of intimacy evolved, with more friendly conversation around the opening and ending of the group as well as an awareness of the upcoming end of the group. Questions of whether participants could make progress in their lives, and whether or not they could succeed in applying what they had learned in everyday situations after the group ended, were brought up and discussed. As the group came closer to its end, a range of feelings emerged, including a sense of pride and accomplishment, as well as fear and sorrow, while the facilitators encouraged all the voices in the group to be heard. Facilitators then encouraged group members to keep practicing what they had learned and achieved with important people in their lives, after the group ended, which they argued would help them to continue their progress along their recovery journey.

Before wrapping up, in the last part of NECT, participants were invited to look back and reflect on their journey, what they had learned about themselves and what they wished to take with them into the future. Just like at the beginning of the group, participants were asked again how they described themselves at this point in their lives, having the chance to check if anything had changed since they set off on this journey. After looking back at what he had written in the first session, Danny said some things had changed for him and some had not. He did not feel quite as much as a "loser" any more, due to the support he had got from the group, what he had learned about himself, and some of the strategies he had begun to apply in his everyday life. Also, he felt proud for having attended almost all of the group sessions. And yet, Danny shared that he was sad it had ended, uncertain of what lay ahead in the future, and uncertain he could find the motivation to apply for a new job. Other group members shared what they had written about themselves at this point, reflecting on the process they had gone through in the group.

In the closing session, after inviting each participant to say what he or she would take with them or leave behind, group facilitators took some time to share how they had been moved by the participation of each group member and to say that they had learned so much about the human spirit, about coping with injustice and about finding ways to make sense of times of trouble and challenge in life. They also conveyed their hope that people would use what they had learned and practised in the group, in future situations, while facing stigma and injustice.

Research on NECT

To date, NECT has been translated into seven languages (Hebrew, Russian, Danish, Dutch, Swedish, Spanish, and Chinese) and its acceptability and feasibility has been successfully demonstrated in different countries and settings as detailed later. Research on the impact of NECT has been carried out in Israel, the US, and Sweden.

In a small (n=18) qualitative study (Roe, Hasson-Ohayon, Derhy, Yanos, & Lysaker, 2010) conducted in Israel, NECT completers reported positive change in hope and the ability to actively cope with psychosocial challenges, as well as changes in self-experience such as the ability to notice and think about their thoughts and emotions. Five controlled trials of NECT have been conducted to date. The first (Yanos, Roe, West, Smith, & Lysaker, 2012), conducted in New York and Indianapolis, included a sample of 39 people with severe mental illness randomly assigned to NECT or treatment as usual. Possibly due to low statistical power, the study found no statistically significant difference between participants in NECT vs. treatment as usual at post-treatment, but noted a trend favoring NECT for self-stigma and insight with effect sizes of .3–.5 (Yanos et al., 2012). The second study (Roe et al., 2014), a quasi-experiment conducted in Israel with 119 public mental health service recipients, found that participants in NECT improved significantly, compared with participants receiving treatment as usual, in measures of self-stigma, self-esteem, and perceived quality of life, with small to moderate effect sizes of 0.3 to 0.6 (Roe et al., 2014). A third study, a randomized controlled trial (RCT) conducted in Sweden, compared NECT to treatment as usual in a sample of 87 people with psychotic disorders (Hansson, Lexen, & Holmen, 2017). This study found that participants in NECT improved significantly in self-stigma and self-esteem in contrast to participants in treatment as usual, with an effect size of roughly 0.5. Furthermore, improvements were sustained at six-month follow-up, and sustained improvement in self-stigma was significantly associated with the number of NECT sessions attended.

A recent RCT in the US (Yanos et al., 2019) included 170 participants who were randomly assigned to NECT or supportive group therapy and interviewed at four time points over the course of nearly a year. This study found that NECT participants improved significantly compared to supportive group therapy participants over the study period in the social withdrawal aspect of self-stigma. Further, NECT participants in outpatient sites improved significantly more over time in self-stigma in comparison to supportive group therapy participants in outpatient sites (with an effect size of .4), while NECT participants in day treatment sites improved significantly more in hopelessness and narrative insight than other participants at those sites. NECT participants overall decreased their use of avoidant coping strategies. Considering its growing evidence-base, NECT has recently been included in the Swedish treatment guidelines for psychosis in 2018 (Swedish National Board of Health and Welfare, 2018; Malortie et al., 2019).

NECT and enhancement of reflectivity

As evident from the outlined description of NECT, facilitators use cognitive restructuring and narration techniques to induce and maintain a positive sense of self amongst group members. Cognitive restructuring aims to challenge stigmatized aspects of self-perception and includes reflecting on the way participants perceive themselves. Although cognitive restructuring is considered a cognitive rather than metacognitive technique, it does include a "meta" view on one's cognition (Moritz & Lysaker, 2018). Thus, during participation in NECT, participants are asked to reflect on the stigmatizing attribution they are enacting toward themselves. In addition, they are encouraged to comment and reflect on other participants' shared experience, which enhances not only their self-reflectivity, but also the awareness of the other (see Chapter 1, for presentation of metacognition domains).

In addition to these two aspects, this widely used definition of metacognition includes decentration, which refers to the ability to take a non-egocentric view of the mind of others and recognize that others' mental states are influenced by a range of factors, and mastery, which refers to the ability to use complex metacognitive knowledge in order to cope with psychological problems (Lysaker & Klion, 2017). Notably, using cognitive restructuring in a group format enables one to practice decentration, as feedback from others may be used to create perspective from one's egocentric view. It also allows persons to practice mastery as group discussion may include reflecting on ways to react to stigma, that is, using the reflective knowledge on self and others to respond to challenges.

The narrative techniques in NECT are highly related to the concept of metacognition. As emphasized in developmental theories and phenomenological literature (e.g. Cortina & Liotti, 2010), reflective abilities and the capacity to narrate are co-occurring. Thus, for a person to create a story, he or she needs to reflect on their own thoughts and feelings and the thoughts and feelings of other people. Similar to the intersubjective processes described in another chapter discussing group Therapeutic Alliance Focused Therapy (Chapter 10), the group context provides a unique intersubjective space for the creation of shared meaning, enabling narratives to evolve. Accordingly, each participant's narrative is continually developed through ongoing group dialogue. Enhancing metacognition while doing NECT can be further done by integrating intersubjective elements. For example, as suggested by Hasson-Ohayon (2012), self-disclosure of the therapist may facilitate the reflective subjectivity of the participants in NECT. Accordingly, the therapist may share his or her thoughts and feelings in the group or share their own experiences of stigma.

Although NECT does not address metacognition explicitly and directly, it involves techniques directed to enhance a positive self-identity via increased reflection. As described in the clinical presentation outlined, participants needed to reflect upon themselves with regard to the experience of psychosis and stigma, in order to create a positive sense of self. As NECT is delivered in a group format, awareness of the other is also part of the process.

Conclusions

Public stigma about mental illness can lead to self-stigma, which can then erode a person's foundational sense of self as an agent in the world or valuable member of their community. In this chapter we have described a group-based approach to addressing self-stigma and sense of self among adults diagnosed with serious mental illness. We have detailed its three stages and provided an illustration of how this can unfold in a real-life setting and noted how this aligns with research suggesting that NECT can lead to meaningful improvements in subjective outcomes related to recovery in controlled studies. Finally, we have suggested that a core mechanism of NECT may go beyond the correction of specific beliefs or the acquisition of skills and involve the growth of metacognition capacity or a transformation in a person's ability to form integrated ideas about him/herself and others, so allowing them to participate in their own communities in more intricate and integral ways. Importantly, there are limitations and future directions to pursue. For example, studies are needed in a broader range of contexts including with persons experiencing a first episode psychosis as well as those who refuse mental health services. More nuanced theoretical and qualitative work is also needed to more carefully understand how different processes, including therapeutic alliance and empowerment, influence changes in sense of self and long-term outcomes.

References

Bruner, J. (1987). Life as narrative. *Social Research, 54*, 11–32.
Corrigan, P. W., & Watson, A. C. (2002). The paradox of self-stigma and mental illness. *Clinical Psychology: Science and Practice, 9*(1), 35–53.

Cortina, M., & Liotti, G. (2010). The intersubjective and cooperative origins of consciousness: An evolutionary-developmental approach. *Journal of the American Academy of Psychoanalysis and Dynamic Psychiatry, 38*(2), 291–314.

Deegan, P. E. (1993). Recovery of sense of value after being labeled. *Journal of Psychosocial Nursing, 31*, 7–11.

Estroff, S. (1981). *Making it crazy.* Berkeley, CA: University of California Press.

Estroff, S. (1989). Self, identity, and subjective experiences of schizophrenia: In search of the subject. *Schizophrenia Bulletin, 15*, 189–196.

Hansson, L., Lexen, A., & Holmen, J. (2017). The effectiveness of narrative enhancement and cognitive therapy: A randomized controlled study of a self-stigma intervention. *Social Psychiatry and Psychiatric Epidemiology, 52*, 1415–1423.

Hasson-Ohayon, I. (2012). Integrating cognitive behavioral-based therapy with an intersubjective approach: Addressing metacognitive deficits among people with schizophrenia. *Journal of Psychotherapy Integration, 22*(4), 356.

Hasson-Ohayon, I. (2018). Overlap and distinction between measures of insight and self-stigma. *Psychiatry Research, 266*, 47–64.

Link, B. G., Cullen, F. T., Struening, E. L., Shrout, P. E., & Dohrenwend, B. P. (1989). A modified labeling theory approach to mental disorders: An empirical assessment. *American Sociological Review, 54*, 400–423.

Lysaker, P. H., & Klion, R. E. (2017). *Recovery, meaning-making, and severe mental illness: A comprehensive guide to metacognitive reflection and insight therapy.* London: Routledge.

Lysaker, P. H., Kukla, M., Vohs, J. L., Schnakenberg Martin, A. M., Buck, K. D., & Hasson Ohayon, I. (2019). Metacognition and recovery in schizophrenia: From research to the development of metacognitive reflection and insight therapy. *Journal of Experimental Psychopathology, 10*(1), 2043808718814992.

Lysaker, P. H., & Lysaker, J. T. (2010). Schizophrenia and alterations in self-experience: A comparison of 6 perspectives. *Schizophrenia Bulletin, 36*(2), 331–340.

Lysaker, P. H., Wickett, A. M., Wilke, N., & Lysaker, J. T. (2003). Narrative incoherence in schizophrenia: The absent agent-protagonist and the collapse of internal dialogue. *American Journal of Psychotherapy, 57*, 153–166.

Malortie, S. et al. (2019). National guidelines for care and support regarding Schizophrenia emphasize on recovery perspective. Rehabilitation in combination with medication may enhance quality of life. *Läkartidningen, 116*:FFPU. (In Swedish).

McCarthy-Jones, S., Marriott, M., Knowles, R., Rowse, G., & Thompson, A. R. (2013). What is psychosis? A meta-synthesis of inductive qualitative studies exploring the experience of psychosis. *Psychological, Social and Integrative Approaches, 5*(1), 1–16.

Mead, G. H. (1934). *Mind, self and society.* Chicago, IL: University of Chicago Press.

Moritz, S., & Lysaker, P. H. (2018). Metacognition – What did James H. Flavell really say and the implications for the conceptualization and design of metacognitive interventions. *Schizophrenia Research, 201*, 20–26.

Roe, D., & Davidson, L. (2005). Self and Narrative in schizophrenia: Time to author a new story. *Journal of Medical Humanities, 31*, 89–94.

Roe, D., Hasson-Ohayon, I., Derhy, O., Yanos, P. T., & Lysaker, P. H. (2010). Talking about life and finding solutions to different hardships: A qualitative study on the impact of narrative enhancement and cognitive therapy on persons with serious mental illness. *Journal of Nervous and Mental Disease, 198*(11), 807–812.

Roe, D., Hasson-Ohayon, I., Kravetz, S., Yanos, P. T., & Lysaker, P. H. (2008). Call it a monster for lack of anything else: Narrative insight in psychosis. *JNMD, 196*, 859–865.

Roe, D., Hasson-Ohayon, I., Mashiach-Eizenberg, M., Derhy, O., Lysaker, P. H., & Yanos, P. T. (2014). Narrative Enhancement and Cognitive Therapy (NECT) effectiveness: A quasi-experimental study. *Journal of Clinical Psychology, 70*, 303–312.

Swedish National Board of Health and Welfare. (2018). *National guidelines for care and support regarding schizophrenia and similar conditions, Self-stigma-Psychosocial intervention to decrease self-stigmatization according to the NECT-method.* Retrieved from https://roi.socialstyrelsen.se/riktlinjer/nationella-riktlinjer-for-vard-och-stod-vid-schizofreni-och-schizofreniliknande-tillstand/4/schizofreni-eller-schizofreniliknande-tillstand-sjalvstigmatisering-psykosocial-insats-for-att-minska-sjalvstigmatisering-enligt-nect-metoden/4.65

Thoits, P. A. (2011). Resisting the stigma of mental illness. *Social Psychology Quarterly, 74*(1), 6–28. https://doi.org/10.1177/0190272511398019.

Van Os, J., Linscott, R. J., Myin-Germeys, I., Delespual, P., & Krabbendam, M. (2009). A systematic review and meta-analysis of the psychosis continuum: Evidence for a psychosis proneness – persistence – impairment model of psychotic disorder. *Psychological Medicine, 39*, 179–195.

Yanos, P. T. (2018). *Written off: Mental health stigma and the loss of human potential.* New York: Cambridge University Press.

Yanos, P. T., Lucksted, A., Drapalski, A., Roe, D., & Lysaker, P. H. (2015). Interventions targeting mental health self-stigma: A review and comparison. *Psychiatric Rehabilitation Journal, 38*, 171–178.

Yanos, P. T., Lysaker, P. H., Silverstein, S. M., Vayshenker, B., Gonzales, L., West, M. L., & Roe, D. (2019). A randomized controlled-trial of treatment for self-stigma among persons diagnosed with schizophrenia-spectrum disorders. *Social Psychiatry and Psychiatric Epidemiology, 54*(11), 1363–1378.

Yanos, P. T., Roe, D., & Lysaker, P. H. (2011). Narrative enhancement and cognitive therapy: A new group-based treatment for internalized stigma among persons with severe mental illness. *International Journal of Group Psychotherapy, 61*, 577–595.

Yanos, P. T., Roe, D., & Lysaker, P. H. (2013). *Narrative enhancement and cognitive therapy for self-stigma.* Unpublished Manual.

Yanos, P. T., Roe, D., West, M. L., Smith, S. M., & Lysaker, P. H. (2012). Group-based treatment for internalized stigma among persons with severe mental illness: Findings from a randomized controlled trial. *Psychological Services, 9*, 248–258.

9

THE RECOVERY OF SENSE OF SELF WHILE COPING WITH NEGATIVE SYMPTOMS

Hamish J. McLeod, Nicola McGuire and
Andrew Gumley

Abstract: *Negative symptoms, such as diminished motivational drive, anhedonia, social withdrawal, apathy, and reduced emotionality, are the subject of increasing clinical and research attention. It has become clearer that negative symptoms can be subdivided into experiential and expressive elements, with a variety of phenomenological and metacognitive correlates. In particular, metacognitive difficulties in self-reflectivity around one's wants, interests, and emotional responses play a major role in anhedonia and diminished motivation. This chapter will analyse a range of correlates of negative symptoms including metacognition, neuropsychological, and developmental factors. We will explore how metacognitive difficulties are related to experiences of persistent negative symptoms, and how enhancing metacognitive capacities might support self-recovery. We will also examine how psychological treatments that focus on understanding and responding in an attuned way to the self-experience of people suffering from negative symptoms may increase the chance of meaningful recovery for those who have not benefited from standard approaches to treatment such as medication and generic mental health support.*

The disabling impact of negative symptoms

The notion of negative symptoms is a clinical concept adopted from classical neurology to denote the absence or diminution of functions and abilities (Messinger et al., 2011). Their typical behavioural manifestations include reduced volition, altered experience of pleasure, and difficulties with social functioning. These phenomena have long been recognised in psychosis, but are somewhat overshadowed by positive symptoms such as hearing hostile and critical voices or experiencing distressing persecutory ideas. Yet, Kraepelin referred to the "weakening of the wellsprings of volition" as one of the key features of schizophrenia, reflecting on the characteristic loss of motivational drive and agency commonly displayed by the people he worked with (Carpenter, Heinrichs, & Wagman, 1988; Kraepelin, 1971). More recent analyses suggest that primary negative symptoms are exhibited by 20–25% of people with psychosis across clinical sample studies, studies of people diagnosed with psychosis drawn from the general population returns prevalence rates of 15–20% (Kirkpatrick, Fenton, Carpenter, & Marder, 2006). These problems are commonly unmet treatment needs reported by service users, with loss of motivation standing out as a key area of concern when people with psychosis are asked to rate subjectively important areas of difficulty (Byrne & Morrison, 2015; Moritz, Berna, Jaeger, Westermann, & Nagel, 2017; Sterk, Winter, Muis, & de Haan, 2013). Negative symptoms can also be a source of considerable concern and distress to family members (Provencher & Mueser, 1997; Roick et al., 2007). As these problems have garnered more research attention, it has become clear that their prevalence, and that of related disabling impacts, may be greater than previously assumed. A comprehensive study of 7,678 clinical records in the UK national health service found that 40% of people with a schizophrenia spectrum diagnosis experienced two or more negative symptoms (Patel et al., 2015). This higher rate of negative symptom prevalence is also borne out by a recent meta-analysis of specific negative symptoms observed across the stages of psychotic illness (Sauvé, Brodeur, Shah, & Lepage, 2019). When negative symptom rates are examined across stages of illness from ultrahigh risk groups through to people who have experienced multiple psychotic episodes, some specific negative symptoms, such as anhedonia, are experienced by more than 70% of people. Although these figures are not adjusted for iatrogenic and secondary causes of negative symptom behaviours, they provide an indication of the scope of negative symptoms as a significant clinical problem (Sauvé et al., 2019).

In this chapter, we will explore how psychological treatments, that focus on understanding and responding in an attuned way to the self-experience of people suffering from negative symptoms, may increase the chance of meaningful recovery for those who have not benefitted from usual treatment (Chapter 1; Leonhardt et al., 2017). We argue that this work is sorely needed because we are a long way from having a clear set of negative symptom treatment options that can reliably reduce suffering and support recovery (Barnes et al., 2016; Fusar-Poli et al., 2014; Priebe et al., 2016). Much of the available evidence for individual psychotherapies, such as CBT, is of insufficient quality to say with any certainty what should be added to standard care to produce meaningful improvements for most service users (Bighelli et al., 2018; Jones et al., 2018). Also, early data suggesting a beneficial effect of standard CBT on negative symptoms have not been borne out by later reviews (Velthorst et al., 2014) and it has been suggested that effective negative symptom therapies will need to be augmented with techniques that stimulate metacognition and reflective functioning (Hasson-Ohayon, Kravetz, & Lysaker, 2017). Given the accumulating evidence that metacognitive ability is an important factor in the development and maintenance of negative symptoms, a therapy approach that addresses these difficulties has more potential to overcome the current lack of effective therapeutic options. We also argue that more progress will be made if we carefully consider how different subtypes of negative symptoms may require tailored approaches to formulation and treatment (Velthorst et al., 2014). Symptom-focused approaches are becoming common in psychotherapy for psychosis as we acquire more evidence about the specific processes that underpin the maintenance of specific symptoms (Freeman & Garety, 2014; Lincoln & Peters, 2018).

Subtyping negative symptoms

Much of the recent literature on psychological treatments for psychosis has focused on improved positive symptoms as the key therapeutic outcome (Bighelli et al., 2018) and an increasing number of studies have now tested positive symptom specific processes (e.g. rumination, sleep hygiene, and appraisals of worry) that can be targeted in psychological treatment protocols (Brown, Waite, & Freeman, 2019). This is consistent with the general finding that focusing on specific symptoms can help make significant advances in the understanding of these symptoms and the factors precipitating them (Lincoln & Peters, 2018). In order to apply a similar approach to negative symptoms, it is relevant to look at how they are currently sub-typed and characterised (Galderisi, Färden, & Kaiser, 2016; Galderisi, Mucci, Buchanan, & Arango, 2018). Previous dichotomies, such as primary vs. secondary negative symptoms and deficit vs non-deficit presentations (Carpenter et al., 1988), have been replaced by more nuanced distinctions that separate experiential negative symptoms (e.g. anhedonia and amotivation) from expressive negative symptoms (e.g. affective flattening, poverty of speech) (Foussias & Remington, 2010).

Focusing therapeutic attention on subtypes of negative symptoms is also compatible with current approaches to modelling mental health problems based on more readily observable and measurable processes rather than abstracted and reified diagnostic labels (Cuthbert, 2014). The Research Domain Criteria (RDoC) classification system is the most prominent example that has emerged as an alternative to standard diagnostic schemes for mental health conditions (Insel et al., 2010). Although RDoC is not free from criticism (Lilienfeld, 2014; Lilienfeld & Treadway, 2016), it does encourage an approach to understanding mental illness that builds on specified processes and capacities (e.g. understanding one's own mind, attentional processes, reward sensitivity, arousal regulation) (Cuthbert, 2014). This move away from therapies based on broad diagnostic categories addresses a key problem with schizophrenia as a diagnosis; namely that people with very different symptom profiles are often unhelpfully placed together under the same diagnosis (APA, 2013; World Health Organization, 1992). Under factor analyses, amotivation, anhedonia, and asociality cluster together as "experiential deficits" and poverty of speech and affective blunting reflect a "diminished expression" subdomain (Kirkpatrick et al., 2006; Messinger et al., 2011; Kring & Barch, 2014). Indirect evidence suggests that experiential and expressive negative symptoms are linked to different aspects of functioning (Strauss et al., 2013). These symptoms might also have different clinical impacts, for example; *expressive* deficits increase the likelihood of longer hospital admission, whereas people with greater *experiential* deficits have typically poorer work-related outcomes (Barch & Dowd, 2010; Foussias et al., 2015).

Consistent with the topic of this book, there is also growing evidence of a contribution of metacognitive functioning to negative symptoms, both at the level of combined negative symptom scores (McLeod, Gumley, MacBeth, Schwannauer, & Lysaker, 2014a) and for specific symptoms such as anhedonia (Buck et al., 2014). Before examining these links in more detail, it will help to examine the key conceptual issues that are relevant to understanding the relationship between disrupted self-experience and negative symptoms.

The self and negative symptoms: some key conceptual issues

In this section we discuss four main sets of evidence that shed some light on how negative symptoms may emerge and be maintained. Our argument is that fragmentation of the self, autobiographical memory (AM) deficits, early developmental factors, and disconnectivity in large-scale brain networks all affect self-experience in ways that need to be considered when developing new approaches to supporting negative symptom recovery.

Fragmented self-experience and negative symptoms

A major challenge to applying standard psychological therapies, such as CBT, in the treatment of negative symptoms is the assumptions made about the capacity of people with psychosis to reflect on and modify thoughts about the self as an agent in the world (McLeod, Gumley, & Schwannauer, 2014b). For example, identifying and challenging self-defeating thoughts about personal competence, the likelihood of acceptance by others, and the probability of experiencing pleasure are the key targets in standard CBT for negative symptoms (Grant, Huh, Perivoliotis, Stolar, & Beck, 2012; Klingberg et al., 2011; Rector, Beck, & Stolar, 2005; Staring, Huurne, & van der Gaag, 2013). However, many people with negative symptoms find it very difficult to reflect on their own mental experiences in a way that can support testing of their assumptions and beliefs about the world (McLeod et al., 2014a). So, treatments based on thought challenging have substantial difficulty in gaining any traction because even the process of identifying and exploring one's thoughts in therapy may be confusing or overwhelming. In recognition of this issue, other approaches have focused on attempting to re-stimulate the capacity to experience the self in an embodied way through techniques such as body-oriented psychotherapy which are less reliant on verbal-linguistic modes of expression (Priebe et al., 2016). Hence, before assumptions and beliefs about the world can be tested and modified, many people with negative symptoms will first need support to reassemble their fragmented self-experience so that they can regain a coherent understanding of who they are and what is important and meaningful to them.

Creating the circumstances to support the assembly of fragmented self-experience can quickly appear highly complex and overwhelming for both the service user and the therapist. As an antidote to this threat, many treatment protocols emphasise attaining narrowly defined, focused, treatment goals such as symptom reduction, acquisition of specific social skills, or development of mood regulation strategies (Elis, Caponigro, & Kring, 2013; Favrod, Giuliani, Ernst, & Bonsack, 2010; Johnson et al., 2009). While some of these protocols may support recovery for a few, there is a substantial number who struggle to obtain any recovery-relevant benefits from these approaches. Our proposal is that subjective recovery that encompasses a wider range of outcomes, not just symptom change, will need a therapeutic approach that acknowledges and addresses the complex nature of constructing a coherent sense of self. This requires creating enough time and opportunity for the person to be helped to re-assemble the fragments of their experience so that they can meet both life's challenges and joys. While some approaches have been designed to help people develop the metacognitive capacity needed to cope with the good and bad of human experience (Lysaker & Klion, 2017), there is still work to be done on understanding how these processes could be targeted for change to support recovery from negative symptoms. We also need to harness the benefits of a precise symptom-focused approach but not at the expense of losing sight of the whole person and their experience of psychosis. One way to achieve this reassembly of the fragments of self-experience is to use the therapeutic relationship to stimulate sufficient intersubjective awareness for the person to begin to produce and reflect on their experiences (Hasson-Ohayon, 2012; Salvatore, Dimaggio, & Lysaker, 2007). The narrative that is constructed as we examine our past and current experiences relies heavily on the operation of the autobiographical memory system and so in the next section we provide an account of key aspects of AM function that are relevant to negative symptom expression.

Autobiographical memory and the self

Autobiographical information is the fundamental substrate of many theories of the phenomenology and teleology of the self (Conway, 2005; Conway & Pleydell-Pearce, 2000; Conway, Singer, & Tagini, 2004). The study of autobiographical memory now encompasses an extensive literature, drawing on evidence and theories spanning neuroscience, clinical sciences, philosophy, and cognitive psychology. It is generally argued that AM grounds and constrains the versions of self that can be accessible to consciousness/working memory (Conway, 2005; Sutin & Robins, 2007) and it is clear that the types of AM available to consciousness can vary in conjunction with contextual factors such as mood state, eliciting cues, and threats to self-coherence (Berna et al., 2011; Conway et al., 2004; Singer, Blagov, Berry, & Oost, 2013; Williams et al., 2007). Hence, AM recall can be affected by motivational factors (e.g. when recall of painful memories is avoided) or can break down (e.g. as in amnesia where access to personal information is impaired due to neurological factors).

One emerging theory addressing the interface between AM functioning and anhedonia is that when access to *specific* personally experienced past events is disrupted (e.g. difficulty responding to the question "Can you tell me about a recent social situation you enjoyed?"), the default response is to access personal semantic information in the form of rules or identity-related beliefs that have been shaped by multiple experiences over time (e.g. "I'm not a sociable person – I don't enjoy social events") (Strauss & Gold, 2012). This access to semantic personal information may be habitual, over-generalised, and not routinely subjected to scrutiny and reconsideration. As a result, the output from this exploration of potential sources of pleasure could be either a stereotyped response ("I don't enjoy social events") or a failure to access either a specific AM or an identity-related belief (e.g. "I don't know" or no response at all).

This superficially simple process of judging our own preferences, based on prior experience of the world, has a number of complexities that emerge developmentally at around three to six years of age and are heavily reliant on the reflective capacity for awareness of one's unique experience of the world over time – a human capacity referred to as autonoesis or mental time travel (Tulving, 2005). This capacity requires the development of a subjective sense of a personal "me" that has experiences that occur at different points in time but happen to the same agent or identity. The stimulation of such capacity may well be linked to early experiences that occur in key developmental contexts (particularly interactions with attachment figures). We turn now to examining some of these processes.

Developmental factors in autobiographical memory and self-awareness

One of the features of early relationships is that infants and young children do not start life with the capacity to differentiate a boundary between the self and others, particularly attachment figures who provide a source of affect regulation and nurturance (Schore, 1997). In multiple ways, attachment figures facilitate the co-regulation of affects, and safe exploration of the social and physical world, and in normal development this promotes the capacity to learn about the self as an independent agent with mental experiences that are separable from the mental experiences of others. Infants who are faced with unavailable, hostile, or erratic attachment figures may experience significant disruptions to the development of a stable and secure sense of self. As with other forms of learning, repeated exposure to patterns of interpersonal relating will affect the internal working models/ schemas that are used to guide predictions about the social-interpersonal world (see Griffiths and McLeod (2019) for a review of attachment in relation to negative symptoms). Those who go on to develop insecure attachment patterns may learn to avoid thinking about and seeking contact with the mental states of other individuals, which in people experiencing negative symptoms may manifest in asociality, social withdrawal, and disinterest in personal closeness.

The role of AM processes in this emerging awareness of the self and others is beginning to extend beyond a theoretical understanding, as more data are acquired about how children transition out of the period of childhood amnesia and begin to exhibit the capacity to encode and then retrieve autobiographical events from memory. Ross, Hutchison, and Cunningham (2019) used a paradigm that exploited the fact that AM information tends to be more readily encoded when it is self-referent and applied this to a large sample of three- to six-year-olds, along with measures of AM and the ability to monitor the source of memory information (i.e. internally versus externally generated) (Ross et al., 2019). As predicted, AM, source monitoring, and self-knowledge all increased with age. In addition, there was a bidirectional relationship between growth in autobiographical knowledge capacity (the volume of retrieved episodes) and self-concept. In essence, these data suggest that the ability to encode and retrieve personal AM events depends on the development of self-concept and that once this has formed, the ongoing stimulation of AM further promotes self-awareness. A potential corollary of this, for people with disrupted early relationships, is that this process of self-identity consolidation and development of AM processing capacities may become disrupted. There is evidence from adult samples that avoidance of recall of specific AMs is associated with greater negative symptoms, particularly in people with a history of traumatic admissions to hospital (Harrison & Fowler, 2004). What remains to be determined is whether these patterns of AM function may first emerge in early developmental contexts and then lead to elevated risk of negative symptoms with the onset of illness. As noted above, there is some evidence that once negative symptoms become established, recovery may require the formation of a therapeutic relationship that supports intersubjectivity (Hasson-Ohayon, 2012; Salvatore et al., 2007).

A final step in our consideration of conceptual issues that could inform our understanding of the relationship between the self and negative symptoms is to examine the possible contribution of perturbed functioning of large-scale brain networks.

The Default Mode Network (DMN) and the self

As the techniques and theoretical brain models used in functional neuroimaging have evolved there has been an increasing recognition that the brain is never truly "at rest" (Raichle et al., 2001). Functional imaging of the brain in states of assumed mental inactivity (e.g. eyes closed and resting quietly) reveals coordinated patterns of large-scale and widely distributed networks, the activity of which is associated with complex mental functions such as autobiographical remembering, thinking about the future, and self-reflection (Whitfield-Gabrieli & Ford, 2012). Hence, it appears that if left without salient stimuli to respond to, the typical mode of operation, for most people, is to engage in mental tasks that entail exploration of one's own mind (e.g. remembering events and thinking about the future). This has implications for people with marked negative symptoms as it seems plausible that reduced activity in the brain systems involved in self-reflection, recall of personal experiences, and future planning will have downstream consequences such as avolition, low self-awareness, and potentially anhedonia. There is preliminary neuroimaging evidence that components of the DMN (comprising mPFC, PFC, and precuneus) are functionally less active in people who display lower metacognitive ability (Francis et al., 2017). It will be for future studies to replicate this finding but these results do raise the possibility that disruption of the DMN (or its sub-parts) contributes to the types of metacognitive deficits that worsen negative symptoms.

This development of large-scale network models of brain-mind interaction has encouraged a theoretical shift away from lesion-based aetiological models that propose psychosis is wholly explained by damage to brain regions (e.g. the striatum; Chung & Barch, 2016) or structures (e.g. white matter tracts; Sigmundsson et al., 2001). Instead, there is accumulating evidence that psychosis can be more helpfully understood as being associated with functional dysconnectivity in brain circuits and neuromodulatory processes (Friston, Brown, Siemerkus, & Stephan, 2016). This conceptualisation is consistent with Bleuler's view that loss of associative functions and disruptions of the ability to synthesise thoughts were at the heart of schizophrenia (Dollfus & Lyne, 2017). This view has the very important implication that disruption in the ability to make adaptive predictions about the state of the world and form integrated models of the self over time can vary depending on potentially modifiable contextual factors (Friston et al., 2016). This approach has been used to explain the *positive* symptoms of psychosis, such as delusional beliefs, as a misfiring of the usually adaptive processes of Bayesian inference that close the gap between what we expect to see in the world and our actual sensory experiences (Friston, 2005). In this prediction-error model the argument is that brain systems are working to generate and test hypotheses about the state of the world but that this process disintegrates and causes aberrantly salient experiences that the person needs to integrate into their understanding of the world. These integrative and associative processes are also relevant to the understanding of how fragmentation of self-experience may underpin negative symptoms. One plausible functional impairment is that the default mode network becomes less likely to generate stimulus-independent thought, autobiographical recollections, and willed intentions to act (Frith, 1992). Hence, rather than making unhelpful or inaccurate predictions about the state of the world, some negative symptom presentations could reflect a failure of the natural generative activity of the DMN. This could give rise to phenomenological experiences such as alogia, reduced motivational drive, diminished interest, and lower spontaneous sensation seeking. It would be interesting to see if future studies can map the recovery trajectories and fluctuations in negative symptoms to changes in the functional connectivity of the DMN. This kind of information might help with pacing treatment and ensuring that the level of intervention matches the metacognitive profile of the service user.

Potential treatment implications

Before examining ways that recovery can be supported in people experiencing persistent negative symptoms, it is worth highlighting that despite the lack of reliably effective drugs or psychotherapies for negative symptoms, there is evidence that negative symptoms can and do change over time. Previous pessimistic assumptions about the inevitable long-term deterioration of negative symptoms have been modified in light of evidence that most outpatients show some improvement in negative symptom scores over time, irrespective of treatment exposure (Savill, Banks, Khanom, & Priebe, 2014; Strauss, Harrow, Grossman, & Rosen, 2010). The question then is, what can be done via psychological means to stimulate recovery from negative symptoms? Our analysis suggests a number of avenues.

First, treatment strategies need to be tailored to the level of metacognition exhibited by the person. This is done by carefully observing the kinds of mental operations that they are capable of during the therapeutic session. Using the typology applied in Metacognitive Reflection and Insight Therapy (MERIT; see (Lysaker & Klion, 2017)), people experiencing reduced levels of awareness of their own mind will have difficulty identifying their own thoughts or differentiating between types of cognitive operations (e.g. memories, fantasies, perceptions). People with negative symptoms who have few thoughts and experience their mental world as more barren, empty, or unidimensional will first need to be helped to label and explore their own mental states in a safe and supportive way. Hence, the therapist may need to start by providing comments and observations that re-stimulate the person's awareness of and curiosity about their own mind. For other people, their negative symptoms will arise from experiences of being overwhelmed when they begin to explore their mind and the mind of others. Based on the literature reviewed above, this presentation will be common in people who have traumatic autobiographical memories that they have learned to cope with by avoidance. In both scenarios, the key task for the therapist is to sensitively match the level of intervention to the metacognitive capacity that the service user currently displays.

A second key strategy hinges on helping the person to generate autobiographical recollections that they can use to make sense of their life, their wants and desires, and the personal meanings that they have derived from their experiences. This capacity may be used in a targeted way to address experiential negative symptoms such as anhedonia (e.g. by recollecting previous sources of pleasure), or in a more general way (e.g. in supporting discussions about the links between the meaning of personally experienced events and current personal identity). It remains to be demonstrated whether helping to re-stimulate autobiographical recollection capacities can also restore functional connectivity in the DMN. If this is the case, it may be possible to triangulate changes in metacognition, DMN connectivity, and negative symptom recovery as therapy progresses.

Finally, it also appears that another key therapeutic task is to create opportunities for people to differentiate between personal semantic knowledge (e.g. abstracted identity beliefs) and experienced-based recollections of events. This is particularly important when the person holds undermining identity beliefs, such as seeing themselves as incompetent or unable to form social connections. By definition, these types of beliefs will be overgeneralised abstractions that are no longer linked to specific autobiographical experiences. Helping the person to notice the difference between their actual current experiences and the personal semantic beliefs they hold (e.g. "I'm incapable of experiencing pleasure") creates the chance to develop a more complex and nuanced view of themselves and their capabilities. For example, such an approach should help diminish the amotivation that arises from problems with anticipating pleasure (Raffard, Esposito, Boulenger, & Van der Linden, 2013). As an increasing body of work addressing anhedonia shows, an increased capacity to recall actual personally experienced events may provide the best source of information about what is personally meaningful and rewarding (Engel, Fritzsche, & Lincoln, 2013; Strauss & Gold, 2012).

In conclusion, it is clear that negative symptoms are a highly salient problem area for persons with psychosis and their families. It also seems that specific subtypes of negative symptoms may be higher priority for care than others so the treatment options we use should be deployed to target the negative symptoms that are most relevant to the person and their recovery needs. There is now extensive evidence, from a number of theoretical and methodological sources, that suggests negative symptoms, self-identity, and metacognitive capacity all interact. In particular, the recovery of a clearer sense of self-identity, bolstered by an integrated narrative sense of one's own history, may be important parts of the process of recovering from negative symptoms. Future studies are needed that examine whether the enhancement of metacognitive ability (e.g. via MERIT; (Lysaker & Klion, 2017)) causes improvements in negative symptoms and reduces fragmentation of self-identity. The evidence reviewed here suggests that this is a highly promising therapeutic pathway to explore and develop.

References

American Psychiatric Association (2013). *Diagnostic and statistical manual of mental disorders (DSM-5)*. Arlington, VA: American Psychiatric Association.

Barch, D. M., & Dowd, E. C. (2010). Goal representations and motivational drive in schizophrenia: The role of prefrontal-striatal interactions. *Schizophrenia Bulletin, 36*(5), 919–934. http://doi.org/10.1093/schbul/sbq068.

Barnes, T. R., Leeson, V. C., Paton, C., Costelloe, C., Simon, J., Kiss, N., . . . Taylor, S. (2016). Antidepressant controlled trial for negative symptoms in schizophrenia (ACTIONS): A double-blind, placebo-controlled, randomised clinical trial. *Health Technology Assessment, 20*(29), 1–46. http://doi.org/10.3310/hta20290.

Berna, F., Bennouna-Greene, M., Potheegadoo, J., Verry, P., Conway, M. A., & Danion, J.-M. (2011). Self-defining memories related to illness and their integration into the self in patients with schizophrenia. *Psychiatry Research, 189*(1), 49–54. http://doi.org/10.1016/j.psychres.2011.03.006.

Bighelli, I., Salanti, G., Huhn, M., Schneider-Thoma, J., Krause, M., Reitmeir, C., . . . Leucht, S. (2018). Psychological interventions to reduce positive symptoms in schizophrenia: Systematic review and network meta-analysis. *World Psychiatry, 17*(3), 316–329. http://doi.org/10.1002/wps.20577.

Brown, P., Waite, F., & Freeman, D. (2019). "Twisting the lion's tail": Manipulationist tests of causation for psychological mechanisms in the occurrence of delusions and hallucinations. *Clinical Psychology Review*, 1–0. http://doi.org/10.1016/j.cpr.2018.12.003.

Buck, K. D., McLeod, H. J., Gumley, A., Dimaggio, G., Buck, B. E., Minor, K. S., . . . Lysaker, P. (2014). Anhedonia in prolonged schizophrenia spectrum patients with relatively lower vs. higher levels of depression disorders: Associations with deficits in social cognition and metacognition. *Consciousness and Cognition*, *29*, 68–75.

Byrne, R., & Morrison, A. P. (2015). Service users' priorities and preferences for treatment of psychosis: A user-led Delphi study. *Psychiatric Services*, *65*(9), 1167–1169. http://doi.org/10.1176/appi.

Carpenter, W. T., Jr, Heinrichs, D. W., & Wagman, A. M. (1988). Deficit and nondeficit forms of schizophrenia: The concept. *American Journal of Psychiatry*, *145*, 578–583.

Chung, Y. S., & Barch, D. M. (2016). Frontal-striatum dysfunction during reward processing: Relationships to amotivation in schizophrenia. *Journal of Abnormal Psychology*, *125*(3), 453–469. http://doi.org/10.1037/abn0000137.

Conway, M. A. (2005). Memory and the self☆. *Journal of Memory and Language*, *53*(4), 594–628. http://doi.org/10.1016/j.jml.2005.08.005.

Conway, M. A., & Pleydell-Pearce, C. W. (2000). The construction of autobiographical memories in the self-memory system. *Psychological Review*, *107*(2), 261. http://doi.org/10.1037//0033-295X.

Conway, M. A., Singer, J. A., & Tagini, A. (2004). The self and autobiographical memory: correspondence and coherence. *Social Cognition*, *22*(5), 491–529. http://doi.org/10.1521/soco.22.5.491.50768.

Cuthbert, B. N. (2014). The RDoC framework: Facilitating transition from ICD/DSM to dimensional approaches that integrate neuroscience and psychopathology. *World Psychiatry*, *13*(1), 28–35.

Dollfus, S., & Lyne, J. (2017). Negative symptoms: History of the concept and their position in diagnosis of schizophrenia. *Schizophrenia Research*, *186*, 3–7.

Elis, O., Caponigro, J. M., & Kring, A. M. (2013). Psychosocial treatments for negative symptoms in schizophrenia: Current practices and future directions. *Clinical Psychology Review*, *33*(8), 914–928. http://doi.org/10.1016/j.cpr.2013.07.001.

Engel, M., Fritzsche, A., & Lincoln, T. M. (2013). Anticipatory pleasure and approach motivation in schizophrenia-like negative symptoms. *Psychiatry Research*, *210*(2), 422–426. http://doi.org/10.1016/j.psychres.2013.07.025.

Favrod, J., Giuliani, F., Ernst, F., & Bonsack, C. (2010). Anticipatory pleasure skills training: A new intervention to reduce anhedonia in schizophrenia. *Perspectives in Psychiatric Care*, *46*(3), 171–181. http://doi.org/10.1111/j.1744-6163.2010.00255.x.

Foussias, G., & Remington, G. (2010). Negative symptoms in schizophrenia: Avolition and Occam's razor. *Schizophrenia Bulletin*, *36*(2), 359–369. http://doi.org/10.1093/schbul/sbn094.

Foussias, G., Siddiqui, I., Fervaha, G., Agid, O., & Remington, G. (2015). Dissecting negative symptoms in schizophrenia: Opportunities for translation into new treatments. *Journal of Psychopharmacology*, *29*(2), 116–126. http://doi.org/10.1177/0269881114562092.

Francis, M. M., Hummer, T. A., Leonhardt, B. L., Vohs, J. L., Yung, M. G., Mehdiyoun, N. F., . . . Breier, A. (2017). Association of medial prefrontal resting state functional connectivity and metacognitive capacity in early phase psychosis. *Psychiatry Research: Neuroimaging*, *262*, 8–14. http://doi.org/10.1016/j.pscychresns.2016.12.014.

Freeman, D., & Garety, P. (2014). Advances in understanding and treating persecutory delusions: A review. *Social Psychiatry and Psychiatric Epidemiology*, *49*(8), 1179–1189. http://doi.org/10.1007/s00127-014-0928-7.

Friston, K. J. (2005). Models of brain function in neuroimaging. *Annual Review of Psychology*, *56*(1), 57–87. http://doi.org/10.1146/annurev.psych.56.091103.070311.

Friston, K. J., Brown, H. R., Siemerkus, J., & Stephan, K. E. (2016). The dysconnection hypothesis (2016). *Schizophrenia Research*, *176*(2–3), 83–94. http://doi.org/10.1016/j.schres.2016.07.014.

Frith, C. D. (1992). *The cognitive neuropsychology of schizophrenia*. Sussex, UK: Psychology Press Ltd.

Fusar-Poli, P., Papanastasiou, E., Stahl, D., Rocchetti, M., Carpenter, W., Shergill, S., & McGuire, P. (2014). Treatments of negative symptoms in schizophrenia: Meta-analysis of 168 randomized placebo-controlled trials. *Schizophrenia Bulletin*, *41*(4), 892–899. http://doi.org/10.1093/schbul/sbu170.

Galderisi, S., Färden, A., & Kaiser, S. (2016). Dissecting negative symptoms of schizophrenia: History, assessment, pathophysiological mechanisms and treatment. *Schizophrenia Research*, *186*, 1–2. http://doi.org/10.1016/j.schres.2016.04.046.

Galderisi, S., Mucci, A., Buchanan, R. W., & Arango, C. (2018). Negative symptoms of schizophrenia: New developments and unanswered research questions. *The Lancet Psychiatry*, *5*(8), 664–677. http://doi.org/10.1016/S2215-0366(18)30050-6.

Grant, P. M., Huh, G. A., Perivoliotis, D., Stolar, N. M., & Beck, A. T. (2012). Randomized trial to evaluate the efficacy of cognitive therapy for low-functioning patients with schizophrenia. *Archives of General Psychiatry*, *69*(2), 121.

Griffiths, H., & McLeod, H. J. (2019). Promoting recovery from negative symptoms. An attachment theory perspective. In K. Berry, S. Bucci, & A. N. Danquah (Eds.), *Attachment theory and psychosis: Current perspectives and future directions*. London: Routledge.

Harrison, C. L., & Fowler, D. (2004). Negative symptoms, trauma, and autobiographical memory. *The Journal of Nervous and Mental Disease*, *192*(11), 745–753. http://doi.org/10.1097/01.nmd.0000144693.12282.11.

Hasson-Ohayon, I. A. (2012). Integrating cognitive behavioral-based therapy with an intersubjective approach: Addressing metacognitive deficits among people with schizophrenia. *Journal of Psychotherapy Integration*, *22*(4), 356–374. http://doi.org/10.1037/a0029576.

Hasson-Ohayon, I. A., Kravetz, S., & Lysaker, P. H. (2017). The special challenges of psychotherapy with persons with psychosis: Intersubjective metacognitive model of agreement and shared meaning. *Clinical Psychology & Psychotherapy*, *24*(2), 428–440. http://doi.org/10.1002/cpp.2012.

Insel, T., Cuthbert, B., Garvey, M., Heinssen, R., Pine, D.S., Quinn, K., . . . Wang. P. (2010). Research domain criteria (RDoC): Toward a new classification framework for research on mental disorders. *American Journal of Psychiatry*, *167*(7), 748–751. http://doi.org/10.1176/appi.ajp.2010.09091379.

Johnson, D. P., Penn, D. L., Fredrickson, B. L., Meyer, P. S., Kring, A. M., & Brantley, M. (2009). Loving-kindness meditation to enhance recovery from negative symptoms of schizophrenia. *Journal of Clinical Psychology*, *65*(5), 499–509. http://doi.org/10.1002/jclp.20591.

Jones, C., Hacker, D., Xia, J., Meaden, A., Irving, C. B., Zhao, S., . . . Chen, J. (2018). Cognitive behavioural therapy plus standard care versus standard care for people with schizophrenia. *Cochrane Database of Systematic Reviews*, *158*(10), 1706–330. http://doi.org/10.1002/14651858.CD007964.pub2.

Kirkpatrick, B., Fenton, W. S., Carpenter, W. T., & Marder, S. R. (2006). The NIMH-MATRICS consensus statement on negative symptoms. *Schizophrenia Bulletin*, *32*(2), 214–219. http://doi.org/10.1093/schbul/sbj053.

Klingberg, S., Wolwer, W., Engel, C., Wittorf, A., Herrlich, J., Meisner, C., . . . Widemann, G. (2011). Negative symptoms of schizophrenia as primary target of cognitive behavioral therapy: Results of the randomized clinical TONES study. *Schizophrenia Bulletin*, *37*(suppl 2), S98–S110. http://doi.org/10.1093/schbul/sbr073.

Kraepelin, E. (1971). *Dementia praecox and paraphrenia*. Melbourne, FL: Robert E. Krieger Publishing Co Inc.

Kring, A. M., & Barch, D. M. (2014). The motivation and pleasure dimension of negative symptoms: Neural substrates and behavioral outputs. *European Neuropsychopharmacology*, *24*(5), 725–736. http://doi.org/10.1016/j.euroneuro.2013.06.007.

Leonhardt, B. L., Huling, K., Hamm, J. A., Roe, D., Hasson-Ohayon, I., McLeod, H. J., & Lysaker, P. H. (2017). Recovery and serious mental illness: A review of current clinical and research paradigms and future directions. *Expert Review of Neurotherapeutics*, *17*(11), 1117–1130.

Lilienfeld, S. O. (2014). The Research Domain Criteria (RDoC): An analysis of methodological and conceptual challenges. *Behaviour Research and Therapy*, *62*(C), 129–139. http://doi.org/10.1016/j.brat.2014.07.019.

Lilienfeld, S. O., & Treadway, M. T. (2016). Clashing diagnostic approaches: DSM-ICD Versus RDoC. *Annual Review of Clinical Psychology*, *12*(1), 435–463. http://doi.org/10.1146/annurev-clinpsy-021815-093122.

Lincoln, T. M., & Peters, E. (2018). A systematic review and discussion of symptom specific cognitive behavioural approaches to delusions and hallucinations. *Schizophrenia Research*, 1–14. http://doi.org/10.1016/j.schres.2017.12.014.

Lysaker, P. H., & Klion, R. E. (2017). *Recovery, meaning-making, and severe mental illness*. London: Routledge.

McLeod, H. J., Gumley, A. I., MacBeth, A., Schwannauer, M., & Lysaker, P. H. (2014a). Metacognitive functioning predicts positive and negative symptoms over 12 months in first episode psychosis. *Journal of Psychiatric Research*, *54*, 109–115. http://doi.org/10.1016/j.jpsychires.2014.03.018.

McLeod, H. J., Gumley, A. I., & Schwannauer, M. (2014b). The impact of metacognition on the development and maintenance of negative symptoms. In *Social cognition and metacognition in schizophrenia* (pp. 115–135). San Diego, CA: Elsevier. http://doi.org/10.1016/B978-0-12-405172-0.00007-7.

Messinger, J. W., Trémeau, F., Antonius, D., Mendelsohn, E., Prudent, V., Stanford, A. D., & Malaspina, D. (2011). Avolition and expressive deficits capture negative symptom phenomenology: Implications for DSM-5 and schizophrenia research. *Clinical Psychology Review*, *31*(1), 161–168. http://doi.org/10.1016/j.cpr.2010.09.002.

Moritz, S., Berna, F., Jaeger, S., Westermann, S., & Nagel, M. (2017). The customer is always right? Subjective target symptoms and treatment preferences in patients with psychosis. *European Archives of Psychiatry and Clinical Neuroscience*, *267*(4), 335–339. http://doi.org/10.1007/s00406-016-0694-5.

Patel, R., Jayatilleke, N., Broadbent, M., Chang, C.-K., Foskett, N., Gorrell, G., . . . Stewart, R. (2015). Negative symptoms in schizophrenia: A study in a large clinical sample of patients using a novel automated method. *BMJ Open, 5*(9), e007619. http://doi.org/10.1136/bmjopen-2015-007619.

Priebe, S., Savill, M., Wykes, T., Bentall, R. P., Reininghaus, U., Lauber, C., . . . Röhricht, F. (2016). Effectiveness of group body psychotherapy for negative symptoms of schizophrenia: Multicentre randomised controlled trial. *The British Journal of Psychiatry, 209*(1), 54–61. http://doi.org/10.1192/bjp.bp.115.171397.

Provencher, H. L., & Mueser, K. T. (1997). Positive and negative symptom behaviors and caregiver burden in the relatives of persons with schizophrenia. *Schizophrenia Research, 26*(1), 71–80.

Raffard, S., Esposito, F., Boulenger, J. P., & Van der Linden, M. (2013). Impaired ability to imagine future pleasant events is associated with apathy in schizophrenia. *Psychiatry Research, 209*(3), 393–400. http://doi.org/10.1016/j.psychres.2013.04.016.

Raichle, M. E., MacLeod, A. M., Snyder, A. Z., Powers, W. J., Gusnard, D. A., & Shulman, G. L. (2001). A default mode of brain function. *Proceedings of the National Academy of Sciences, 98*(2), 676–682. http://doi.org/10.1073/pnas.98.2.676.

Rector, N. A., Beck, A. T., & Stolar, N. (2005). The negative symptoms of schizophrenia: A cognitive perspective. *Canadian Journal of Psychiatry. Revue Canadienne De Psychiatrie, 50*(5), 247–257.

Roick, C., Heider, D., Bebbington, P. E., Angermeyer, M. C., Azorin, J. M., Brugha, T. S., . . . EuroSC Research Group (2007). Burden on caregivers of people with schizophrenia: Comparison between Germany and Britain. *The British Journal of Psychiatry, 190*(4), 333–338. http://doi.org/10.1192/bjp.bp.106.025353.

Ross, J., Hutchison, J., & Cunningham, S. J. (2019). The me in memory: The role of the self in autobiographical memory development. *Child Development, 28*, 1–16. http://doi.org/10.1111/cdev.13211.

Salvatore, G., Dimaggio, G., & Lysaker, P. H. (2007). An intersubjective perspective on negative symptoms of schizophrenia: Implications of simulation theory. *Cognitive Neuropsychiatry, 12*(2), 144–164. http://doi.org/10.1080/13546800600819921.

Sauvé, G., Brodeur, M. B., Shah, J. L., & Lepage, M. (2019). The prevalence of negative symptoms across the stages of the psychosis continuum. *Harvard Review of Psychiatry, 27*(1), 15–32. http://doi.org/10.1097/HRP.0000000000000184.

Savill, M., Banks, C., Khanom, H., & Priebe, S. (2014). Do negative symptoms of schizophrenia change over time? A meta-analysis of longitudinal data. *Psychological Medicine*, 1–15. http://doi.org/10.1017/S0033291714002712.

Schore, A. N. (1997). Early organization of the nonlinear right brain and development of a predisposition to psychiatric disorders. *Development and Psychopathology, 9*(4), 595–631.

Sigmundsson, T., Suckling, J., Maier, M., Williams, S. R., Bullmore, E. T., Greenwood, K. E., . . . Toone, B. (2001). Structural abnormalities in frontal, temporal, and limbic regions and interconnecting white matter tracts in schizophrenic patients with prominent negative symptoms. *American Journal of Psychiatry, 158*, 234–243.

Singer, J. A., Blagov, P., Berry, M., & Oost, K. M. (2013). Self-defining memories, scripts, and the life story: Narrative identity in personality and psychotherapy. *Journal of Personality, 81*(6), 569–582. http://doi.org/10.1111/jopy.12005.

Staring, A. B. P., Huurne, ter, M.-A. B., & van der Gaag, M. (2013). Cognitive Behavioral Therapy for negative symptoms (CBT-n) in psychotic disorders: A pilot study. *Journal of Behavior Therapy and Experimental Psychiatry, 44*(3), 300–306. http://doi.org/10.1016/j.jbtep.2013.01.004.

Sterk, B., Winter, R. I., Muis, M., & de Haan, L. (2013). Priorities, satisfaction and treatment goals in psychosis patients: An online consumer's survey. *Pharmacopsychiatry*. http://doi.org/10.1055/s-0032-1.

Strauss, G. P., & Gold, J. M. (2012). A new perspective on anhedonia in schizophrenia. *American Journal of Psychiatry, 169*(4), 364–373.

Strauss, G. P., Harrow, M., Grossman, L. S., & Rosen, C. (2010). Periods of recovery in deficit syndrome schizophrenia: A 20-year multi-follow-up longitudinal study. *Schizophrenia Bulletin, 36*(4), 788–799. http://doi.org/10.1093/schbul/sbn167.

Strauss, G. P., Horan, W. P., Kirkpatrick, B., Fischer, B. A., Keller, W. R., Miski, P., . . . Carpenter, W. T. (2013). Deconstructing negative symptoms of schizophrenia: Avolition-apathy and diminished expression clusters predict clinical presentation and functional outcome. *Journal of Psychiatric Research, 47*(6), 783–790. http:doi.org/10.1016/j.jpsychires.2013.01.015.

Sutin, A. R., & Robins, R. W. (2007). Phenomenology of autobiographical memories: The Memory Experiences Questionnaire. *Memory, 15*(4), 390–411. http://doi.org/10.1080/09658210701256654.

Tulving, E. (2005). Episodic memory and autonoesis: Uniquely human? In H. S. Terrace & J. Metcalfe (Eds.), *The missing link in cognition: Origins of self-reflective consciousness* (pp. 1–54). Oxford, UK: Oxford University Press.

Velthorst, E., Koeter, M., van der gaag, M., Nieman, D. H., Fett, A. K. J., Smit, F., & de Haan, L. (2014). Adapted cognitive-behavioural therapy required for targeting negative symptoms in schizophrenia: Meta-analysis and meta-regression. *Psychological Medicine*, 1–13. http://doi.org/10.1017/S0033291714001147.

Whitfield-Gabrieli, S., & Ford, J. M. (2012). Default mode network activity and connectivity in psychopathology. *Annual Review of Clinical Psychology, 8*(1), 49–76. http://doi.org/10.1146/annurev-clinpsy-032511-143049.

Williams, J. M. G., Barnhofer, T., Crane, C., Hermans, D., Raes, F., Watkins, E., & Dalgleish, T. (2007). Autobiographical memory specificity and emotional disorder. *Psychological Bulletin, 133*(1), 122–148. http://doi.org/10.1037/0033-2909.133.1.122.

World Health Organization. (1992). *International statistical classification of diseases and related health problems* (10th revision ed.). Geneva: World Health Organization.

10

THE RECOVERY OF THE SELF THROUGH THERAPEUTIC ALLIANCE FOCUSED GROUP THERAPY

Ilanit Hasson-Ohayon, Adi Lavi-Rotenberg, Libby Igra, Steven de Jong and David Roe

Abstract: *Therapeutic alliance is an essential aspect and meaningful mechanism for change in psychotherapy. In addition to mediating the outcome of therapy, therapeutic alliance is considered important as it enables the enhancement of metacognitive abilities. However, although considered beneficial, it is broadly assumed that forming a therapeutic alliance with clients who have been diagnosed with psychosis might be especially challenging. Therefore, several therapeutic approaches were developed in order to specifically focus on this construct in the context of recovery from psychotic disorders. One such approach is Therapeutic Alliance Focused Therapy (TAFT), which is a group adaptation based on the manual for Therapeutic Alliance Focused Family Intervention. The TAFT aimed to address the challenges to therapeutic alliance by emphasizing the use of interventions that enhance agreement on goals and feeling a positive emotional bond, as well as safety, in the therapy context. The current chapter presents the TAFT's four therapeutic elements, and later discusses the enhancement of metacognitive abilities that might be achieved throughout the reflections on self and other as part of the intervention. A group case study is presented to illustrate the elements of the TAFT and group's dynamics, followed by a critical discussion on challenges in implementation.*

Introduction

The therapeutic alliance (TA) has been consistently shown to be one of the most important factors common to psychotherapy across approaches (Flückiger, Re, Wampold, & Horvath, 2018). Research has consistently shown a robust association between alliance and outcome across a broad range of psychotherapy approaches (Horvath & Bedi, 2002; Horvath, Del Re, Flückiger, & Symonds, 2011; Martin, Garske, & Davis, 2000). The classic theoretical definitions of TA refer to it as an active collaboration between the healthy parts of the client's ego and the therapeutic process (Greenson, 1965; Zetzel, 1956). According to Bordin's broadly used pantheoretical definition (1979), it consists of the quality and strength of the affective bond between therapist and client, an agreement on the goals of therapy, and a consensus on how to attain those goals. In the overall field of mental health there has been a long-standing interest in the construct of TA as a mechanism for change in therapy, with extensive evidence linking the strength of TA with treatment outcomes (Ahn & Wampold, 2001; Horvath et al., 2011; Zilcha-Mano, Dinger, McCarthy, & Barber, 2014).

In the field of psychotherapy with people who experience psychosis, there is growing evidence of the possibility of good therapeutic relationships between clients and therapists (Evans-Jones, Peters, & Barker, 2009; Shattock, Berry, Degnan, & Edge, 2017), and also that TA is a meaningful mechanism for change (Davis & Lysaker, 2007; Goldsmith, Lewis, Dunn, & Bentall, 2015; Lecomte, Laferrière-Simard, & Leclerc, 2012). A recent systematic review found preliminary evidence that TA ratings predicted symptomatic improvement for early psychosis, fewer re-hospitalizations, and reduced medication use (Shattock et al., 2017). Importantly, it has been shown that not only is there a positive relationship between TA and treatment outcome among persons diagnosed with psychotic disorders (i.e. a better alliance leads to more improvement in psychotherapy), but also that a poor therapeutic alliance can be actively detrimental to the client (Goldsmith et al., 2015).

Focusing on TA with persons with psychosis seems important as it may serve to enhance reflectiveness regarding self-goals and interpersonal relationships. In other words, focusing on agreement of goals and tasks as well as on the feelings that are experienced in the sessions (i.e. the three related components of TA) requires one to reflect about self and other, enhancing metacognitive capacities.

Accordingly, psychotherapeutic approaches that emphasize TA allow persons to form new ideas about themselves and others. Most importantly, these approaches are also expected to help people to have a new or renewed sense of self and others that differ from the one they previously had, not just in terms of content, but also in the quality of being more flexible and integrated. Considering outcomes such as more complex and integrated representations of self and others is in line with recent conceptualizations of metacognition (Lysaker & Klion, 2017) and its recognition as an important part of the recovery process (Lysaker, Gagen, Moritz, & Schweitzer, 2018). Accordingly, metacognition is regarded as consisting of four related aspects: 1. self-reflectivity, which refers to the comprehension of one's own mental states, 2. understanding others' minds, which refers to the comprehension of others' mental states, 3. decentration, which refers to the ability to take a non-egocentric view of the mind of others and recognizes that others' mental states are influenced by a range of factors, and 4. mastery, which refers to the ability to use complex metacognitive knowledge in order to cope with psychological problems (Lysaker & Klion, 2017).

It is generally assumed that, for clients who have been diagnosed with psychosis, forming a TA can be especially challenging due to difficulties in the formation of interpersonal relationships (e.g. the client's confusion about interpersonal boundaries, Lysaker, Davis, Buck, Outcalt, & Ringer, 2011). Another assumption is that this group of people are more prone to early traumatic relational experiences which impact adult relationships, creating challenges with service engagement and adherence (Kreyenbuhl, Nossel, & Dixon, 2009; Varese et al., 2012). In addition, the views that these clients hold of their problems and abilities might differ from the views held by their therapists (Amador & Johanson, 2000; Themistocleous et al., 2009). Concerning these possible differing views, Hasson-Ohayon, Kravetz, and Lysaker (2017) proposed an intersubjective model of psychotherapy that defines the possible barriers for developing TA with such clients: Specifically, it posits that the client and therapist may hold different narratives with regard to their roles, different descriptions of the condition or problem that they are dealing with, and different views towards mental illness and/or other mental illness-related topics.

For example, clients who have psychotic disorders may experience the mental health system as oppressing, demeaning, and impeding their personal autonomy (Adame & Knudson, 2007; Deegan, 1997), whereas their therapists may view the same system as a necessary step towards recovery. This issue is important because higher perceived coercion by the client is related to a more negative client–therapist relationship; perceived loss of autonomy goes hand in hand with a more negative view of the treatment (Theodoridou, Schlatter, Ajdacic, Roessler, & Jaeger, 2012). Another example is the different attitudes held towards psychiatric medications. Whereas the therapist may perceive his/her role as being responsible for the client's adherence, the client may be ambivalent about the prescribed medications and their side effects (Hasson-Ohayon et al., 2017).

With these challenges to TA in mind, as well as the importance of TA for outcome, it seems important to consider therapeutic approaches that are specifically focused on developing TA in the context of recovery from psychotic disorders. One such approach is Therapeutic Alliance Focused Therapy (TAFT), which is a group adaptation of the manual for Therapeutic Alliance Focused Family Intervention (Friedlander et al., 2006). This intervention enhances agreement on goals and feeling positive emotional bond and safety in the therapy context. It was previously used as an intervention for parents of people with severe mental illness (Levy-Frank, Hasson-Ohayon, Kravetz, & Roe, 2011, 2012) and was shown to be beneficial in reducing family burden – that is, reducing the negative objective and subjective implications of being an informal caregiver. Therapeutic Alliance Focused Therapy will be discussed here as a group therapy for persons diagnosed with psychotic disorders that addresses the challenges to TA described above. The current chapter presents the basic principles of TAFT following a group case study accompanied by a critical discussion on challenges in implementation.

Therapeutic Alliance Focused Therapy (TAFT) for persons diagnosed with psychotic disorders

As mentioned above, TAFT represents an adaptation of a family therapy format (see Friedlander et al., 2006) to a group therapy format, and attends to the four elements of the TA according to the family alliance intervention. These therapeutic elements include: 1. a commitment to the therapeutic process, meaning a commitment to work towards change, and a belief that change is possible; 2. an emotionally authentic relationship with the therapist, meaning an open and direct dialogue between all group members, including therapists; 3. a feeling of safety and security in the therapeutic setting that allows for expressing thoughts and emotions and discussing conflicts within the group; and 4. a sense of agreement about goals that allows for group work to take place with a common aim. The four therapeutic elements are related to each other, but each in its own right provides information regarding the strength of the TA. With these four TA elements in mind, TAFT also offers guidelines for each of the elements, that is, the therapist manual consists of detailed guidelines regarding factors that can either enhance or impair each of the TA elements.

Regarding the first element, therapist interventions that might enhance engagement in the therapeutic process may be sharing the format of the therapy with the group, explaining the rationale behind the group, and asking participants to share their goals, questions, and thoughts about the therapy. By contrast, therapists who pressure clients to participate or who are critical of participants might negatively affect the participants' commitment. Positive indications from the participants that this element is working would be the sharing of goals with group members and expressing optimism, whereas negative indications would include complaints regarding the group or the therapeutic process. Regarding the second element, therapists who express empathy towards the participants, share their thoughts and feelings regarding the situation, or normalize participants' vulnerability might enhance the relationship between them. Sarcasm, criticism, or hostile interactions, on the other hand, are likely to harm the emotional connection. Positive indications from the participants that this element is working would be, for example, expressing affection and trust towards other group members and the therapist/s, whereas negative indications would include avoiding eye contact or enacting hostile behaviours toward the therapist/s. Regarding the third element, therapists who identify negative reactions or hostility between participants and handle them properly – for example, by helping participants better communicate, or shifting the discussion towards a less heated topic – would enhance participants' feelings of safety and security in the sessions. By contrast, a failure to detect or address problems might make the therapeutic system feel less safe and secure for participants. Positive indications from the participants that this element is working would be, for example, expressing emotional vulnerability or sharing intimate information with group members, whereas negative indications would include expressing non-verbal anxiety or refusing to participate. Last, regarding the fourth element, therapists who encourage participants to compromise and to ask one another about their perspectives might facilitate a shared sense of purpose within the group. On the other hand, therapists who do not intervene when participants become argumentative about goals, values, or their need for treatment could negatively affect this element. Positive indications from the participants that this element is working would be, for example, a suggestion to compromise or a validation of other group members' perspectives, whereas negative indications would include expressing disrespect for other perspectives or displaying sarcastic and hostile reactions toward other participants.

As is evident from this description of the TA elements in TAFT, the intervention is minimally structured, allowing for the content and agenda to emerge naturally from the group, based on participants' preferences. Thus, this group therapy intervention is focused on the group dynamic and not on participants' psychopathology (e.g. symptoms or deficits), as other more structured protocols are (e.g. cognitive behavioural therapy (CBT) for psychosis, social cognition and interaction training (SCIT), Roberts, Penn, & Combs, 2013). Notably, the first two sessions of TAFT are relatively structured and focus on developing a group identity and common goal. Accordingly, the therapist or therapists (groups can be led by one or two therapists) stimulate a discussion about expectations, developing group rules and a format. The rest of the sessions usually have a flexible structure, beginning with a joint decision on the day's agenda, an open discussion, and a summary. If a request from clients, which is in line with TA elements (i.e. an agreed-upon request about which all participants feel positive), refers to the inclusion of structured interventions, such interventions will be included. For example, if the clients ask to learn more about their diagnosis/es, then a psychoeducational intervention will be put in place; if the clients ask for job interview training, then behavioural techniques will be applied. In other words, although the general TAFT structure is dynamically oriented, the assimilation of content and techniques from other psychotherapeutic approaches is suitable as long as they adhere to the TA elements.

Therapeutic alliance, TAFT, and metacognition

In the context of the main topic of this book (i.e. mentalization and metacognitive based psychotherapies), it is evident that TAFT does not explicitly focus on the enhancement of metacognitive abilities. However, focusing on the elements of TA, in a reflective exploratory way, is assumed to enhance metacognition. Each element may be used as a fruitful basis for joint reflection, assuming that the therapist pays close attention to the level of metacognitive functioning of each individual group member, and of the group as a whole. In TAFT, the group provides a space profoundly characterized by intersubjectivity. While working within the intersubjective space, the enhancement of metacognition is expected to take place, as intersubjectivity and metacognition are assumed to co-occur (Lysaker et al., 2013; Hasson-Ohayon et al., 2017).

For instance, the first and fourth elements (commitment to the therapeutic process and joint agreement on goals) are closely related to Mastery, one of the four subscales of the metacognition scale. In brief, metacognitive Mastery is a term used to refer to a person's ability to identify psychological stressors and find adaptive methods of coping. At the first level, M1, the person is able to recognize that psychological stressors are present, but the stressors identified are implausible. Someone may, for instance, mention that they are feeling tense (a psychological stressor), but that this is because the FBI is watching them (implausible). At the second level, M2, the person offers a plausible stressor.

Just as each member of the group individually may fluctuate in their ability to recognize plausible psychological difficulties and adaptive ways of coping with them, so may the group as a whole. By opening with a joint discussion of why each group member has come to the meeting that day, the therapist can determine whether M1 or M2 is present (i.e. the recognition of psychological distress and the plausibility of the identified stressor) and what form of coping the group members recommend to one another.

It is important to note that it is not the task of the therapist to correct a participant who explains his/her presence in the session in terms of M1 (e.g. "I was ordered by a secret society to come") or even lacks awareness of any psychological suffering ("I am doing great!" said by a person who appears highly distressed). Rather, the role of the therapist is to observe how the group responds, and only then to offer reflective comments or questions that may stimulate further discussion. In other words, the task of the therapist is to elicit metacognitive acts from the group members, *not* to perform metacognitive acts for them. A therapist may, for instance, ask the group members if they want to ask questions or comment on what another group member has said.

The group setting is a profoundly intersubjective space as it consists of interacting subjects. Tolerating the presence of other minds, and tolerating the process of constructing a joint narrative, is a metacognitively taxing activity whose challenges should not be underestimated. The therapist should pay particular attention to moments when participants agree or disagree profoundly, and offer reflections during such occurrences. Doing so will stimulate reflection both on oneself ("what am I thinking?") and on the other ("what are they thinking?"). For example, statements such as "It seems to me like we are all thinking the same thing", "Wow, Mary, you and Joe really seem to be on the same wavelength today", or "Gosh, Max and Bill, you just can't seem to agree on anything today, huh?" are intended to stimulate reflection and address therapeutic alliance challenges such as differing views of the session agenda.

Similarly, moments of harmony or conflict in the group (elements two and three of TAFT) can be addressed via metacognitive reflections by the therapist. Through asking reflective questions ("It seems to me that the situation is a little tense . . . am I sensing that correctly?"), the therapist not only stimulates metacognitive activity (each participant reflects on his/her emotions, which would be considered Level 4 of Self-Reflectivity in the MAS-A, which assesses metacognition), he/she also models a behaviour for the group. It is likely that, if such questions were posited frequently, the group would adopt this same reflective attitude and, as such, each individual in the group might begin to adopt it as well. Although for the therapist it might be tempting to offer such reflections only during moments of tension, it could be especially worthwhile to do so when spirits are high. It may be just as important for group members to reflect on situations that are pleasurable.

It could be helpful for therapists to consider, before each remark, whether their remark will invite metacognitive reflectivity, who by and about whom. Most relevant are the domains of Self-Reflectivity: Self (does the participant think about their own thinking and feeling?); Other (does the participant think about the other's thinking and feeling?); and Mastery (is the participant reflecting on identifying and coping with stressors?). In group therapy terms, these ideas could be phrased as follows: Self (the purpose of any reflection is to call an individual's attention to his/her own internal world); Other (the individual's ideas about what the group or individuals in the group are thinking and feeling); and Mastery (the way in which the current interaction within the group is causing or reducing psychological stressors).

Illustrative group example

The following description of a TAFT group is provided to illustrate its elements, dimensions, and possible dynamics. The described group was part of a research trial comparing SCIT with TAFT (Hasson-Ohayon, Mashiach-Eizenberg, Lavi-Rotenberg, & Roe, 2019) in psychiatric community settings in Israel.[1] Approval for the study was obtained from the ethics committee of the Department of Psychology at Bar-Ilan University, as well as from two psychiatric hospital committees. After receiving a detailed explanation of the study, all research participants provided their written informed consent. In the following group illustration, details have been changed so that participants are not identifiable and to best illustrate the TAFT elements, and all names are pseudonyms. As such, although parts of the described exchanges are fictional, they are based on the processes that took place in the group.

Nine clients (seven men and two women, age range 25–48) attended the group with various levels of attendance, with six clients completing 24 weekly sessions (range of attendance 15–24 sessions). Two female therapists, one of whom was a psychologist and one a social worker, supervised the group in a psychiatric rehabilitation centre located in central Israel. Supervision meetings took place every other week with a senior psychologist. The group was open to new clients during the first two weeks and closed to new participants after that.

As previously mentioned, the first two TAFT sessions are dedicated to building TA, discussing group expectations, and developing rules. Six participants attended the first session, an additional two attended the next session, and one more attended the third. During the introduction period, one of the therapists encouraged the clients to share their expectations from the group and their current feelings. As each of the participants shared his or her expectations, the therapist reflected that there appeared to be similarities between them. Daniel expressed the wish that the group would meet his social needs, as he struggled with loneliness.

Mia expressed confusion regarding understanding what people felt towards her and hoped that the group would be able to help her "understand people better". Sophia shared that she wished to be more assertive and less shy with people, and others mentioned additional social challenges. Accordingly, one of the therapists said: "It seems that all of you are interested in working on social relationships" and invited the group to comment on this by asking them: "Am I right? What do you think about what I've said?" After the group members agreed that this issue was indeed an important one for all of them, and that they would like for it to be a focus of the group work, rules were established.

In accordance with TAFT Element 1, the therapists shared with the group the format of the therapy (e.g. place, time, frequency of meetings, privacy) and explained the rationale behind the group: "We will work here together on agreed-upon joint goals. Agreement is not always easy, and we will learn together the processes of agreement, listening, and negotiating." The group members were invited to comment, and the discussion continued the following session. At that session, after welcoming new participants, one of the group members named Mia said, "I thought about the group and I think that I want to talk about what is happening in the group and not social things outside the group." After she elaborated on this point a bit more, the rest of the group members began to offer their opinions. Daniel, for example, said that he wanted to talk about his experiences in the yeshiva (a Jewish day school where Ultraorthodox boys and men study), where he was feeling lonely. Mia was not pleased by the fact that others had different opinions, and she began to talk without leaving space for others to talk. That began a dynamic in which Mia, Daniel, and Toby (who also thought that experiences from outside the group should be shared) were talking over each other, potentially damaging participants' feelings of safety and security within the therapeutic system.

In line with the TAFT framework, the therapists viewed this unproductive dialogue as an indication of a problem in the TA element of feeling secure within the therapeutic setting and a positive emotional relationship in the group. As a way of coping with these issues, the therapists asked the participants if they would like to pause the discussion temporarily in order to formulate rules for dialogue so that people could listen productively to each other. All of the group members except for Mia responded in a positive way, indicating a joint wish to create a dialogical environment. When sensing Mia's displeasure, one of the therapists asked her if she would like to share her thoughts and feelings with the group. Mia responded by saying angrily that she understood that there needed to be rules, but she really wanted to talk about the group dynamic and felt that nobody was interested. The therapist responded by saying: "It seems that first we need to find a good way of speaking with each other before deciding on the content of the meeting. What do you think?" Positive indications were then forthcoming from all, including Mia. Sophia made a suggestion that anyone who wished to talk should hold a pen in his or her hand, to ensure a process of taking turns. Daniel and Toby said they felt that this pen-holding would interfere with spontaneity, and others agreed with them, saying that they too would like to have a more natural conversation. Harry, who usually took the role of "listener" and sat quietly, commented that the discussion reminded him of "survival games" where each person needed to fight for his or her place. The second session ended without a productive agreed-upon decision.

In the next session the therapists, in accordance with TAFT elements, worked to overcome the conflict within the group, and specifically to enhance participants' feeling of safety within the therapeutic system. Accordingly, they asked participants how they wished to solve the question of using (or not using) a pen as a concrete expression of one's turn to talk; expressed empathy with the frustration of a few of the participants; and expressed sadness with regard to Harry's metaphor of survival. These comments led Sophia to suggest that perhaps they could start by using the pen and then stop when they did not need it anymore. One of the therapists remarked on the positivity and hope reflected in Sophia's suggestion and asked the participants how they felt about this idea; they all agreed to try. Max said that now they could talk about the important things on their minds, and suggested that each member could share how his or her week had been, from the time of the last meeting. In order to ensure the engagement of all of the group members, the therapists checked that everyone was on board with this idea, and a round began. This session format was accepted well, and it became the group routine. Each session opened with an update round during which each member could mention a topic that he or she wished to discuss more fully at a later point in the session.

The content of the sessions revolved around social challenges both within the group and outside it. The therapists continually verified that the goal of improving social life was of interest to all and paid attention to indications of a positive TA versus ruptures. Attending to ruptures in the group alliance included inviting participants to explore feelings and thoughts regarding their understanding of the self and the other (i.e. metacognitive processes). For example, at the beginning of the sixth session Mia asked to speak with the therapist alone outside the room because she wasn't feeling comfortable in the group. The therapist replied by inviting her to talk about these feelings in the group and explained that the session had already begun. Mia responded to this invitation with frustration and talked about feeling attacked because of the way one of the group members, Denis, was looking at her. Denis responded in a defensive manner, saying that he was a curious person and that this was simply the way he looks at people. The group seemed to be divided in their support of the two. The therapists reminded everyone of the joint goals and rules, and emphasized that everyone needed to feel secure in order to share personal things with the group. This response reduced the tension in the group, and Denis said that he felt bad about being attacked. He continued by saying that he was sorry if he had hurt Mia's feelings, and that his staring had come from a place of good intentions. Mia then responded by saying that when she felt under attack, she tended to attack back. At that point, other members joined the dialogue and gave examples from their own private lives of acting aggressively when feeling under attack. When the therapists summarized the session and invited participants to share their current thoughts and feelings, it was revealed that everyone was happy that they had discussed the previously un-discussed tension in the group.

An additional example of rupture management was provided at Session 10, a session which included the attendance of a few participants who had missed some previous sessions. A discussion began regarding commitment to the group and reasons for not attending. The therapists did not interfere with the emerging dialogue, and the participants began arguing and interrupting each other. Max said that it was not easy to open up to strangers and that he was angry for people not committing to the group. Ron said that sometimes there were reasons for not attending, which Max and others could not be aware of; therefore, they could not understand.

One of the therapists suggested that perhaps not coming was related not only to external events but also to things that had happened in the group. This comment led to a pause in the dialogue, which ended when Ron said that, in fact, he had felt hurt when Mia commented during an earlier session that he had eaten too many cookies. This comment fuelled an argumentative and unpleasant atmosphere, leading one of the therapists to say: "In this kind of situations we feel ambivalent about intervening. On one hand, we would like you all to express your feelings; on the other hand, we don't want anyone to get hurt." This comment was in line with the therapist's responsibility, in accordance with TAFT, to ensure a secure environment. The therapist's manifestation of sincere caring deactivated the aggressive atmosphere and participants went on to talk about their expectations that the therapists would protect them from getting hurt. One of the therapists then suggested that maybe each group member could help achieve this goal. At the end of this session, it was apparent that participants were more able to see the other. For example, Sophia said to the therapist, "It must be hard for you when we are shouting at each other."

During the later sessions, the TA seemed to have improved, enabling the group to work on social challenges. During one session for example, Max shared his disappointment in himself for having had the opportunity to ask someone out and not taking it. The group responded by asking questions that helped him understand that he was afraid of rejection. Others shared similar experiences and talked about having a mental illness and being in a "normal" environment versus being in places with other people who had mental illnesses. Although the focus was increasingly put on social challenges that took place outside the group, attention was also paid – in tandem – to the group's processes, their relationships with each other, and the possibility that the way they behaved in the "outside" world mirrored the way they behaved in the group. This awareness was expressed in several incidents, for instance when Mia, acting out her anger during a session by playing with her phone, acknowledged that she often did the same thing with friends when going out.

The theme of commitment to the group, rules regarding when and how to speak, and aggressiveness in dialogue continued to constitute much of the content of the group's sessions. Working with these themes, the therapist used the TAFT elements as a framework and sensitively addressed indications of ruptures. Indications of a positive TA were reinforced, for instance by the therapist commenting: "It was nice to see everybody sharing his and her feelings today, and we could really listen to each other", or: "It seems that you were really able to use the feedback that your friends here in the group gave you; well done!" At the final group session, summarizing the experience, participants shared how important the group had been to them, specifically mentioning how meaningful the social aspects were and the new things they had learned about themselves. For example, Daniel talked about the changes in his goals and what he wished to receive from the group, sharing that at, first, he had wanted to work on feelings of belonging and now he felt he needed the group to help him with his existential depression. Mia said that she had learned about the "other", about other people's feelings, and was able now to focus not only on herself but on others as well. She also said she felt sad that a few people had left the group and that not all of them felt they had accomplished their goals. Others talked about continuing to have challenges in the area of dating, but said that the group had helped them with this issue, and they also talked about the meaning of having a mental illness in the context of different social interactions.

Summary and conclusions

In this chapter we discussed the importance of TA in psychotherapy and psychosocial interventions conducted with persons diagnosed with psychotic disorders or other serious mental illnesses. In addition to mediating the outcome of therapy, TA is considered an important focus of therapy as a positive TA enables the enhancement of metacognitive abilities. Different frameworks for addressing and enhancing TA were suggested (e.g. Chapter 6; Hasson-Ohayon et al., 2017), with a focus on the challenges of building a TA with persons who have psychotic disorders. One approach for addressing TA challenges described in this chapter is TAFT, which provides a list of possible interventions for therapists working in a group format.

Although TAFT is not defined as a metacognitive approach, it naturally seems to stimulate reflections on self and other, and as such involves metacognitive acts. It does not, however, systematically use interventions that are in accordance with the client's level of metacognition, as for example MERIT does. Further developing the TAFT approach to more specifically apply metacognitive elements and address clients' levels of metacognition may have benefits for clients who struggle with metacognitive functioning. Notably, applying metacognitive approaches to a group format would require an adaptation of elements from individualized approaches (see detailed description of MERIT and mentalization-based therapy, described in this book). Clients in a group may vary profoundly in terms of their levels of metacognition, a factor which could create an additional challenge for the therapist in an already challenging setting given that he/she would need to apply interventions that are individually tailored to the various clients' levels of metacognitive capacity. Accordingly, clinicians should consider ways in which more explicit metacognitive approaches could be implemented in a group format to address TA. Elements of TAFT integrated with elements of MERIT may serve as a starting point for the formulation of a group metacognitive therapy.

Note

1 Clinicaltrail.gov ID NCT02380885) and was funded by the Israel Science Foundation (grant 329/13

References

Adame, A. L., & Knudson, R. M. (2007). Beyond the counter-narrative: Exploring alternative narratives of recovery from the psychiatric survivor movement. *Narrative Inquiry*, *17*(2), 157–178.

Ahn, H. N., & Wampold, B. E. (2001). Where oh where are the specific ingredients? A meta-analysis of component studies in counseling and psychotherapy. *Journal of Counseling Psychology*, *48*(3), 251.

Amador, X. F., & Johanson, A. L. (2000). *I am not sick, I don't need help!*. New York: Vida Press.

Bordin, E. S. (1979). The generalizability of the psychoanalytic concept of the working alliance. *Psychotherapy: Theory, Research & Practice*, *16*(3), 252.

Davis, L. W., & Lysaker, P. H. (2007). Therapeutic alliance and improvements in work performance over time in patients with schizophrenia. *Journal of Nervous and Mental Disease*, *195*(4), 353–357.

Deegan, P. E. (1997). Recovery and empowerment for people with psychiatric disabilities. *Social Work in Health Care*, *25*(3), 11–24.

Evans-Jones, C., Peters, E., & Barker, C. (2009). The therapeutic relationship in CBT for psychosis: Client, therapist and therapy factors. *Behavioural and Cognitive Psychotherapy*, *37*(5), 527–540.

Flückiger, C., Del Re, A. C., Wampold, B. E., & Horvath, A. O. (2018). The alliance in adult psychotherapy: A meta-analytic synthesis. *Psychotherapy*, *55*(4), 316–340.

Friedlander, M. L., Escudero, V., Horvath, A. O., Heatherington, L., Cabero, A., & Martens, M. P. (2006). System for observing family therapy alliances: A tool for research and practice. *Journal of Counseling Psychology*, *53*(2), 214.

Goldsmith, L. P., Lewis, S. W., Dunn, G., & Bentall, R. P. (2015). Psychological treatments for early psychosis can be beneficial or harmful, depending on the therapeutic alliance: An instrumental variable analysis. *Psychological Medicine*, *45*(11), 2365–2373.

Greenson, R. R. (1965). The working alliance and the transference neurosis. *The Psychoanalytic Quarterly*, *34*(2), 155–181.

Hasson-Ohayon, I., Kravetz, S., & Lysaker, P. H. (2017). The special challenges of psychotherapy with persons with psychosis: Intersubjective metacognitive model of agreement and shared meaning. *Clinical Psychology & Psychotherapy*, *24*(2), 428–440.

Hasson-Ohayon, I., Mashiach-Eizenberg, M., Lavi-Rotenberg, A., & Roe, D. (2019). Randomized controlled trial of adjunctive Social Cognition and Interaction Training (SCIT), adjunctive Therapeutic Alliance Focused Therapy (TAFT) and treatment as usual among persons with serious mental illness. *Frontiers in Psychiatry*, *10*, 364.

Horvath, A. O., & Bedi, R. P. (2002). The alliance. In C. Norcross (Ed.), *Psychotherapy relationships that work: Therapist contributions and responsiveness to patients* (pp. 37–69). New York, NY: Oxford.

Horvath, A. O., Del Re, A. C., Flückiger, C., & Symonds, D. (2011). Alliance in individual psychotherapy. *Psychotherapy, 48*(1), 9.

Kreyenbuhl, J., Nossel, I. R., & Dixon, L. B. (2009). Disengagement from mental health treatment among individuals with schizophrenia and strategies for facilitating connections to care: A review of the literature. *Schizophrenia Bulletin, 35*(4), 696–703.

Lecomte, T., Laferrière-Simard, M., & Leclerc, C. (2012). What does the alliance predict in group interventions for early psychosis? *Journal of Contemporary Psychotherapy, 42*, 55–61.

Levy-Frank, I., Hasson-Ohayon, I., Kravetz, S., & Roe, D. (2011). Family psychoeducation and therapeutic alliance focused interventions for parents of a daughter or son with a severe mental illness. *Psychiatry Research, 189*(2), 173–179.

Levy-Frank, I., Hasson-Ohayon, I., Kravetz, S., & Roe, D. (2012). A narrative evaluation of a psychoeducation and a therapeutic alliance intervention for parents of persons with a severe mental illness. *Family Process, 51*(2), 265–280.

Lysaker, P. H., Buck, K. D., Fogley, R. L., Ringer, J., Harder, S., Hasson-Ohayon, I., . . . & Dimaggio, G. (2013). The mutual development of intersubjectivity and metacognitive capacity in the psychotherapy for persons with schizophrenia. *Journal of Contemporary Psychotherapy, 43*(2), 63–72.

Lysaker, P. H., Davis, L. W., Buck, K. D., Outcalt, S., & Ringer, J. M. (2011). Negative symptoms and poor insight as predictors of the similarity between client and therapist ratings of therapeutic alliance in cognitive behavior therapy for patients with schizophrenia. *The Journal of Nervous and Mental Disease, 199*(3), 191–195.

Lysaker, P. H., Gagen, E., Moritz, S., & Schweitzer, R. D. (2018). Metacognitive approaches to the treatment of psychosis: A comparison of four approaches. *Psychology Research and Behavior Management, 11*, 341–351.

Lysaker, P. H., & Klion, R. E. (2017). *Recovery, meaning-making, and severe mental illness: A comprehensive guide to metacognitive reflection and insight therapy.* London: Routledge.

Martin, D. J., Garske, J. P., & Davis, M. K. (2000). Relation of the therapeutic alliance with outcome and other variables: A meta-analytic review. *Journal of Consulting and Clinical Psychology, 68*(3), 438.

Roberts, D. L., Penn, D. L., & Combs, D. R. (2013). *Social cognition and interaction training SCIT: Treatment manual.* New York: Oxford University Press.

Shattock, L., Berry, K., Degnan, A., & Edge, D. (2017). Therapeutic alliance in psychological therapy for people with schizophrenia and related psychoses: A systematic review. *Clinical Psychology & Psychotherapy, 25*(1), e60–e85.

Themistocleous, M., McCabe, R., Rees, N., Hassan, I., Healey, P. G. T., & Priebe, S. (2009). Establishing mutual understanding in interaction: An analysis of conversational repair in psychiatric consultations. *Communication & Medicine, 6*(2), 165–176.

Theodoridou, A., Schlatter, F., Ajdacic, V., Roessler, W., & Jaeger, M. (2012). Therapeutic relationship in the context of perceived coercion in a psychiatric population. *Psychiatry Research, 200*(2–3), 939–944.

Varese, F., Smeets, F., Drukker, M., Lieverse, R., Lataster, T., Viechtbauer, W., . . . & Bentall, R. P. (2012). Childhood adversities increase the risk of psychosis: A meta-analysis of patient-control, prospective-and cross-sectional cohort studies. *Schizophrenia Bulletin, 38*(4), 661–671.

Zetzel, E. R. (1956). Current concepts of transference. *International Journal of Psychoanalysis, 37*, 369–376.

Zilcha-Mano, S., Dinger, U., McCarthy, K. S., & Barber, J. P. (2014). Does alliance predict symptoms throughout treatment, or is it the other way around? *Journal of Consulting and Clinical Psychology, 82*(6), 931.

11

TRAUMA AND MEANING-MAKING IN THE RECOVERY OF THE SELF

Implications for Metacognitive Reflection and Insight Therapy (MERIT)

Jay A. Hamm, PsyD, Rhianna E. Beasley, M.A. and Yael Mazor

Abstract: *People experiencing psychosis often suffer inordinately high rates of trauma associated with functional impairments and difficulties forming an integrated sense of self. Given these high rates, there is a need for treatments that can flexibly address the impact of trauma in the context of psychosis. This may entail attending to fragmented narrative episodes and alterations in metacognitive capacity. Past work on Metacognitive Reflection and Insight Therapy (MERIT) has suggested a role for metacognitive psychotherapy in assisting individuals experiencing psychosis with a history of trauma to pursue self-directed recovery. The literature related to MERIT has identified a focus on assisting people to make sense of their experiences and has highlighted the treatment's ability to be tailored for individuals in various states of disorder and recovery. To date though, there has been limited direct exploration of how MERIT might be adapted to specifically address trauma. In this chapter, we offer a brief overview of the research concerning the intersection of trauma and psychosis, then explore how MERIT might be used to effectively address trauma in psychotherapy with individuals experiencing psychosis. We highlight considerations for the application of both the general preconditions for MERIT, as well as the eight practice elements, in psychotherapy with individuals with psychosis and trauma histories.*

Introduction

Individuals experiencing psychosis, including those diagnosed with schizophrenia, experience high rates of past and ongoing trauma, which have important implications for their lives (e.g. Newman, Turnbull, Berman, Rodrigues, & Serper, 2010). This points to the importance of developing appropriate forms of professional support and therapeutic interventions that effectively address trauma and its consequences in people's lives, including interventions specifically designed to help people to make sense of trauma and determine how to best live with or overcome it. One treatment approach that may be of unique use for this purpose is Metacognitive Reflection and Insight Therapy (MERIT), which aims to promote the capacities through which people reflect upon and integrate their subjective experiences. As discussed at greater length in the introductory chapter (Chapter 1), MERIT views recovery as a highly individualised process and posits that persons experiencing even the most severe states of distress and dysfunction can find ways to make sense of their experiences, develop an improved sense of self, and pursue meaningful life goals. Given the high rates of trauma in populations diagnosed with serious mental illnesses (Van Dam et al., 2015), this process of meaning-making inevitably involves uncovering and making sense of past traumatic experiences. To date, several case reports have illustrated the course of MERIT with individuals with trauma histories (e.g. Buck, Vertinski, & Kukla, 2018; Hillis, Bidlack, & Macobin, 2018), but these have not fully elaborated the conceptual and technical considerations of how MERIT attends to the presence of trauma histories.

Accordingly, in this chapter we explore how MERIT might be used to effectively address trauma and its varied sequelae in individuals' lives. We first offer a brief overview of key findings relevant to the intersection of trauma and psychosis. We then attend to potential tensions within contemporary psychotherapy for persons with both psychosis and histories of trauma, regarding the potential benefits or intended outcomes of therapy. Following this, we suggest a set of general principles, as well as more specific technical considerations, for utilising the MERIT framework with persons with trauma histories.

Psychosis and trauma: empirical findings

Research has revealed that trauma is a significant factor influencing the lives of persons with psychosis. Robust evidence has established that individuals diagnosed with schizophrenia experience disproportionately high rates of trauma (e.g. Gilbert et al., 2009). Traumatic events may include victimisation during adulthood as well as extremely high rates of childhood trauma. While exposure to traumatic events ranges from 51.2% to 60.7% in the general population, approximately 75% of individuals diagnosed with schizophrenia have been exposed to trauma (Kessler, Sonnega, Bromet, Hughes, & Nelson, 1995; Resnick, Bond, & Mueser, 2003). According to a meta-analysis of 46 studies on the subject, childhood trauma rates in individuals diagnosed with schizophrenia range from 28% to 73%. The variability in childhood trauma rates across these studies may be explained by actual differences across surveyed groups (e.g. first-episode psychosis versus prolonged psychosis, inpatient populations versus outpatient community mental health populations) or by methodological issues including errors due to retrospective reporting of childhood trauma, varying assessment measures, and different methods of assessment (e.g. interviews versus questionnaires) (Bendall, Jackson, Hulbert, & McGorry, 2007). Childhood sexual abuse, physical abuse, emotional abuse, and neglect have consistently emerged as significantly associated with psychosis (Arseneault et al., 2011; Bebbington et al., 2004; Janssen et al., 2004; Read, van Os, Morrison, & Ross, 2005; Spauwen, Krabbendam,

Lieb, Wittchen, & Van Os, 2006; Varese et al., 2012). Similarly, rates of comorbid posttraumatic stress disorder (PTSD) in populations with severe mental illness are substantially higher than the lifetime prevalence rate of PTSD in the general population (Mueser et al., 2008). Even when not leading to the full diagnostic criteria for PTSD, the ramifications of trauma in individuals' lives can be devastating. These higher rates of trauma are also linked with significant disruption of life roles, and poorer social and occupational functioning over time (Gilbert et al., 2009). Specifically, childhood abuse and neglect have been linked with a variety of difficulties that often persist into adulthood, including mental illness, suicide attempts, substance abuse, risky sexual behaviour, poor educational achievement, lower rates of skilled employment, obesity, delinquency, and criminal behaviour (Gilbert et al., 2009).

There is some evidence to suggest that particular types of trauma may be stronger risk factors for the later development of psychosis, as well as to suggest that certain types of trauma might be more likely to predict certain types of psychotic symptoms. Specifically, childhood sexual abuse and neglectful care appear to have a stronger relationship with the development of psychosis when compared to other kinds of maltreatment or adversity (Bebbington et al., 2011; Janssen et al., 2004; Read et al., 2005), with childhood sexual abuse being strongly associated with positive symptoms (especially auditory hallucinations) and neglectful care both predictive of negative and positive symptoms (Read et al., 2005; Van Dam et al., 2015). The relationship between childhood maltreatment and psychosis remains statistically significant even when controlling for other risk factors including gender, socioeconomic status, IQ, childhood mental health problems, cannabis use, and genetic risk for schizophrenia (Arseneault et al., 2011; Varese et al., 2012). Others have supported these findings and suggested that childhood abuse is a causal risk factor for psychosis (Read et al., 2005), specifically for hallucinations and delusions, and have pointed to thematic similarities between the content of these phenomena and the traumatic events in childhood (Hardy et al., 2005; Read et al., 2005). Individuals with a history of childhood sexual or physical abuse have also been found to have earlier, longer, and more frequent hospitalisations, spend more time in restrictive interventions such as seclusion rooms, receive higher medication doses, engage in more self-harm and suicide attempts, and have more severe symptoms (Read et al., 2005). Thus, childhood adversity appears to not only increase the likelihood of psychosis in adulthood, but also to negatively impact the course of psychosis.

Childhood trauma and psychosis appear to have a "dose-response effect", wherein more severe, earlier, or more frequent episodes of childhood maltreatment lead to a higher risk for later psychosis (Janssen et al., 2004; Read et al., 2005; Spauwen et al., 2006; Varese et al., 2012). This is important in light of findings that one episode of maltreatment tends to be associated with a risk for additional further episodes of victimisation (Gilbert et al., 2009; Varese et al., 2012). Adults with serious mental illnesses experience higher rates of victimisation than the general population, and trauma in adulthood has been identified as a media-tor in the link between childhood trauma and adult psychosis (Bebbington et al., 2004; Read et al., 2005). In other words, although child abuse can predict psy-chotic symptoms in the absence of adult victimisation, a combination of child and adult victimisation appears most strongly predictive of psychosis (Read, Agar, Argyle, & Aderhold, 2003).

In summary, the research on trauma and psychosis has established a number of clear trends: these include evidence that trauma is associated with an increased risk for later psychosis, that the frequency and severity of traumatic experiences are positively correlated with that risk, that trauma has a number of adverse con-sequences on functioning, and that certain types of trauma are more commonly linked with specific types of psychotic phenomena. Trauma, thus, is an important factor associated with marked disruption of persons' lives.

Trauma, metacognition and fragmentation

One way that trauma may particularly disrupt persons' lives, beyond its obvious immediate impact, is found in its connections with metacognition and psycho-logical fragmentation. Metacognition is a construct referring to the capacities by which persons form ideas and integrate information about self and others, and ultimately use this information to respond to life challenges. Metacognition, as considered here, has conceptual links to Bleuler's early formulations regarding the centrality in psychosis of difficulties integrating thoughts, affects, and desires (Lysaker et al., 2020). A large body of empirical work has attended to metacogni-tion and associated constructs such as social cognition (see chapters 1 and 3, Lysa-ker et al., 2020 for overview). Within this broader body of research, a few studies have directly investigated the relationship between trauma and metacognition. For instance, people diagnosed with PTSD demonstrate metacognitive impairments, though to a lesser degree than is found in people diagnosed with schizophre-nia (Lysaker et al., 2015). Additionally, and perhaps more directly pertinent to considerations of therapy for people with psychosis and a trauma history, Leon-hardt, Hamm, Belanger, and Lysaker (2015) report that in a sample of individuals diagnosed with schizophrenia and with histories of trauma, higher levels of one dimension of metacognition – self-reflectivity – were associated with heightened emotional distress. These findings converge with other research linking a higher capacity for self-reflection with distress (Hasson-Ohayon et al., 2015). These find-ings may support the possibility that certain features of psychosis are protective, with impaired self-reflection effectively functioning for many with childhood trauma as a buffer from emotional pain.

Consistent with this contention, preliminary conceptual work has drawn links between metacognition, trauma, and dissociative phenomena (Pec, Bob, & Lysa-ker, 2015). Others have examined the role of dissociation in the link between trauma and psychosis to explain findings that dissociative processes in trauma, such as depersonalisation, are associated with psychotic symptoms, especially hallucinations (Kilcommons & Morrison, 2005). It is possible that trauma-induced dissociation impairs reality-testing and fosters a sense of disconnection from the self which may, or may not lead to psychosis (Kilcommons & Morrison, 2005).

Indeed, trauma narratives are often "dissociated", fragmented, or "unelaborated" (Boulanger, 2007; Gumley & Shwannauer, 2006). This fragmentation may be amplified in the case of earlier life trauma which "yields increasingly incoherent and fragmented memories that are at greater risk of becoming distorted, elaborated, and disconnected from the traumatic event itself" (Morrison, Frame, & Larkin, 2003, p. 345). In other words, it is possible that early trauma memories are fragmented and become more distorted over time, yielding a confusing and disjointed life narrative that individuals struggle to integrate and utilise in the face of life's challenges, thereby impeding their metacognitive capacities even before psychosis sets in. Consistent with these ideas, cognitive perspectives have pointed to common biases including tendencies to rely on culturally unacceptable or self-defeating appraisals of autobiographical memory in individuals diagnosed with PTSD as well as in persons experiencing psychosis (Morrison et al., 2003). Lysaker and colleagues similarly described the profound "difficulty ordering and communicating their life stories" found in persons diagnosed with schizophrenia and link this to a sense of isolation and distress (Lysaker, Wickett, Wilke, & Lysaker, 2003, p. 153). Similarly, Boulanger (2007) has described trauma as spurring a "collapse of the self" even in the absence of psychosis (p. 132).

However, not all research investigating meaning-making processes in trauma has focused on dysfunction and debility. There is an emerging body of work that has instead explored the possibility for meaning-making and personal growth resulting from trauma, referring to this phenomenon as posttraumatic growth (PTG) (Mazor, Gelkopf, Mueser, & Roe, 2017). PTG, as originally conceptualised by Tedeschi and Calhoun (1995, 1996), is the result of struggle and the attempt to cope with adverse trauma, and is hypothesised to occur when a highly stressful life event forces people to reexamine their core beliefs and life narrative. PTG is facilitated by the reduction of emotional distress associated with traumatic experiences, which allows rumination to transform into deliberate thinking about the trauma and its aftermath (Tedeschi & Calhoun, 1995; Tedeschi, Cann, Taku, Senol- Durak, & Calhoun, 2017). As a result, people may sense a positive change following their traumatic experience (Tedeschi & Calhoun, 2004), or act in a new and different way (Hobfoll, Canetti-Nisim, & Johnson, 2006; Hobfoll, Tracy, & Galea, 2006). Indeed, research shows that meaning-making and coping self-efficacy mediate posttraumatic growth, providing evidence that even individuals experiencing severe forms of trauma and psychosis are capable of growing from their adverse experiences, particularly if efforts are made to improve coping self-efficacy and making meaning from such experiences (Mazor et al., 2017). Viewed from this perspective, psychotherapy may provide an avenue for shared meaning-making, reconstruction of life narratives, and posttraumatic growth.

Psychosis, trauma, and psychotherapy

The links between trauma and meaning-making, including difficulties in the capacities that give rise to meaning-making, pose a challenge for trauma treatment. Specifically, psychotherapies for persons experiencing psychosis naturally need to take account of the role of trauma in clients' lives, and assist people in making sense of what they have experienced. In order to do so, though, two questions emerge related to basic assumptions about psychotherapy for persons experiencing trauma and psychosis: namely, what are the primary intended objectives of psychotherapy, and when is it appropriate to use psychotherapy to address trauma in persons who experience psychosis?

Concerning the aims of psychotherapy, a number of contemporary treatment approaches for individuals experiencing psychosis have generally operated with the, implicit or explicit, assumption that the primary objective of therapy is the elimination of certain discrete phenomena or problems and that subsequent progress can be viewed in terms of gains in objective markers of symptom severity or functional impairment. These approaches can roughly be considered to have been developed in, or sustained by, a "medical model" of psychotherapy, wherein persons with identified problems are seen within the context of a medical setting and offered intervention aimed at treating or "curing" these discrete problems (see Elkins, 2009). In the case of trauma, these symptom – or illness – focused approaches are intended primarily to contribute to the lessening or amelioration of posttraumatic stress symptoms (e.g. reduced arousal or avoidance, decreased frequency of re-experiencing phenomena) or other discrete distressing manifestations of trauma history (e.g. depression, maladaptive interpersonal patterns).

Consistent with this, recent decades have witnessed the proliferation of cognitive behavioural interventions aimed at targeting specific trauma responses including those associated with diagnoses such as PTSD. Randomized controlled trials (RCTs) have supported the effectiveness of cognitive behavioural therapy (CBT) in reducing the severity of PTSD symptoms. However, despite extensive evidence of high rates of trauma in individuals diagnosed with schizophrenia spectrum disorders, traumatic experiences and PTSD symptoms often go unrecognised in people experiencing psychosis (Seow et al., 2016). In light of recent trends towards trauma-informed care, it was recently suggested that clinicians should be more vigilant in recognising signs of PTSD in people diagnosed with psychotic disorders, rather than assuming such signs are part of the psychosis (Morrison et al., 2003; Read & Fraser, 1998; Seow et al., 2016). Moreover, most randomized controlled trial (RCT research on specialised therapies for trauma has been investigated in populations explicitly seeking treatment to address trauma and therefore are unlikely to identify individuals with comorbid PTSD, seeking treatment for other issues including psychosis (Mueser et al., 2008). Such treatments also often have strict exclusionary criteria that make many individuals with psychosis ineligible.

Despite the popularity of these symptom-focused psychotherapy approaches, especially within frameworks of care that privilege medical models of distress and psychiatric disorder that prioritise the amelioration of discrete signs and symptoms, other approaches to psychotherapy have long taken a different conceptual approach to the intended aims of psychotherapy. Rather than viewing the therapist as an expert who treats symptoms, psychotherapy has also been conceptualised as a place to promote shared meaning-making, understanding, and the cultivation of insight, growth, and acceptance. Such an approach is suggested to include re-allocating psychotic experiences "in their human contexts" and encourage clinicians to "listen, hear, and connect for mutual learning, healing, and wholeness" (Britz, 2017, p. 121). Consistent with this view are contentions that narratives, and the meaning-making associated with them, are inherently an intersubjective process and that the psychotherapist's presence and participation is key to the integration of trauma narratives. These aims have long been reflected in certain threads within the humanistic, existential, interpersonal, and psychodynamic traditions (Boulanger, 2007; Laing, 1978; Searles, 1965; Sullivan, 1962), as well as in current integrative psychotherapy approaches for people experiencing psychosis (e.g. Hamm, Hasson-Ohayon, Kukla, & Lysaker, 2013; Hasson-Ohayon et al., 2015). Additionally, there are examples of models that offer integration in which psychotherapy is posited to treat symptoms as well as to promote meaning-making and personal growth (e.g. Garrett & Turkington, 2011; Gumley & Schwannauer, 2006; Hasson-Ohayon, 2012).

Regardless of the primary aim of psychotherapy, a second essential question arises concerning when psychotherapy targeting trauma might be most appropriately offered to individuals with experiences of psychosis. Some authors have suggested that specific treatments should target discrete problems and as such have advised that, for individuals with psychosis, trauma treatments should be postponed until clients are no longer actively experiencing symptoms of psychosis (Fuller, 2010). Specifically, Fuller (2010) suggests that, consistent with the importance of reinforcing safety in trauma models, clinicians should not explore thoughts or feelings associated with trauma while clients are still in an unsafe situation or experiencing psychosis. This step-wise or phased approach to offering psychotherapy presents immediate obstacles to real-world clinic settings, however, as individuals diagnosed with serious mental illness are likely to present with extensive cumulative trauma, as well as other forms of disenfranchisement including homelessness, poverty, medical problems, disability, and others (Mueser et al., 2008). In other words, utilising these phased approach treatment models, that postpone trauma work until the other barriers are eliminated, may lead to some clients with psychosis never being considered eligible for treatment.

This kind of approach is also potentially at odds with alternative views of psychosis and the role of treatment, which suggest that psychotic experiences are not merely problems to be eliminated, but are also meaningfully connected to life events, including traumatic experiences (Britz, 2017). Additionally, offering these kinds of treatments, targeting discrete pathologies, would appear to undermine calls for holistic, recovery-oriented approaches that target the whole person and support meaning-making and self-direction, and would furthermore risk colluding with the fragmentation associated with both psychosis and accompanying treatment approaches (Hamm et al., 2017). In the section that follows, we will explore how MERIT may serve as a treatment option that can effectively address the treatment challenges presented by these issues.

Metacognitive Reflection and Insight Therapy and trauma

MERIT appears to be an example of a treatment approach well-suited to the challenges presented by trauma and psychosis. MERIT's integrative treatment framework is intended to be flexible enough to accommodate individual preferences and capacities, and is designed for use with individuals at any stage of recovery (Lysaker & Klion, 2017). MERIT aims to promote integration and meaning-making, while its emphasis on metacognitive mastery is designed to support improved self-management of life challenges, which often include the sequelae of trauma. However, despite rich reported case descriptions applying MERIT in psychotherapy with individuals with trauma, to date there has not been a full examination of what MERIT might entail when working with individuals with histories of trauma and psychosis. In what follows, we describe how MERIT is well-positioned to support meaning-making through both its foundational conceptual assumptions, as well as more specific practice considerations linked with MERIT's treatment framework.

MERIT suggests that a key objective of treatment is to engage in meaning-making, at a pace appropriate to an individual's capacity, with aims of metacognitive growth, increased integration, narrative coherence, and enhanced sense of personal agency (Lysaker & Klion, 2017). The research supporting MERIT suggests that metacognition may offer a construct that helps operationalise long-standing observations about disruptions in narrative and loss of coherence (Hamm & Lysaker, 2015). Viewed in this way, more severe decrements in metacognitive capacity may be understood as reflecting increasingly fragmented ways of experiencing self, others, and the world, and are also suggested to be amenable to change and thus viable targets for therapeutic intervention.

Consistent with the link between trauma and psychosis discussed above, for many people life experiences discussed in therapy involve past trauma. As Hardy (2017) points out, the degree to which psychotherapy is directly focused on historical trauma may be moderated by disruptions in autobiographical memory and by overall metacognitive abilities. Consistent with this idea, and with the literature reviewed above, establishing links between trauma, metacognition, and fragmentation, MERIT uses a method of assessing clients' metacognitive capacities as a way to operationalise the degree of fragmentation, as well as a guide for tailoring interventions. This assessment method enables MERIT practitioners to tailor interventions to each client's metacognitive abilities at any given time. As an individual's metacognitive capacities improve, clients should be increasingly able to consider alternative attributions and interpretations of events, including being able to acknowledge that the therapist has independent and valid thoughts (even if they do not necessarily agree with them), and may be better able to tolerate distress associated with recalling traumatic events. In other words, rather than viewing fragmentation merely as a barrier to helping clients address trauma, instead it becomes the direct focus of therapy and effort is made to support the person in reflecting upon their lives at whatever level is possible at that time, even in states of substantial fragmentation.

Of note, the early clinical work that informed the development of MERIT was also attentive to the importance of trauma in persons' histories as it emerged and was reflected upon within the consulting room. One of the early MERIT case reports (Lysaker, Buck, & LaRocco, 2007) described a man who in therapy progresses from a state of disorganisation to a state in which he can discuss and start to make sense of his experience of childhood sexual abuse. In this particular case, as has been observed so commonly in clinical practice (e.g. Buck et al., 2013), the process of meaning-making was accompanied by emotional distress as the man developed increased awareness and ability to process his painful history.

Given these factors, MERIT seems particularly well-suited to responding to the often-profound consequences of trauma in individuals' lives. We now will elaborate general and specific considerations for applying the MERIT framework in work with individuals with trauma histories.

MERIT general assumptions as relevant to trauma

As detailed in the MERIT guidebook (Lysaker & Klion, 2017), successful application of MERIT rests on a series of assumptions that serve as preconditions for effective treatment: i) Psychotic experiences can be understood, ii) meaning-making is best accomplished in psychotherapy through a consultative treatment relationship, iii) recovery from serious mental illness is possible and should be self-directed, iv) improved awareness is often accompanied by emotional pain, and v) stigma remains a pervasive barrier to recovery. Each of these assumptions has particular bearing on psychotherapy with individuals with psychosis and trauma history.

Psychotic experiences can be understood and an important role for psychotherapy is consultative meaning-making

The idea that interpretations and attributions of events are pivotal in the manifestation of both PTSD and psychosis sets the stage for renewed exploration and shared meaning-making. Given the complex and interwoven aetiologies and symptoms of PTSD and psychotic disorders differentiating between the two is often difficult. MERIT offers an alternative approach, not dependent on diagnosis but focused instead on the client-identified psychological problem that may include past trauma, current distressing symptoms, or something else entirely, and which may evolve over the course of therapy. The use of MERIT provides a comprehensive and flexible framework through which to address trauma and psychosis in a person-centered, recovery-oriented manner.

Rather than viewing hallucinations, delusions, and disorganised behaviours as necessarily problems that should be minimised or better managed, MERIT instead suggests that these phenomena can be understood, and encourages mutual reflection and shared meaning-making between therapist and client. Given findings that such symptoms (e.g. disorganisation, content of hearing voices or delusions) can be symbolic of past trauma (Hardy et al., 2005; Read et al., 2005), this assumption would indicate that MERIT therapists adopt similar efforts to understand and pursue meaning-making in the face of reported trauma or expressed content that appears to indirectly signal undisclosed trauma.

Recovery is possible and should be self-determined

MERIT also holds that recovery, even from the most profoundly fragmented or disordered states, is possible, and must be self-determined. As such, the therapist should be open to understanding where the client is in the process, and offering interventions that assist clients in taking charge of their own recovery. This includes not specifying a particular order or curriculum to follow that would dictate when therapy addresses each issue. Applied to trauma in particular, this would suggest that clients should also be supported in moving at their own pace in regard to whether, when, and to what depth they discuss past trauma.

MERIT therapists strive to establish a non-hierarchical, consultative relationship in which client and therapist mutually identify the psychological problem to be addressed. In doing so, MERIT therapists recognise inherent power differentials that exist in therapy relationships, as well as additional disempowering social factors such as poverty and discrimination that commonly affect clients. Recognising these, though, every effort is made to forge a relationship based on mutuality and collaboration, resisting historical tendencies that position the therapist as "knowing best". From this perspective, clients can move at their own pace and are empowered to drive the direction of treatment. Similarly, MERIT recognises that recovery involves deeply subjective elements that may manifest differently for each client and which can reflect meaningful improvements even in the face of persistent symptoms. In this way, clients are encouraged to find their own means of recovery from trauma, psychosis, or any other psychological problem.

Improved awareness may be accompanied by increased pain and distress

Lysaker et al. (2007) point out that mental health practitioners sometimes believe that individuals diagnosed with schizophrenia should not delve into their pasts, but for many this process is essential to their ability to make sense of what has happened in their lives and make decisions about how to move forward in recovery. However, making sense of trauma is often a painful process and clinicians should be aware that working through these experiences may be followed by an increase in distress, or a retreat into psychosis. In light of this, it is important to consider clients' tolerance for the pain associated with the trauma narratives, but also to recognise that, even in the face of distress, meaning-making can occur in which persons can better observe their lives after trauma, acknowledge that they wish the trauma had not happened, and integrate the experience into ongoing pursuits of meaning and personal growth. However, when clinicians assume the authority for determining at what point it is best to discuss trauma, they risk erring on either end, by avoiding trauma or by forcing discussion about trauma before clients are ready. MERIT's client-driven open stance allows clients to bring trauma into the room when they are ready or when it surfaces naturally within the context of the intersubjective processes in therapy. Similarly, exploration of interpersonal processes provides a space for clients (or therapists) to comment on how fast therapy is moving, how they are experiencing the relationship, and what they think is occurring in the therapeutic context.

Stigma remains pervasive and should be addressed in therapy

A final general tenet of MERIT is the recognition that stigma toward mental illness remains prevalent in all areas of society and that this must be recognised and challenged. Stigmatising beliefs are myriad, though there are several specific notions that are relevant to the contextualisation of trauma histories. First, individuals receiving a diagnosis of schizophrenia should be believed when they report trauma. Historically, people diagnosed with schizophrenia were commonly viewed to be unreliable historians of their own trauma histories, but this is belied by evidence that trauma reports by people with psychosis are generally reliable and accurate (Goodman et al., 1999). Second, individuals should be viewed as capable of finding meaning and confronting distress associated with trauma. In other words, distress should not be seen as inherently dangerous or to be avoided. Benevolence stigma may prompt therapists to avoid discussion of trauma, based on beliefs that clients should be protected from pain (Hasson-Ohayon, Kravetz, & Lysaker, 2017). Relatedly, stigmatising notions of incompetence or ability to experience a wide range of emotions might lead a therapist to making a decision about whether and at what point to discuss trauma. Contrary to these ideas, within the MERIT framework individuals experiencing psychosis are viewed as agents able to decide on their own when they are ready to discuss trauma with a therapist. Third, clients themselves also hold stigmatising beliefs about mental illness (i.e. internalised stigma). High levels of internalised stigma can contribute to increased comfort with sick role, disavowal of personal agency or responsibility, or diminished hope that the emotional distress associated with engaging in these meaning-making discussions could support meaningful change and recovery, and may thereby inhibit full participation in treatment (Corrigan, 2004; Ritsher & Phelan, 2004; West, Yanos, Smith, Roe, & Lysaker, 2011). If clients hold such views, this may naturally run counter to the previous three preconditions, and explicit discussion in session may be necessary to address the presence and impact of these beliefs.

Specific practice-based considerations

In addition to the general assumptions or preconditions detailed above, MERIT offers a practice framework for assisting clinicians in partnering with individuals with psychosis to make meaning of life experiences and develop improved mastery strategies. Although it provides flexibility to individualise treatment, and to account for differing backgrounds and theoretical orientations of diverse therapists, the framework does call for eight activities that should be present in each session. The application of these practice elements will be considered specifically for individuals with trauma histories. The eight elements can be broken down into the content elements (attending to agenda, insertion of therapist's mind, elicitation of narrative episode, identification of psychological problem), process elements (intersubjective focus, attention to progress), and superordinate elements (offering interventions aimed at stimulating metacognition and tailored to the person's capacity). Next we address considerations for these three subdomains of the MERIT practice framework while working with persons with trauma history.

Content elements

The first MERIT practice element calls for attention to the client's agenda throughout the session. Consistent with the discussion above, clients' agendas may be related to desires to either address trauma directly in session, avoid reflection on trauma, or potentially competing desires to do both. Consistent attention to the client's evolving agendas in therapy commonly leads to discussion of these wishes to approach or avoid reflecting on past trauma. Therapists should be attentive to cues that traumatic experiences are on clients' minds and may bring the issue into the room themselves by "inserting" their own minds. Complementary to the therapist attending to the client's agenda, the second content element involves promotion of dialogue through the explicit introduction of the therapist's mind in the discussion. At times, clients may want therapists to forget about trauma, a process which likely parallels their own wishes to forget about it. While the therapist continues to hold narratives in mind, calling attention to efforts to erase the therapist's memory of the trauma may lead to valuable discussion about interpersonal processes. The other two MERIT practice elements focused on content are: elicitation of narrative episodes and identification of psychological problems (Chapter 1). In terms of eliciting and exploring narrative episodes, the episodic memories that emerge in therapy naturally involve a wider range of life experiences, some of which involve memories of traumatic life experiences. Therapists should be prepared for recollections of trauma to emerge in response to their efforts to elicit narrative content. It is important to reinforce the idea that the identified psychological problem may be unrelated to the client's diagnosis or trauma, and it is critical that the client identify their own psychological problem.

From a practical perspective, the first step in effectively working with trauma in therapy is for clinicians to be curious about traumatic experiences. This communicates that these experiences are important and invites clients to discuss them further. The manner in which it is discussed, with emphasis on mutual dialogue and attention to the client's agenda, reinforces the consultative stance and lends to a more collaborative consideration of when it might be safe and most useful to explicitly process past trauma.

It is important for the therapist to recognise the links between trauma and fragmentation, and to be attentive to the possibility that narratives may become particularly fragmented with intense emotion or as self-esteem and sense of self are threatened, as is common in traumatic events (Lysaker et al., 2003). Depending on the circumstances, therapists can call attention to the distress, but of course should not abandon the general consultative stance by insisting that clients continue to discuss trauma. It is also the case that depending upon the person's metacognitive capacity and tolerance for distress, these narratives may be more or less fragmented. For example, initially fragments of trauma narratives may emerge, but they may be confusing or tangled in delusional ideas. MERIT views the task of the therapist as to assist in reflecting upon this narrative material, at the level the client is capable of. Regarding trauma narratives, this may involve reflecting merely upon specific fragments, rather than rushing forward by providing a more synthesised interpretation of the impact of trauma on self-esteem, avoidance, arousal, and so on. (for instance, by providing psychoeducation about a model of trauma). Clinicians should expect trauma narratives to often be disorganised initially and it may take considerable time, patience, and repeated exploration of narrative episodes before the trauma becomes clear and accessible to work through.

Identification of a psychological problem may or may not be linked directly with trauma history, and may change or evolve over time (within or across sessions). It is not uncommon for clients with psychosis not to identify trauma as their major psychological problem, and many may not even disclose it until much later in therapy, as trust is developed and at least basic levels of metacognitive integration have been established. As a client's personal narrative gains coherence and their metacognitive knowledge develops, the psychological repercussions of trauma (e.g. fear, anger, insecurity) may emerge as central psychological problems for reflection in therapy.

Process elements

MERIT's process elements stress the fundamentally intersubjective nature of psychotherapy and encourage direct dialogue about what is happening between client and therapist in and across sessions, and also invite discussion about perceived progress. Trauma may influence these processes in a variety of ways. For one, trauma often has a profound impact on interpersonal relationships which may affect the therapeutic dynamic in many ways, and this should be matter for mutual reflection. For instance, fears of abandonment, trust/mistrust dynamics, difficulties with interpersonal boundaries, or fears of honestly expressing emotion linked with past trauma may all emerge in the interpersonal processes between client and therapist.

In addition, as the person begins to disclose and process their trauma history, therapists should be prepared both for clients to desire to share with the therapist what has happened to them, but also to have this be rejected as potentially threatening, resulting in clients' attempts to "destroy all bridges to understanding" (Lysaker et al., 2003, p. 162). This pattern of approach-withdraw is common as clients test, perhaps for the first time, the implications of closeness and inter-subjectivity. In such cases, therapists must remain steady and manage their own eagerness, feelings of rejection, and wishes for the client's progress as they continue to work to establish consensus on the goals for therapy and facilitate shared meaning-making (Hasson-Ohayon et al., 2017).

Superordinate elements: tailoring trauma interventions to a person's given metacognitive level

The superordinate practice elements of MERIT call for therapists to offer interventions that stimulate reflection on self and others, and to use that metacognitive knowledge to inform response to life challenges (i.e. mastery). A critical feature of this involves the therapist tailoring interventions according to the client's current metacognitive capacity. As a general point, we believe that the sense-making of trauma, that we have argued is central to therapy, occurs throughout the process, even when the person has quite impaired metacognitive capacity. In other words, even if trauma has contributed to substantial emotional numbing, or highly disorganised and fragmented narratives, the conversations occurring throughout therapy are intended to support shared meaning-making of the person's life, which includes the factors that have contributed to their current difficulties. When processing trauma, much like other matters, it is essential that the therapist attempts to offer interventions that match the person's current capacity for reflection.

For instance, although people with trauma histories may have a significant degree of anxious arousal or emotional distress, individuals with metacognitive capacities may not initially have the ability to identify and distinguish between different emotional states, and so reflections commenting on or asking them to describe their emotions may be too complicated to be successful and it would be more appropriate to use language identifying different cognitive functions (e.g. "You are remembering . . .", "Your thoughts keep turning to . . ." etc.). These kinds of interventions may even be too advanced for others who struggle to distinguish their own mental contents from other forces in the environment, which would indicate the need for even simpler interventions, aimed at helping a person achieve the level of integration to more effectively establish the boundaries of their own mind as distinct from the minds of others. We recognise the strong temptation to manifestly explore emotion inherent in trauma narratives and which therapists may observe or feel themselves in the moment, but remind therapists of the importance of meeting the client at their metacognitive capacities. Promoting mastery likewise involves adjusting interventions to the appropriate level and stimulating higher levels. An important consideration for many is whether the individual currently has met the threshold of being able to identify a plausible psychological problem (versus denial of all problems or for instance explaining problems exclusively in terms of delusional content) to which one might respond with a mastery strategy. If this level of mastery has not been achieved, then mastery interventions are recommended to be aimed at promoting this capacity.

These subtle technical indications may contrast from many traditional trauma interventions that rely heavily on discussion of affective arousal, links between thoughts and emotion, and explicit discussion of coping strategies. In general, though, these superordinate elements underscore the central aim of joining the whole person in sense-making at their current ability level, recognising that trauma has often profoundly affected the course of their lives as well as their current difficulties in integrating information.

Summary and conclusions

Extensive research and clinical evidence have established important links between trauma and psychosis, both in regards to prevalence as well as in the subjective experience of self. In contrast to some conventional approaches to trauma treatment, MERIT views psychotherapy as fundamentally an opportunity to assist people in making sense of their lives and developing improved abilities to self-determine their response to life challenges. The general assumptions and specific practice elements of MERIT are both compatible with, and offer some guidance for, assisting individuals to respond to the wide range of effects trauma can have on lives. MERIT can thus be viewed as one type of trauma-informed treatment and is an approach that can be offered to and accepted by individuals experiencing a wide range of complex mental health concerns and who are in various stages of disorder and recovery.

References

Arseneault, L., Cannon, M., Fisher, H. L., Polanczyk, G., Moffitt, T. E., & Caspi, A. (2011). Childhood trauma and children's emerging psychotic symptoms: A genetically sensitive longitudinal cohort study. *American Journal of Psychiatry, 168*(1), 65–72.

Bebbington, P. E., Bhugra, D., Brugha, T., Singleton, N., Farrell, M., Jenkins, R., . . . & Meltzer, H. (2004). Psychosis, victimisation and childhood disadvantage. *The British Journal of Psychiatry, 185*(3), 220–226.

Bebbington, P. E., Jonas, S., Kuipers, E., King, M., Cooper, C., Brugha, T., . . . & Jenkins, R. (2011). Childhood sexual abuse and psychosis: Data from a cross-sectional national psychiatric survey in England. *The British Journal of Psychiatry, 199*(1), 29–37.

Bendall, S., Jackson, H. J., Hulbert, C. A., & McGorry, P. D. (2007). Childhood trauma and psychotic disorders: A systematic, critical review of the evidence. *Schizophrenia Bulletin, 34*(3), 568–579.

Boulanger, G. (2007). *Wounded by reality: Understanding and treating adult onset trauma.* Mahwah, NJ: The Analytic Press.

Britz, B. (2017). Listening and hearing: A voice hearer's invitation into relationship. *Frontiers in Psychology, 8*, 387.

Buck, K. D., Roe, D., Yanos, P., Buck, B., Fogley, R. L., Grant, M., . . . & Lysaker, P. H. (2013). Challenges to assisting with the recovery of personal identity and wellness for persons with serious mental illness: Considerations for mental health professionals. *Psychosis: Psychological, Social, and Integrative Approaches, 5*(2), 134–143.

Buck, K. D., Vertinski, M., & Kukla, M. (2018). Metacognitive reflection and insight therapy (MERIT): Application to a long-term therapy case of borderline personality disorder. *American Journal of Psychotherapy, 71*(4), 145–154.

Corrigan, P. W. (2004). How stigma interferes with mental health care. *American Psychologist, 59*(7), 614.

Elkins, D. N. (2009). The medical model in psychotherapy: Its limitations and failures. *Journal of Humanistic Psychology, 49*(1), 66–84.

Fuller, P. R. (2010). Applications of trauma treatment for schizophrenia. *Journal of Aggression, Maltreatment & Trauma, 19*(4), 450–463.

Garrett, M., & Turkington, D. (2011). CBT for psychosis in a psychoanalytic frame. *Psychosis, 3*(1), 2–13.

Gilbert, R., Widom, C. S., Browne, K., Fergusson, D., Webb, E., & Janson, S. (2009). Burden and consequences of child maltreatment in high-income countries. *The Lancet, 373*(9657), 68–81.

Goodman, L. A., Thompson, K. M., Weinfurt, K., Corl, S., Acker, P., Mueser, K. T., & Rosenberg, S. D. (1999). Reliability of reports of violent victimization and posttraumatic stress disorder among men and women with serious mental illness. *Journal of Traumatic Stress, 12*(4), 587–599.

Gumley, A., & Schwannauer, M. (2006). *Staying well after psychosis: A cognitive interpersonal approach to recovery and relapse prevention.* West Sussex, UK: John Wiley & Sons.

Hamm, J. A., Buck, B., Leonhardt, B. L., Wasmuth, S., Lysaker, J. T., & Lysaker, P. H. (2017). Overcoming fragmentation in the treatment of persons with schizophrenia. *Journal of Theoretical and Philosophical Psychology, 37*(1), 21.

Hamm, J. A., Hasson-Ohayon, I., Kukla, M., & Lysaker, P. H. (2013). Individual psychotherapy for schizophrenia: Trends and developments in the wake of the recovery movement. *Psychology Research and Behavior Management, 6*, 45.

Hamm, J. A., & Lysaker, P. H. (2015). Psychoanalytic accounts of the phenomenology of schizophrenia: Synthetic metacognition as a construct for guiding investigation. *Psychoanalytic Psychology, 33*(1), 147–160.

Hardy, A. (2017). Pathways from trauma to psychotic experiences: A theoretically informed model of posttraumatic stress in psychosis. *Frontiers in Psychology, 8*, 697.

Hardy, A., Fowler, D., Freeman, D., Smith, B., Steel, C., Evans, J., . . . & Dunn, G. (2005). Trauma and hallucinatory experiences in psychosis. *Journal of Nervous and Mental Disease, 193*(8), 501–507.

Hasson-Ohayon, I. (2012). Integrating cognitive behavioral-based therapy with an intersubjective approach: Addressing metacognitive deficits among people with schizophrenia. *Journal of Psychotherapy Integration, 22*(4), 356–374.

Hasson-Ohayon, I., Avidan-Msika, M., Mashiach-Eizenberg, M., Kravetz, S., Rozencwaig, S., Shalev, H., & Lysaker, P. H. (2015). Metacognitive and social cognition approaches to understanding the impact of schizophrenia on social quality of life. *Schizophrenia Research, 161*(2–3), 386–391.

Hasson-Ohayon, I., Kravetz, S., & Lysaker, P. H. (2017). The special challenges of psychotherapy with persons with psychosis: Intersubjective metacognitive model of agreement and shared meaning. *Clinical Psychology & Psychotherapy, 24*(2), 428–440.

Hillis, J., Bidlack, N., & Macobin, B. (2018). Metacognitive reflection and insight therapy (MERIT) for persons with a schizophrenia spectrum disorder and interpersonal trauma. *American Journal of Psychotherapy*, *71*(4), 186–195.

Hobfoll, S. E., Canetti-Nisim, D., & Johnson, R. J. (2006). Exposure to terrorism, stress-related mental health symptoms, and defensive coping among Jews and Arabs in Israel. *Journal of Consulting and Clinical Psychology*, *74*(2), 207.

Hobfoll, S. E., Tracy, M., & Galea, S. (2006). The impact of resource loss and traumatic growth on probable PTSD and depression following terrorist attacks. *Journal of Traumatic Stress*, *19*(6), 867–878.

Janssen, I., Krabbendam, L., Bak, M., Hanssen, M., Vollebergh, W., Graaf, R. D., & Os, J. V. (2004). Childhood abuse as a risk factor for psychotic experiences. *Acta Psychiatrica Scandinavica*, *109*(1), 38–45.

Kessler, R. C., Sonnega, A., Bromet, E., Hughes, M., & Nelson, C. B. (1995). Posttraumatic stress disorder in the National Comorbidity Survey. *Archives of General Psychiatry*, *52*(12), 1048–1060.

Kilcommons, A. M., & Morrison, A. P. (2005). Relationships between trauma and psychosis: An exploration of cognitive and dissociative factors. *Acta Psychiatrica Scandinavica*, *112*(5), 351–359.

Laing, R. D. (1978). *The divided self.* New York: Penguin Books.

Leonhardt, B.L., Hamm, J. A., Belanger, E. A., & Lysaker, P. H. (2015). Childhood sexual abuse moderates the relationship of self-reflectivity with increased emotional distress in schizophrenia. *Psychosis*, *7*(3), 195–205.

Lysaker, P. H., Buck, K. D., & LaRocco, V. A. (2007). Clinical and psychosocial significance of trauma history in the treatment of schizophrenia. *Journal of Psychosocial Nursing and Mental Health Services*, *45*(8), 44–51.

Lysaker, P. H., Dimaggio, G., Wickett-Curtis, A., Kukla, M., Luedtke, B., Vohs, J., . . . & Davis, L. W. (2015). Deficits in metacognitive capacity are related to subjective distress and heightened levels of hyperarousal symptoms in adults with posttraumatic stress disorder. *Journal of Trauma & Dissociation*, *16*(4), 384–398.

Lysaker, P. H., & Klion, R. (2017). *Recovery, meaning-making, and severe mental illness: A comprehensive guide to metacognitive reflection and insight therapy.* London: Routledge.

Lysaker, P. H., Minor, K. S., Lysaker, J. T., Hasson-Ohayon, I., Bonfils, K., Hochheiser, J., & Vohs, J. L. (2020). Metacognitive function and fragmentation in schizophrenia: Relationship to cognition, self-experience and developing treatments. *Schizophrenia Research Cognition*, *19*. https://doi.org/10.1016/j.scog.2019.100142.

Lysaker, P. H., Wickett, A. M., Wilke, N., & Lysaker, J. (2003). Narrative incoherence in schizophrenia: The absent agent-protagonist and the collapse of internal dialogue. *American Journal of Psychotherapy*, *57*(2), 153–166.

Mazor, Y., Gelkopf, M., Mueser, K. T., & Roe, D. (2017). Posttraumatic growth in psychosis. *Frontiers in Psychiatry*, *7*, 202.

Morrison, A. P., Frame, L., & Larkin, W. (2003). Relationships between trauma and psychosis: A review and integration. *British Journal of Clinical Psychology*, *42*(4), 331–353.

Mueser, K. T., Rosenberg, S. D., Xie, H., Jankowski, M. K., Bolton, E. E., Lu, W., . . . & Wolfe, R. (2008). A randomized controlled trial of cognitive-behavioral treatment for posttraumatic stress disorder in severe mental illness. *Journal of Consulting and Clinical Psychology*, *76*(2), 259–271.

Newman, J. M., Turnbull, A., Berman, B. A., Rodrigues, S., & Serper, M. R. (2010). Impact of traumatic and violent victimization experiences in indivdiuals with schizophrenia and schizoaffective disorder. *The Journal of Nervous and Mental Disorder*, *198*(10), 708–714.

Pec, O., Bob, P., & Lysaker, P. H. (2015). Trauma, dissociation and synthetic metacognition in schizophrenia. *Activitas Nervosa Superior*, *57*(2), 59–70.

Read, J., Agar, K., Argyle, N., & Aderhold, V. (2003). Sexual and physical abuse during childhood and adulthood as predictors of hallucinations, delusions and thought disorder. *Psychology and Psychotherapy: Theory, Research and Practice*, *76*(1), 1–22.

Read, J., & Fraser, A. (1998). Abuse histories of psychiatric inpatients: To ask or not to ask? *Psychiatric Services*, *49*(3), 355–359.

Read, J., van Os, J., Morrison, A. P., & Ross, C. A. (2005). Childhood trauma, psychosis and schizophrenia: A literature review with theoretical and clinical implications. *Acta Psychiatrica Scandinavica*, *112*(5), 330–350.

Resnick, S. G., Bond, G. R., & Mueser, K. T. (2003). Trauma and posttraumatic stress disorder in people with schizophrenia. *Journal of Abnormal Psychology*, *112*(3), 415–423.

Ritsher, J. B., & Phelan, J. C. (2004). Internalized stigma predicts erosion of morale among psychiatric outpatients. *Psychiatry Research*, *129*(3), 257–265.

Searles, H. F. (1965). *Collected papers of schizophrenia and related subjects*. New York: International Universities Press.

Seow, L. S. E., Ong, C., Mahesh, M. V., Sagayadevan, V., Shafie, S., Chong, S. A., & Subramaniam, M. (2016). A systematic review on comorbid post-traumatic stress disorder in schizophrenia. *Schizophrenia Research*, *176*(2–3), 441–451.

Spauwen, J., Krabbendam, L., Lieb, R., Wittchen, H. U., & Van Os, J. (2006). Impact of psychological trauma on the development of psychotic symptoms: Relationship with psychosis proneness. *The British Journal of Psychiatry*, *188*(6), 527–533.

Sullivan, H. S. (1962). *Schizophrenia as a human process*. New York: Norton.

Tedeschi, R. G., & Calhoun, L. G. (1995). *Trauma & transformation: Growing in the aftermath of suffering*. Thousand Oaks, CA: Sage.

Tedeschi, R. G., & Calhoun, L. G. (1996). The posttraumatic growth inventory: Measuring the positive legacy of trauma. *Journal of Traumatic Stress*, *9*(3), 455–471.

Tedeschi, R. G., & Calhoun, L. G. (2004). Posttraumatic growth: Conceptual foundations and empirical evidence. *Psychological Inquiry*, *15*(1), 1–18.

Tedeschi, R. G., Cann, A., Taku, K., Senol-Durak, E., & Calhoun, L. G. (2017). The posttraumatic growth inventory: A revision integrating existential and spiritual change. *Journal of Traumatic Stress*, *30*(1), 11–18.

Van Dam, D. S., van Nierop, M., Viechtbauer, W., Velthorst, E., van Winkel, R., Bruggeman, R., . . . & Myin-Germeys, I. (2015). Childhood abuse and neglect in relation to the presence and persistence of psychotic and depressive symptomatology. *Psychological Medicine*, *45*(7), 1363–1377.

Varese, F., Smeets, F., Drukker, M., Lieverse, R., Lataster, T., Viechtbauer, W., Read, J., . . . & Bentall, R. P. (2012). Childhood adversities increase the risk of psychosis: A meta-analysis of patient-control, prospective -and cross-sectional cohort studies. *Schizophrenia Bulletin*, *38*(4), 661–671.

West, M. L., Yanos, P. T., Smith, S. M., Roe, D., & Lysaker, P. H. (2011). Prevalence of internalized stigma among persons with severe mental illness. *Stigma Research and Action*, *1*(1), 3.

12

A COMMON JOURNEY

The recovery of the self in psychosis through therapeutic interactions

Lisa Korsbek

Abstract: *This chapter describes a lived experience of the recovery of the self in psychosis, which unfolded as part of a therapeutic relationship in long-term psychotherapy. In the discussion, the beginning of recovery is situated in a decisive experience of relatedness and interconnectedness in the therapeutic encounter. This experience laid the foundation for the development of an actual relationship and was a turning point for proceeding into experiences of the reciprocity of the therapeutic interplay. As the therapy evolved, the journey was increasingly experienced as a common journey; as a shared process of understanding and meaning making in the interpersonal and intersubjective space of interactions that gradually turned into, also, a process of recovery. The chapter illustrates how profound feelings of being fundamentally isolated and separated can, in the process of recovery, gradually develop into an experience of oneself as also a relational self. The chapter frames the account of lived experience predominantly in interpersonal theory and relational therapy and relies on the work of Sullivan, Winnicott, and the French psychoanalyst André Green. The experience of relatedness and interconnectedness is described in the tradition of person-centred therapy. Following the recovery paradigm as defined by William Anthony, the concept of recovery is a personal experience but also facilitated by interpersonal processes. The final parts of the chapter draw on narrative theory and on the reflections by Winnicott on the fear of breakdown. As recovery is experienced as a process of both growth and loss, loss is described as the loss of personal identity within a diagnosis, the loss of one's illness identity when transcending diagnosis, and fear of the profound loss of self-protection in the recovery of the self in psychosis.*

Introduction

This chapter is based on the lived experience of psychosis and psychotherapy. It illustrates aspects of my personal recovery process that gradually unfolded within the interpersonal context of a long-lasting therapeutic relationship. The process depended on both my therapist and me. It demanded the willingness of both of us to engage, and the courage of my therapist to situate herself as an active partner in the interplay.

In the chapter, I stress the interpersonal field of helping and healing. I frame aspects of my recovery process in the relational therapeutic thinking of D. W. Winnicott and of the French psychoanalyst André Green, who elaborated further on D. W. Winnicott. I also recount experiences of relatedness and interconnectedness in the therapeutic encounter that are central to the person-centred tradition of therapy.

Experiences of relatedness and interconnectedness in the therapeutic interplay are sometimes vital in forming a helping therapeutic relationship in people with experiences of profound loss of meaning in episodes of psychosis. In my own process, the experience of therapeutic togetherness helped to convey to me a sense of being and belonging. It also made apparent to me that the process fundamentally was a shared process and that recovery, within the interpersonal context of a therapeutic relationship, is a process of mutual experiences and mutual understanding: a common journey of interaction and meaning making, reflecting also the metacognitive model of therapy portrayed elsewhere in this book (e.g. Chapter 3; Chapter 11).

Recovery is, however, not only a process of recovery from a state of inner isolation or psychosis. Recovery is also a process of recovery towards a new self-understanding and new ways of experiencing oneself and others. The process requires that it be possible to make new and valuable narratives of oneself in the world. If the central narrative of oneself has been a narrative of a lifelong illness, recovery can imply a fundamental reorganisation of one's identity.

Sometimes, recovery is a process of both growth and loss and can entail mourning; mourning a loss of one's former experiences and of one's earlier identity. Mourning was in my own recovery process also mourning a radical new sense of my own self as a being in time and mortality.

The missing link of a human connection

Nearly always, at least since adolescence, I had felt enclosed in a private world, separated and fundamentally alienated from other people and from myself. My dreams were dreams about glass. Glass mirrors, glass windows, glass walls. I was behind the glass. Other people were on the other side of the glass. Sometimes, someone broke through the glass. In those dreams, these often were scary people, who wanted to hurt me, to destroy or annihilate me. Some of them were people I could sense also when I was awake. Some of them were always there. Some of them I could see, either completely or partially, and I was terrified.

My basic feeling was emptiness. I did not feel anything. I could not feel myself and could not feel the real existence of other people. The world felt empty of content and very literally emptied. Things around me were things I could see well. They also had some weight and fullness, if I touched them and felt them. But they were mostly meaningless, as I felt unrelated to the world and to myself.

The condition was especially painful, because something told me this was not the way that other people experienced themselves in the world. I felt that I was missing something, a connectedness that could help me relate to a sense of my own self and make me feel alive.

Even when, at the beginning of my thirties, I met my future husband, and we lived together, I still had the fundamental sense of separateness from the world. My profound experience of myself was as a being in a dead state of non-existence, stuck somewhere in the birth canal of existence.

The psychotic experiences, when they were most vivid and directing my thinking, were often preferable to this dead state of non-existence. In psychosis, everything was at least alive. In psychosis, after all, something happened, and things woke up, they fell out of their fixed places and adopted new and vibrant forms. In the psychosis, I often felt that I became much more alive. I became vigilant, frightened, hyper-observant, and reactive. Everything in the world I suddenly felt was connected, but unfortunately, everything also related to me in an often persecuting and intimidating manner, resulting in another hospitalisation.

My thoughts needed to rest somewhere, so that they did not haunt me. My experiences needed a secure place so they could be reflected upon and responded to, and so they did not evolve in different chaotic and overwhelming directions. To feel my own existence and come to life with a growing sense of myself was a demanding job, but it became possible in a therapeutic relationship with a psychiatrist that was to last for 18 years.

In a process of dialogic exchange and interaction, in which the relationship between us gradually developed, my basic feeling of not being part of the world, but fundamentally alienated and separated from it, disappeared. My experience was the experience of a human connectedness that laid the foundation for a growing sense of my own self. The deeply human experience of a human response, thus, became a turning point in my recovery of the self in psychosis.

Recovery as a deeply human experience, facilitated by deeply human responses

Everyone needs a place to belong, and people in recovery sometimes need the invitation to enter into a relationship that helps facilitate and support a feeling of belonging in the world. Anthony was in fact very clear when he defined recovery as "a deeply human experience, facilitated by the deeply human responses of others" (Anthony, 1993, p. 531), implying that, although personal, recovery often is facilitated by *interpersonal* processes and unfolds as a response to human processes *between* people.

Anthony defined recovery, in close association with the narratives of people with lived experience, as "deeply personal, unique process of changing one's attitudes, values, feelings, goals, skills, and/or roles" (Anthony, 1993, p. 527). This definition deviated decisively from the traditional, clinical understanding of the main objective of mental health care, namely to help people get rid of their symptoms. The definition was central to a growing recognition that the voices of people with lived experience are indispensable to our understanding of recovery, and must be included in transforming mental health care systems into spaces of truly supportive recovery-oriented practice (Schrank & Slade, 2007; Slade, Amering, & Oades, 2008; Piat & Sabetti, 2009). Today, the concept of recovery profoundly permeates the political agenda around mental health in many countries (Sowers, 2005; Davidson, O'Connell, Tondora, Styron, & Kangas, 2006; Farkas, 2007; Slade et al., 2008; Piat, Sabetti, & Bloom, 2010; Le Boutillier et al., 2011; Waldemar, Arnfred, Petersen, & Korsbek, 2016). Anthony's vision that recovery would pull the field of practice into the future and be the guiding vision of the mental health service system in the years to come (Anthony, 1993, p. 535–36) is now a broadly shared vision of mental health care.

The concept of recovery as personal is also the focal point of much literature and research on recovery today (Leonhardt et al., 2017). The model of CHIME, based on a narrative synthesis of published descriptions and models of personal recovery, has pointed to five categories for personal recovery in mental health: Connectedness, Hope and optimism about the future, Identity, Meaning in life, and Empowerment, which give the acronym CHIME (Leamy, Bird, Le Boutillier, Williams, & Slade, 2011; Williams et al., 2015). The model is, in recent time, one of the widely used conceptual frameworks to comprehend what it is important to support in people's personal recovery processes (Eriksen, Arman, Davidson, Sundfør, & Karlsson, 2014; Brijnath, 2015; Slade, Oades, & Jarden, 2017).

Recovery, although personal, seldom unfolds in a vacuum or takes place in isolation. Qualitative research illuminates that people with lived experience often point to recovery as a journey that involves important contributions from others, and other people, whether family, friends or professionals, are, directly or indirectly, often seen as a necessary part (Topor, Borg, Di Girolamo, & Davidson, 2011). Some qualitative research also shows that it is more the rule than the exception that mental health professionals can play an important role; sometimes people in recovery have deemed the role of professionals as decisive (Schön, Denhov, & Topor, 2009).

A study of which attitudes and approaches, on the part of professionals, people in mental health services experience as most helpful to their recovery showed that these are seldom attributed to any specific method or treatment procedure undertaken by the professionals. Often, what is most helpful seems rooted in authenticity when professionals show an interest in and involvement with the person over and beyond the diagnosis (Schön et al., 2009). This can imply professionals are doing more for the person than is regarded as standard practice, when they give more attention than is expected, sometimes doing things other than what is customary or expected in terms of the professional role, sometimes bending the rules (Denhov & Topor, 2012). The attitudes and approaches often contain and convey some element of "extraness" (Schön et al., 2009; Denhov & Topor, 2012), that contributes to the person's experience of being a real and valued person (Schön et al., 2009; Denhov & Topor, 2012). The attitudes and approaches of the professionals that people in recovery often experience as being most helpful are professionals interacting in ways that address the human quality of their relationship, which seems close to Anthony's understanding of recovery as "a deeply human experience, facilitated by the deeply human responses of others" (Anthony, 1993, p. 531).

Experiences of relatedness and interconnectedness in the therapeutic encounter

Anthony does not fully explain, however, how to understand the meaning of deeply human experiences, facilitated by the deeply human responses. But deep human experiences in human interactions are well-known experiences within many interpersonal therapeutic orientations and are often seen as reciprocal experiences of relatedness and interconnectedness in the therapeutic relationship (Hasson-Ohayon, Kravetz, & Lysaker, 2017).

In the person-centred tradition of therapy and counselling, Mearns introduced the term relational depth (Mearns & Cooper, 2005). He related the term to Rogers' notion of presence, which Rogers had described as the moments in therapy when the therapist's innermost self is reaching out to touch the innermost self of the person in therapy (Rogers, 1957; Mearns & Cooper, 2005). Accordingly, Mearns defined relational depth as "a state of profound contact and engagement between two people, in which each person is real with the Other, and able to understand and value the Other's experiences at a high level" (Mearns & Cooper, 2005, p. xii).

Ehrenberg has emphasised the interactive nature of the therapeutic relationship, seeing it as always a mutual, authentic, collaborative, and deeply human experience of relatedness. She describes therapy as working at an intimate edge of relatedness, and she characterized the deeply human experiences of relatedness as "the point of maximum and acknowledged contact at any given moment in a relationship without fusion, without violation of the separateness and integrity of each participant" (Ehrenberg, 1974, pp. 424–425). Psychiatrist and psychoanalytic theorist Stern has also recognised the experiences of relatedness and interconnectedness in the therapeutic encounter. He termed these "moments of meetings" and described them as the moments in which two people make a special kind of mental contact that involves an experience of a "mutual interpenetration of minds" (Stern, 2004, p. 75). For Ehrenberg, the experiences of relatedness and interconnectedness in the therapeutic relationship "can feel like wonders, and bits of magic" (Ehrenberg, 2010, p. 137) that are "unique to the moment and to the particular relationship" (Ehrenberg, 2010, p. 137). For Stern, these experiences are seen as the nodal experiences for change: "the moments most remembered years later that changed the course of therapy" (Stern, 2004, p. 176).

As always, shared experiences of the therapeutic relationship involve deep emotional qualities including psychological intimacy, mutuality, and presence (Wiggins, Elliott, & Cooper, 2012, p. 2), and, accordingly, cannot be attributed to any specific technique or be the result of any cognitive skills that have been learned (Mearns & Schmid, 2006; Knox, Murphy, Wiggins, & Cooper, 2013).

When they take place in the actual and present meeting between the client and the therapist in a state of togetherness, the experiences often unfold in moments without words. Terms used in the person-centred tradition of therapy to identify the experiences as always shared experiences of togetherness are "co-presence" (Cooper, 2005), "co-resonance", and "in-depth co-creative process of personalization" (Schmid & Mearns, 2006).

Therapeutic togetherness as a turning point of recovery

In my own process, the experience of relatedness and interconnectedness in the therapeutic encounter was decisive, laying the foundation for the therapeutic relationship to develop into actually becoming a relationship. It continued to be of central value as an emotional anchoring point of our relationship, which helped me to understand and accommodate other developments within it. It also helped me to endure other experiences, feelings, and thoughts. In difficult times, I could return to these experiences to maintain momentum, perhaps maintaining momentum in both of us so that we would get through the difficult periods.

Years of work preceded the experience, and the experience was overwhelming and shocking too. It was concrete and immediate. It gave me an image of two separate railway tracks that suddenly met and became connected with each other, leaving me in silence, wondering what had happened. Immediately, I was aware also of it as a radical change, I felt it as being a kind of breakthrough. Nearly instantly I, in my experience, also felt the deep and formative nature of the contact with the person in the chair opposite me.

The feelings that came with the experience were new and strange. The possible implications of them could not be fully comprehended in the actual moment, but I instinctively knew that the experience was vital and that I, in the moment it took place, had a new and radical sense of being and belonging.

This experience was, however, not only a starting point. In giving me a sense of being and belonging, it turned my experience of the relationship between my therapist and me into being gradually an experience of its mutuality, and it brought with it new developments in our interactions that moved me more and more away from my isolated starting point.

In the years that followed this experience, the relationship between my therapist and me developed into being more and more a relationship of shared experiences. Our reflections and understandings were increasingly a shared process of understanding and making meaning from our interactions; increasingly I had the experience that both of us were part of the process and that the journey was a common journey. The experience, thereby, became also a turning point. In giving me a sense of being and belonging, it helped to turn my self-experience into gradually experiencing myself as a relational self and as being part of the world, which in turn gave me an increasing sense of growth as well as a growing sense of myself that eventually also turned the process into a process of recovery.

The interpersonal field of helping and healing

From the perspective of interpersonal and relational therapy my therapist became a significant other: that is, a person in an individual's life who is of sufficient importance to affect the individual's emotions, behaviour, and sense of the self (Anderson & Chen, 2002). The significant other is, in relational theory, a concept encompassing "any individual who is or has been deeply influential in one's life and in whom one is or once was emotionally invested" (Anderson & Chen, 2002). The definition, thus, not only includes one's parents but also all members of one's family, as well as people outside family relations who, either earlier or later, have been important people in one's life. It also includes persons of actual importance in one's life as when a therapist in a therapeutic relationship usually always is of some importance to the person in therapy.

This meaning of the significant other is described in the interpersonal theory of psychiatry of Sullivan. Sullivan saw the self as fundamentally a relational self, and developments in life, as well as in childhood, he defined as emerging predominantly from experiences of the relational self in relating to and interacting with significant others (Sullivan, 1953; Kanter, 2013). Sullivan contrasted interpersonal theory with the objectifying stance of descriptive psychiatry, which he often thought fails to include the professional in the process of helping and healing (Davidson, Rakfeldt, & Strauss, 2010; Kanter, 2013), and argued that the therapist "cannot stand off to the side and apply his sense organs . . . without becoming personally implicated in the operation" (Sullivan, 1954, p. 3). Approaches in interpersonal therapy are, in general, different from approaches in psychoanalysis. In classical psychoanalysis, the first step towards change happens via transferences, or the unconscious redirection by the persons in analysis of former experiences and emotions from his/her earlier relationships onto the present relationship with the therapist (Freud, 1912/1975). In interpersonal therapy, the significant other of the therapist is not only significant because of transference, but also as a real person of importance in the actual interactions of the therapeutic relationship (Sullivan, 1954; Kanter, 2013).

Therapeutic relationships and interactions that might help facilitate a process of recovery in people demand the engagement of both parties in the relationship. They depend on the courage of the professional to take an authentic and active part in the interplay. In an authentic therapeutic relationship both parties help each other and both can be conceived helpers. They can both invite feelings of hope and possibilities to emerge in their shared experience of the therapeutic interplay. They can support one another in interactions and approaches of the therapy that can truly meet and respond to the person in therapy. To be able to truly meet in a therapeutic relationship also implies that both parties are able to leave constricting ideas outside the door, exclude their preconceived understandings of the goal of the therapy and be aware of any bias or prejudices about the illness or the cure (Hasson-Ohayon et al., 2017). The ability of my therapist to do this was decisive to my experience of her as a partner in the process and to develop our ability to help each other in the interplay, so our interactions most continuously supported me in my experiences of our relationships and of the process.

Therapeutic interplay in the potential space of Winnicott

As the relationship between my therapist and me developed and became a shared process, I increasingly also had the experience that our interactions carried investments by both of us. She often stressed the importance of this development in our relationship. She clearly appreciated it, and for a time she even got into the habit of emphasising her experience that I was making immense progress. This felt affirmative, encouraging me to keep going, although emphasising it too much also sometimes could annoy me.

To illustrate some of the dynamics of this part of the process, I find that we must turn to aspects of relational therapeutic thinking of Winnicott (Winnicott, 1991/1971) and of the French psychoanalyst Green (1975, 1978), who elaborated further on Winnicott's thoughts on the potential space.

Although Winnicott focused on child development, he also had a distinct interest in people with severe mental illness (Casher, 2013). Especially regarding therapy with people with episodes of psychosis, he emphasised the importance of creating a real and genuine relationship with the person (Kuriloff, 1998; Casher, 2013).

In general, Winnicott (1991/1971) stressed the importance of real transactions between the two persons of the therapeutic interplay and saw the contributions of the therapist as being profound. He regarded the strong treatment focus in classical psychoanalysis on the intrapsychic dynamics of an individual, placing the therapist as a neutral and predominantly irrelevant person, as mostly ineffective (Casher, 2013). The famous sentence of Winnicott that "if the therapist cannot play, then he is not suitable for the work" (Winnicott, 1991/1971, p. 54) reflects his basic approach. Winnicott saw therapy as an overlapping interplay of interactions in the therapeutic relationship that consists of investments from both parties in the relationship. Understanding therapeutic processes implied understanding the importance and meaning of the both verbal and nonverbal communication that "takes place in the overlap of two areas of playing, that of the patient and that of the therapist" (Winnicott, 1991/1971, p. 54).

As an overlapping of two areas of play, the interplay unfolds in an intermediate area. Winnicott (1991/1971) termed the area a third area and a potential space. The area is an intermediate third area between inner and outer, between fantasy and reality, and between subject and object. This implies that the interactions in the intermediate area cannot be traced back to only one side of the area and be identified as originating in either fantasy or reality, in either subject or object, or in either the person in therapy or in the therapist. In the overlapping of the interplay, the interactions of it belong to both parties of the therapeutic relationship as they are formed by the investments of both.

Winnicott also saw the potential space as a space of possibilities. The overlapping interplay in the intermediate area has the potential to be a transformative interplay. The interplay is not only an interaction of a certain authenticity. As the mutually overlapping dynamics of the interactions belong to neither of two parties of the relationship solely, but only to the intermediate area to which the inner realities and the external life of both the person in therapy and the therapist contribute, it is a unique interplay. It is unique in the specific meaning of the word, as an interplay that exists only in these specific interactions of this specific encounter in this specific relationship. Therefore, the interplay in the intermediate area is also a potential space. It is a potential space of becoming what the person in therapy has never been, namely his or her own self. It is the potential space for the person to discover and develop their own unique, or true, version of the self and grow gradually into being oneself.

Meaning making in the third intermediate area of therapeutic interactions

The thoughts and approaches of the French psychoanalyst Green are embedded in a theoretical-academic tradition of French psychoanalysis, and as a psychoanalyst schooled in classical psychoanalysis, Green is sometimes seen as a true disciple of Freud (Reed & Levine, 2018). But Green also met Winnicott, and early on began to elaborate on Winnicott's concept of potential space (Reed, 2015). In fact, Green proposed that most of the effective therapeutic communication was situated in this intermediate area between reality and fantasy, subject and object, inner and outer. He introduced the term "tertiary" to designate the character of the overlapping processes in the "meeting of two communications in the potential space which lies between them" (Green, 1975, p. 12). By tertiary, Green wanted to stress indisputably that the processes in the potential space are both internal and external with investments from both the client and the therapist in the therapeutic interplay. As processes of both, we cannot identify to whom which part belongs. The processes can only be termed and comprehended as processes belonging to both therapist and client as they unfold in the dynamics of their actual and interpersonal interplay.

Green saw these processes as always unfolding in present time, as an always present meeting of the two persons of the therapeutic interplay in the intermediate area between them, and with neither person being unaffected by this meeting. Meaning in therapy and meaning of therapy, Green saw as being created and constituted as the result of this interplay. Meaning was always the meaning made in the meeting in the third area, the meaning in the potential space made by the actual interactions of the two persons in their interplay.

The understanding described by Winnicott and Green of the therapeutic interplay as two areas of an overlapping communication in a third intermediate area, corresponded with my growing experience that the interactions between my therapist and me were formed by the investments from both of us. As the therapy also gradually brought with it a certain familiarity of its interplay, my therapist often stressed the importance of certain changes to, or developments in, our relationship. Her approach also often signified that she was definitively a "part of it". Sometimes, she showed me that she was affected by our interactions too, demonstrating, thus, that she underwent emotional processes herself. As the reflections were increasingly mutual reflections, and the journey increasingly felt like a common journey, it became clear to me that the meaning of our interplay was one made in the course of it, and that both of us contributed to it. It also became clear that this meaning had not existed before, as if to be found in the course of the therapy. Meaning in the therapeutic process and meaning of the process came into existence only through the therapy and only as result of our continuous and common meaning making. The process also constituted what in the end became a common story of the therapy, a narrative of our therapeutic interplay, its meaning made by and through this specific interplay in this specific relationship.

Narrative meaning and the meaning of a narrative in the end

The most famous formulation on the meaning of narrative is that by the French philosopher Ricoeur: "time becomes human to the extent that it is articulated through a narrative mode, and the narrative attains its full meaning when it becomes a condition of temporal existence" (Ricoeur, 1984, p. 52). Brooks, a professor of the Humanities at Yale in the 1980s, put it more straightforwardly: "Mens sana in fabula sana: Mental health is a coherent life story" (Brooks, 1986, p. 53).

Narrative structuring, as a way of organising and ordering one's existence in time, is vital for situating and understanding ourselves as human beings. It is an ongoing negotiation with reality, in which we give meaning to the past and anticipate things to be expected in the future, making sense of what we have experienced in life, what we have suffered and enjoyed, and, in essence, it sustains our sanity. Illness, on the other hand, whether mental or physical, is a biographical disruption of one's narrative. Illness disrupts how we understand our self in the world; it leads us to question the sense of continuity and inner coherence and to feel disconnected without a sense of personal meaning (Bury, 1982; Charmaz, 1983). Often an illness experience also invokes our need to reconstruct our life story, to give suffering form and to articulate the experience within the framework of one's personal biography (Williams, 1984; Radley, 1993).

To regain control of one's life story, to make meaning again if meaning has been broken, implies that one can construct narratives that support this process. In people with a diagnosis of severe mental illness, the process of reconstructing a personal narrative of one's life experiences can be felt to be complicated by the dominant historical narratives that surround some mental health diagnoses.

The central narrative of my own diagnosis of schizophrenia in my twenties was not a narrative of recovery, not even one of very much hope for the future. The central narrative was a story of a lifelong illness. When the responses and the attitudes of the staff at the inpatient hospital sometimes also reflected the hopelessness of the diagnosis, it was easy to internalise this and confuse it with my personal identity. It took time to reorganise that narrative of hopelessness, to deconstruct the overlap between diagnosis and identity, and get to a point where the world of life could outperform to a wider degree the strong narrative of diagnosis (Yanos, Roe, & Lysaker, 2010; Korsbek, 2013).

In theories of narrative the end of the narrative is decisive. The end is decisive as the final element of the narrative that brings light to our understanding. A narrative is, in reality, not much of a narrative without an end, because the end is ultimately what brings the meaning of the whole story to us. Reading a story is for Brooks (1984) always a reading for an end that ultimately will bring forth the meaning of the whole. In therapy the end is usually also decisive and brings narrative closure too. It brings closure to the therapeutic narrative that has been made by the lines of the stories told and retold in the therapeutic process, often several times in several different forms.

This narrative is also the narrative of the therapeutic relationship. It is a narrative of how the relationship has developed over time and how it is to be understood. It is a narrative of how the meaning of the relationship has been reflected in the therapeutic interplay and come to be constituted as shared meaning. The narrative includes the perceptions, understandings, and all the mutual reflections on the changes in the therapeutic process of what has been important and experienced as integral or fundamental.

This narrative is, at the same time, a product of the therapy. The narrative did not exist before, but only came into existence as the result of the therapeutic interplay. It is a unique narrative, unique in being the narrative of a unique interplay in a unique relationship, existing only in this relationship and only as a narrative of this therapeutic interplay. Ideally, ending therapy, thus, comes when a person has internalised the dynamic interplay of the therapeutic relationship to "take away with him the potential space in order to reconstitute it in the outside world, through cultural experience, through sublimation and, more generally, through the possibility of pairing or (let us rather say) of coupling" (Green, 1978, p. 180).

Recovery as a process of both growth and loss

Experiences of relatedness in therapy might perhaps often be a first essential step toward forming a meaningful therapeutic relationship. In people with experiences of a profound loss of meaning in episodes of psychosis, such experiences might sometimes serve as a fundamental first part of the recovery process. As my own experience of togetherness was the experience that helped convey to me a sense of being and belonging, it also helped to create a common ground of the therapeutic encounter on which a deeper sense of my own self and of meaning gradually could evolve.

The process of recovery is, however, virtually never linear. The process of recovery goes back and forth. Sometimes there are relapses which should not always be classified as relapses, but instead as integral parts of recovery even when such relapses include hospital readmission. Recovery, in the beginning, may be entered from a hesitant or skeptical frame of mind, as if one expects to find, or meet, something that was not expected. Recovery may be experienced as a process of both growth and loss.

My own experience of the recovery process was also of a process of profound loss. Sensing this, I felt deeply ambivalent and confused. Reflecting on what I was perhaps about to lose, I increasingly mourned the prospect of a future in which I perhaps could no longer flee into a more secluded and shielded part of my inner world. I began reflecting more on the meaning of my psychotic experiences. In some periods, I idealised the psychotic experiences, feeling that psychosis had offered me protection. I even, sometimes, expressed that I was not sure that I could stand living a boring, ordinary life. Constantly, I vacillated between wanting and not wanting to proceed further along the direction that had opened up for me.

I began perceiving my direction as being also a choice. My experience was that I had never had access to the choice before. Recovery, I then felt, was a choice also between staying in a world of my own, in which I might still have the possibility to escape, or taking part in the world of others and having no opportunity for escape. It was a choice, indeed, that might have become possible because of the work that preceded it, but it was not an easy choice, and I hesitated. I hesitated for years in a growing sense that if I chose the new direction, it was not only a point of no return, but implied a state of no defence.

In my experience of the potential transforming power of human connectedness, I also experienced it as a loss, a loss of my defences which left me vulnerable. My feeling since adolescence of being enclosed in a private world, separated and fundamentally alienated from other people and from myself, made more sense to me as it resulted perhaps also from an urgent need to protect an important part of my innermost self.

Fear and mourning in the recovery process

If a profound feeling of being in a dead state of non-existence is the manifest experience of a fierce defence of one's innermost self, the experience of the transformative power of human relatedness and interconnectedness can be as critically dangerous as it can be healing.

Winnicott, in his famous 1974 essay, describes the fear of a breakdown as a fear of a breakdown which has in fact already happened but which, because it was so overwhelming, has not yet been experienced. For me, the overwhelming experience of relatedness and interconnectedness in the therapeutic encounter was the decisive moment that transgressed my deadened state of non-existence. It, thereby, not only opened the door into a new experience of myself as being and belonging, but also into the innermost, most vulnerable and protected, part of my innermost self.

Experiences of psychosis may be preferable to the experience of being in a dead state of non-existence, but a dead state of non-existence is preferable to being dead in reality. My fear had never been a fear of a breakdown due to psychosis, but a fear of what might be behind psychosis and may be protected by it. To open myself to the potential transformative power of human connectedness was to take a chance with a potential catastrophic outcome.

I mourned, and had the almost unbearable sense of losing my experience of being stuck somewhere in the birth canal of existence. In some sense, I had an experience of myself as dying. Paradoxically, to be stuck somewhere in the birth canal of existence had been a life-giving experience, as if in a fixed state of being-in-between, as being not really alive, but being not dead either, I, by avoiding life, could also avoid death.

Fear in recovery is a fear that the past not yet experienced will be catastrophic; the fear of being devastated in the very moment of becoming. The experience in my own process was that recovery was a processing forward in time that was also a transgressing backwards in time. It brought me back to a past that was the past, before my past had become the dead state of non-existence in my experience of the present, while the experience of being fundamentally separated and alienated now became distant and constituted itself as my new past.

My experience of coming into life with a sense of my own self was, thus, also a rather radical experience of being now on the other side of the birth channel of existence, and mourning was central to all the transformative parts of my recovery process. I mourned the past, present, and future. I mourned the past that was finally past in the present moment of loss, the present moment of dying in becoming what I had never been, and my new sense of myself as a being in time and mortality that pointed towards new closures: towards the closure of the therapeutic relationship, the closure of the therapeutic narrative, and towards the ultimate closure in the future, which is the closure of death. A recovery of the self in psychosis can be a brutal awakening unto a new reality and sense of oneself, one in which we both celebrate and mourn the emergence of the reality of human existence.

References

Anderson, S. M., & Chen, S. (2002). The relational self: An interpersonal social-cognitive theory. *Psychological Review*, *109*(4), 619–645. https://doi.org/10.1037//0033–295X.109.4.619.

Anthony, W. A. (1993). Recovery from mental illness: The guiding vision of the mental health service system in the 1990s. *Psychosocial Rehabilitation Journal*, *16*(4), 11–23. https://doi.org/10.1037/h0095655.

Brijnath, B. (2015). Applying the CHIME recovery framework in two culturally diverse Australian communities: Qualitative results. *International Journal of Social Psychiatry*, *61*(7), 660–667. https://doi.org/10.1177/0020764015573084.

Brooks, P. (1984). *Reading for the plot: Design and intention in narrative*. Cambridge, MA and London: Harvard University Press.

Brooks, P. (1986). Psychoanalytic constructions and narrative meaning. *Paragraph*, *7*(1), 53–76.

Bury, M. (1982). Chronic illness as biographical disruption. *Sociology of Health & Illness*, *4*(2), 167–182. https://doi.org/10.1111/1467-9566.ep11339939.

Casher, M. (2013). "There's no such thing as a patient": Reflections on the significance of the work of D. W. Winnicott for modern inpatient psychiatric treatment. *Harvard Review of Psychiatry*, *21*(4), 181–187. https://doi.org/10.1097/HRP.0b013e31828ea604.

Charmaz, K. (1983). Loss of self: A fundamental form of suffering in the chronically ill. *Sociology of Health & Illness*, *5*(2), 168–195. https://doi.org/10.1111/1467-9566. ep10491512.

Cooper, M. (2005). Therapists' experiences of relational depth: a qualitative interview study. *Counselling and Psychotherapy Research*, *5*(2), 87–95. https://doi.org/10.1080/17441690500211130.

Davidson, L., O'Connell, M., Tondora, J., Styron, T., & Kangas, K. (2006). The top 10 concerns about recovery encountered in mental health system transformation. *Psychiatric Service*, *57*(5), 640–645. https://doi.org/10.1176/ps.2006.57.5.640.

Davidson, L., Rakfeldt, J., & Strauss, J. (Eds.). (2010). *The roots of the recovery movement in psychiatry*. Oxford, UK: Wiley-Blackwell.

Denhov, A., & Topor, A. (2012). The components of helping relationships with professionals in psychiatry: Users' perspective. *International Journal of Social Psychiatry*, *58*(4), 417–424. https://doi.org/10.1177/0020764011406811.

Ehrenberg, D. B. (1974). The intimate edge in therapeutic relatedness. *Contemporary Psychoanalysis*, *10*(4), 423–437. https://doi.org/10.1080/00107530.1974.10745350.

Ehrenberg, D. B. (2010). Working at the "intimate edge". *Contemporary Psychoanalysis*, *46*(1), 120–141. https://doi.org/10.1080/00107530.2010.10746043.

Eriksen, K. Å., Arman, M., Davidson, L., Sundfør, B., & Karlsson, B. (2014). Challenges in relating to mental health professionals: Perspectives of persons with severe mental illness. *International Journal of Mental Health Nursing*, *23*(2), 110–117. https://doi.org/10.1111/inm.12024.

Farkas, M. (2007). The vision of recovery today: What it is and what it means for services. *World Psychiatry: Official Journal of the World Psychiatric Association (WPA)*, *6*(2), 68–74. PMID: 18235855; PMCID: PMC2219905.

Freud, S. (1912/1975). Zur Dynamik der Übertragung. In Sigmund Freud (Ed.), *Schriften zur Behandlungstechnik, Studienausgabe, Ergänzungsband*. Frankfurt am Main: S. Fischer Verlag.

Green, A. (1975). The analyst, symbolization and absence in the analytic setting (on changes in analytic practice and analytic experience). *The International Journal of Psychoanalysis*, *56*(1), 1–22.

Green, A. (1978). Potential space in psychoanalysis: The object in the setting. In S. Grolnick & L. Barkin (Eds.), *Between reality and fantasy* (pp. 169–189). New York: Jason Aronson.

Hasson-Ohayon, I., Kravetz, S., & Lysaker, P. H. (2017). The special challenges of psychotherapy with persons with psychosis: Intersubjective metacognitive model of agreement and shared meaning. *Clinical Psychology & Psychotherapy*, *24*(2), 428–440. https://doi.org/10.1002/cpp.2012. Epub 2016 Mar 14.

Kanter, J. (2013). Helping, healing and interpreting: Sullivan, the interpersonal school and clinical social work. *Journal of Social Work Practice*, *27*(3), 273–287. https://doi.org/10.1080/02650533.2013.818943.

Knox, R., Murphy, D., Wiggins, S., & Cooper, M. (2013). *Relational depth: New perspectives and developments*. Basingstoke: Palgrave Macmillan.

Korsbek, L. (2013). Illness insight and recovery: How important is illness insight in peo-ples' recovery process? *Psychiatric Rehabilitation Journal, 36*(3), 222–225. https://doi.org/10.1037/prj0000018.

Kuriloff, E. (1998). Winnicott and Sullivan. *Contemporary Psychoanalysis, 34*(3), 379–388. https://doi.org/10.1080/00107530.1998.10746370.

Leamy, M., Bird, V., Le Boutillier, C., Williams, J., & Slade, M. (2011). Conceptual framework for personal recovery in mental health: Systematic review and narrative synthesis. *British Journal of Psychiatry, 199*(6), 445–452. https://doi.org/10.1192/bjp.bp.110.083733.

Le Boutillier, C., Leamy, M., Bird, V. J., Davidson, L., Williams, J., & Slade, M. (2011). What does recovery mean in practice? A qualitative analysis of international recovery-oriented practice guidance. *Psychiatric Services, 62*(12), 1470–1476. https://doi.org/10.1176/appi.ps.001312011.

Leonhardt, B. L., Huling, K., Hamm, J. A., Roe, D., Hasson-Ohayon, I., McLeod, H., & Lysaker, P. H. (2017). Recovery and serious mental illness: A review of current clini-cal and research paradigms and future directions. *Expert Review of Neurotherapeutics, 17*(11), 1117–1130.

Mearns, D., & Cooper, M. (2005). *Working at relational depth in counselling and psycho-therapy*. London: SAGE Publications.

Mearns, D., & Schmid, P. F. (2006). Being-with and being-counter: relational depth: The challenge of fully meeting the client. *Person-Centered & Experiential Psychotherapies, 5*(4), 255–265. https://doi.org/10.1080/14779757.2006.9688417.

Piat, M., & Sabetti, J. (2009). The development of a recovery-oriented mental health system in Canada: What the experience of Commonwealth countries tells us. *Canadian Journal of Community Mental Health, 28*(2), 17–33. https://doi.org/10.7870/cjcmh-2009–0020.

Piat, M., Sabetti, J., & Bloom, D. (2010). The transformation of mental health services to a recovery-orientated system of care: Canadian decision maker perspectives. *The International Journal of Social Psychiatry, 56*(2), 168–177. https://doi.org/10.1177/0020764008100801.

Radley, A. (1993). Introduction. In A. Radley (Ed.), *Worlds of illness: Biographical and cultural perspectives on heaith and disease*. London: Routledge.

Reed, G. S. (2015). André Green on the theory and treatment of "non-neurotic" patients. *Psychoanalytic Review, 102*(5), 649–658. https://doi.org/10.1521/prev.2015.102.5.649.

Reed, G. S., & Levine, H. B. (2018). *André Green revisited: Representation and the work of the negative*. The International Psychoanalytical Association Psychoanalytic Classics Revisited. London: Routledge.

Ricouer, P. (1984). *Time and narrative* (Vol. I). Chicago: Chicago University Press.

Rogers, C. R. (1957). The necessary and sufficient conditions of therapeutic personality change. *Journal of Consulting Psychology, 21*(2), 95–103.

Schmid, P. F., & Mearns, D. (2006). Being-with and being-counter: Person-centered psycho-therapy as an in-depth co-creative process of personalization. *Person-Centered and Expe-riential Psychotherapies, 5*(3), 174–190. https://doi.org/10.1080/14779757.2006.9688408.

Schön, U. K., Denhov, A., & Topor, A. (2009). Social relationships as a decisive factor in recovering from severe mental illness. *International Journal of Social Psychiatry, 55*(4), 336–347. https://doi.org/10.1177/0020764008093686.

Schrank, B., & Slade, M. (2007). Recovery in psychiatry. *Psychiatric Bulletin, 31*(9), 321–325. https://doi.org/10.1192/pb.bp.106.013425.

Slade, M., Amering, M., & Oades, L. (2008). Recovery: An international perspective. *Epidemiologia e Psichiatria Sociale, 17*(2), 128–137. https://doi.org/10.1017/S11211 89X00002827.

Slade, M., Oades, L., & Jarden, A. (Eds.). (2017). *Wellbeing, recovery and mental health*. Cambridge: Cambridge University Press.

Sowers, W. (2005). Transforming systems of care: The American Association of Community Psychiatrists guidelines for recovery oriented services. *Community Mental Health Journal, 41*, 757–774. https://doi.org/10.1007/s10597-005-6433-4.

Stern, D. N. (2004). *The present moment in psychotherapy and everyday life*. New York: W. W. Norton & Company.

Sullivan, H. S. (1953). *The interpersonal theory of psychiatry*. New York: W. W. Norton & Company.

Sullivan, H. S. (1954). *The psychiatric interview*. New York: W. W. Norton & Company.

Topor, A., Borg, M., Di Girolamo, S., & Davidson, L. (2011). Not just an individual journey: Social aspects of recovery. *International Journal of Social Psychiatry, 57*(1), 90–99. https://doi.org/10.1177/0020764010345062.

Waldemar, A. K., Arnfred, S. M., Petersen, L., & Korsbek, L. (2016). Recovery-oriented practice in mental health inpatient settings: A literature review. *Psychiatric Services, 67*(6), 596–602. https://doi.org/10.1176/appi.ps.201400469.

Wiggins, S., Elliott, R., & Cooper, M. (2012). The prevalence and characteristics of relational depth events in psychotherapy. *Psychotherapy Research, 22*(2), 139–158. https://doi.org/10.1080/10503307.2011.629635.

Williams, G. (1984). The genesis of chronic illness: Narrative re-construction. *Sociology of Health & Illness, 6*(2), 175–200. https://doi.org/10.1111/1467-9566.ep10778250.

Williams, J., Leamy, M., Bird, V., Le Boutillier, C., Norton, S., Pesola, F., & Slade, M. (2015). Development and evaluation of the INSPIRE measure of staff support for personal recovery. *Social Psychiatry Psychiatric Epidemiology, 50*(5), 777–786. https://doi.org/10.1007/s00127-014-0983-0.

Winnicott, D. W. (1991/1971). Playing: Creative activity and the search for the self. In *Playing and reality* (pp. 53–64). London: Routledge Paperback.

Winnicott, D. W. (1974). Fear of breakdown. *International Review of Psycho-Analysis, 1*,103–107.

Yanos, P. T., Roe, D., & Lysaker, P. H. (2010). The impact of illness identity on recovery from severe mental Illness. *American Journal of Psychiatric Rehabilitation, 13*(2), 73–93. https://doi.org/10.1080/15487761003756860.

13

THE RECOVERY OF THE SELF IN PSYCHOSIS

A concluding unscientific postscript

Paul H. Lysaker and Ilanit Hasson-Ohayon

Abstract: *In this volume, the collected chapters have described approaches to the treatment of psychosis that have shifted their focus from symptom reduction and skill acquisition to helping persons make their own sense of the challenges they face and how to manage them. While many different approaches have been presented, we suggest that these chapters offer much more than just new concrete ways to intervene. Taken as a whole, they offer at least three insights into how mental health services can directly promote some of the most subjective aspects of personal recovery, namely those related to reclamation of a coherent sense of self. First, the work in this volume illustrates how treatment may promote the integration of embodied, cognitive and affective experience, resulting in a larger and less fragmented sense of oneself and other. With this larger, less fragmented sense of self, the recovering person can have immediately available to them more effective ways to direct their own recovery and act as agents in the world. Second, the mechanism by which treatments may lead to greater integration is necessarily, in part, intersubjective. Meaning made in therapy, regardless of the approach described in each chapter, is jointly made by the diagnosed persons and the clinician. Finally, this work has revealed the neglected complexities of trying to measure outcome. In so doing, it has called for future research to develop ways to take meaning and meaning making into account when trying to understand how the life of someone diagnosed with psychosis is unfolding.*

Introduction

At the outset of this volume we noted that the subjective experience of recovery from the challenges posed by a diagnosis of psychosis requires far more than symptom reduction and skill acquisition (Chapter 1). Instead, it requires persons to develop their own unique sense of those challenges and decide how they want to respond to and/or manage them. Consequently, the kinds of mental health services that could promote recovery need more manifest development. What is needed are services that promote meaning making and an opportunity to experience oneself as having a place in the larger human community. In this volume then, a broad range of approaches which aspire to meet this need have been described. Concretely, this has included interventions that address the need for self-determination and the co-construction of recovery (Chapter 12), metacognition (Chapter 7; Chapter 11; Chapter 3; Chapter 9; Chapter 4; Chapter 6), mentalization (Chapter 5; Chapter 2), therapeutic alliance (Chapter 10) and issues of personal narrative (Chapter 8). Across the volume, these approaches have been demonstrated as viable and also sufficiently flexible to systematically address the complexities encountered in an individual life, whilst also maintaining touch with a fundamental sense of humanity. Also in the chapters we have seen the potential of these approaches to address the unique needs of individuals without recourse to a generic formula, or regression back to a point in which persons diagnosed with psychosis are subtly distanced from managing their own lives.

Taken as a whole, however, we suggest that this volume has done more than establish the viability of these various approaches. It has also gone beyond offering concrete illustrations of how such approaches can be readily delivered across different settings. We feel that it has pointed to at least three related, larger points which are essential for the continued development of research concerned with issues of self-experience and recovery. As more than the sum of its parts, this volume has particularly illustrated important aspects of the phenomenon of recovery of self-experience and its intersubjective nature, as well as various solutions to the complexities of assessing outcome. In this concluding chapter we will explore each of these ideas and discuss their relationship with the treatment models described in the book. Finally, we will discuss limitations and future directions.

The self and its availability though the integration of experience

The first issue that this volume has pointed to concerns what is happening when there are changes to do with self-experience, and related constructs like self-coherence and agency. In the course of a regular day any of us are likely to talk about what we call our self. None of us knows ourselves as objects, however. So what do we mean when we say something about us has changed? We are not reducible to a certain visual image, singular quality, personality trait, specific value or social position. We recognise ourselves in ways that are not equivalent to recognising ourselves in a mirror. Indeed, any of us could drastically alter our appearance and yet feel we are not a different person. Yet, persons diagnosed with psychosis might undergo no drastic alteration in appearance and yet feel something about themselves has fundamentally changed.

William James (1890) famously suggested that we know ourselves when we experience ourselves experiencing the world, that is as we are actively interpreting and responding to the world. Even earlier, the existentialists Nietzsche (1886/1996) and Kierkegaard (1949/1980) noted that we know ourselves through experiencing ourselves acting in the world and they rejected the idea that we have a singular essence. Continuing in this tradition, the different approaches described in this volume are also concerned with how persons experience themselves as they engage as active agents in, and not observers of the world. Explicitly or implicitly concerned with the self, these approaches work towards the recovery of self-experience, which could be described as the return of a healthy, agentic, relatable or coherent sense of self. Each approach must, therefore, offer some kind of activity that enables the recovery of these kinds of self-experience. But what is that activity and how does it produce those effects upon self-experience? Concretely, we argue that the answer to these questions is that each approach in its own way allows persons' experience of themselves in the world to become available to them again in a way that enables them to have a clearer sense of themselves and their relation to others. Each treatment, in a somewhat unique way, facilitates a sense of oneself to again be available, to be recognized and used to respond to life events within the flow of life as persons being better able to integrate their experiences of themselves, others and their larger communities.

As an illustration, in Lewis Carroll's (1923) *Alice's Adventures in Wonderland*, the main character, Alice, encounters a caterpillar who asks her "who are you?" She is uncertain and explains: "I – I hardly know, sir, just at present – at least I know who I WAS when I got up this morning, but I think I must have been changed several times since then. . . . "I can't explain myself, I'm afraid . . . because I'm not myself, you see" (p 37). In this example, Alice looks within, for lack of a better metaphor, and cannot find a being coherently experiencing and interpreting the world, composed of different facets, or one connected to others. It is not that a physical object is absent. It is not that she is failing to look inward sufficiently. Whatever it is that she knows to be herself is not available in the present moment. Naturally, the pieces that make up Alice's sense of self still exist. Nothing tangible has been destroyed and she is not experiencing an irreversible form of dementia. Those pieces, however, are not fitting together in that moment, and so no sense of self is available.

What we have seen then, spread across the chapters in this volume, is the possibility that the recapturing, return or recovery of the self is a matter of the recapturing, return or recovery of the relative availability of self-experience. It is not a process enabled because something physical has been created or constructed. At issue is the reawakening of the processes which allow for the integration of an almost unimaginable amount of information which enables the availability of self-experience in a given moment. Memories, awareness of bodily states, emotions, values, the authority to make sense of one's own experiences, including marginalisation, connection with others and the potential to become are a few examples of what becomes meaningfully integrated in the consciousness of the person diagnosed with psychosis, allowing a sense of self to again be present.

The self and intersubjectivity

The second broad implication that has emerged from the chapters as a whole concerns the foundational role of intersubjectivity in the experience of the self, and therefore in any treatment concerned with self-experience. One century after the work of the early existentialists Nietzsche (1886/1996) and Kierkegaard (1949/1980), the philosopher Martin Buber (1970) described how we know ourselves not only because we are in the world but because, in the world, we are in dialogue with others. For any of us, what we call our self exists through ongoing connections with others. We know ourselves because others have, do or could know us (Bakhtin, 1981). One contemporary term that can describe these kinds of connections, which allow for self-experience, is intersubjectivity. Intersubjectivity, referred to in various chapters, is a spectrum of experiences that can be said to occur *between* people (Beebe, Knoblauch, Rustin, & Sorter, 2005), allowing for the mutual recognition and symbolisation in language of subjective experiences (Stern, 2000). As alluded to in the introduction (Chapter 1), approaches concerned with metacognition and mentalization have long emphasised the importance of recognising the shared nature of meaning making.

Following this, we suggest that the chapters in this book have unmistakably illustrated how thinking about the challenges in one's life is not a concrete cognitive activity that is located within an isolated mind. As is true for anyone, the appraisals described within this volume by recovering persons of their experiences are necessarily shaped by the relative meanings assigned to that experience. Those assigned meanings themselves are always naturally produced or molded by how others do or might respond to those experiences.

As noted by Cortina and Liotti (2010), the ideas that emerge in our minds that are available for reflection require the real *or imagined* presence of other people who could react to our experiences or interpretations of them. A person who might think about an experience that we ourselves have had could include a sibling, partner, friend, rival or colleague. Concretely, any meaning we assign to an experience is affected by: i) how another person has related, or could in the future relate, to that experience and make sense of it and ii) how another person has responded, or could respond, to the meaning we have assigned to that experience (Hasson-Ohayon, McLeod, Gumley, & Lysaker, 2020).

For example, thoughts about a frustrating job interview, date or a recent reoccurrence of symptoms are affected by the meaning one assigns to these experiences. Further, the meanings assigned to those experiences are molded in part by the meanings others have or might attribute to those experiences as well. Whether one blames oneself in the earlier example, for the frustrating interview, sees frustration in job interviews as unavoidable, sees this as a lesson illustrating concrete things to do next time or takes the frustration as a sign to give up, is affected by how others might have responded to and made sense of the same frustration. This is not to say one is defined by the ideas of others. A person could think others might blame him or her for the frustrating interview but reject that and see the responses of others as a function of stigma. From a broader vantage point, developmentally this suggests that there cannot be an isolated human thinker from whom singular thoughts flow.

Turning to psychotherapy, this idea positions the therapeutic relationship as a condition for the possibility of meanings assigned to subjective experience (Hasson-Ohayon, Kravetz, & Lysaker, 2017). As illustrated explicitly in Korsbek (Chapter 12) and Hamm et al. (Chapter 11), pain and emotionally difficult material comes to be jointly understood by two minds, or by a small group of minds in the case of group therapy (Chapter 10), with therapist and client/s in dialogue with each other, and neither in a dominant position. This is true implicitly as well when the experience concerns things usually considered the province of the biological, including medication (Chapter 7). The essential role of intersubjectivity seems to have a range of deeply important consequences and poses questions for work going forwards. To begin, if sense of self is at issue, treatment cannot be fundamentally a matter of teaching or education. Rather, treatment should focus on experience and meaning. The meaning one makes of one's life is an essential part of being an agent and having a coherent sense of self and cannot be granted by someone else or handed down. Treatment must be collaborative, and non-hierarchical. This is not to say that the role of the clinician is unimportant. It does, however, raise questions regarding the relative positions of the clinician and the client as they meet.

Justifiably, many have emphasised that the "diagnosed person" has experiential authority and so care is needed to protect their experience from being co-opted by a more powerful other (Noorani, 2013). While it is true that no one is an expert on the life of another person, it is less clear what it means for anyone to be an expert on their own life when a dialogical understanding of that life is at issue (Zalzala, Gagen, & Lysaker, 2018). Certainly, experiential authority means that the person experiencing psychosis has unique knowledge and a legitimate right to form their own ideas about themselves and to not be coerced into thinking something else. As long emphasised by many (Kierkegaard, 1949/1980), the meaning of the events in a person's life and their place within the human community is never a matter of making a simple observation. In addition, it is only through dialogue that clearer meaning emerges (see Buck, Buck, Hamm, & Lysaker, 2015 for a discussion of the Buber's concept of the between and confirmation). Again, meaning is not made when someone just accepts what others think but occurs following deeply complex exchanges in which multiple meanings are possible.

Indeed, a further point about intersubjectivity and treatment is that dialogue which occurs in the treatment approaches described in this volume is complex and not easily reducible to any kind of simple exchange. Dialogues cannot be predetermined to follow a script. They cannot be conceptualized as entirely supportive or entirely challenging. They must also allow for the recognition by the therapist of what is happening in the moment and so allow simultaneously for a dialogue in which there may be the potential recognition and reflection upon a range of contradictory, complementary and unrelated self-experiences. For example, relating to the whole person must allow within dialogue for self-deception, the underestimation of one's potential and deep wishes which may be aggressive, or other complex aspects to be possible, on both the part of the therapist and recovering person.

Self-experience and outcomes

A third issue, that we believe this volume has pointed to, concerns objective measurement and its illusions. The field of mental health has endured a long history of making claims which are not subject to dispute (Lysaker, Glynn, Wilkness, & Silverstein, 2010). For example, as described in many forums, mental health professionals, on the basis of their own authority, have decided categorically whether a given treatment has worked or is working, whether persons diagnosed with psychosis are well or unwell (Chien, Leung, Yeung, & Wong, 2013). A common remedy to this has been to make sure, scientifically, the processes at issue can be measured and truth be established empirically (Levant et al., 2008).

The chapters in this volume have suggested that an assessment of outcome may be more complex than it might appear. It is reassuring to believe that there are single outcomes which are "good". If so, we can just measure them and determine what "works". But this may be an illusion. If meaning is at play, then the experience of a single outcome by a single person may not always be equivalent to the experience of that outcome by another person. For example, for one person the end of a relationship may be liberating, but for another, an inexpressible loss. The attainment of an entry-level job may feel like a momentous step forward for one person and as capitulating to marginalizing forces for another. Deploying certain social skills can be empowering for some but feel like abandoning a just protest by another. In this way, assessing the meaning of aggregated singular outcomes may be more difficult than one might initially assume.

Furthermore, the path to recovery may be quite predictably unpredictable and not necessarily have a single endpoint. This is to say, as expressed in many places (e.g. Leonhardt et al., 2017), recovery for one person is not the same as recovery for another. Thus, treatments may be limited to the degree to which they begin with a prescribed outcome. If meaning is being made, it may not be predictable what outcomes will emerge as meaningful for a given person. One person may, as things make increasing sense to them, decide to work. Another person might decide to purchase a car. Another person might expand family contact while another person may withdraw. Symptom management may emerge as a key goal for one person while for another, the meanings of symptoms may pale in comparison to the need for social rank.

This is not to call for a reactionary movement backwards or a relativism that allows for anything to be labelled as wellness or its absence. What it does call for is for science to not be limited to simple explanations based on singular outcomes. If meaning is at issue, there may also never be a final meaning and so we need to allow for the evolution of meaning to be an outcome in and of itself.

While there is no clear solution to these dilemmas, some suggestions have emerged from the chapters in this volume. Certainly, one of these is that while meaning cannot be quantified, processes which support experiencing the self and life as meaningful such as metacognition and mentalization can be measured and included in assessments of recovery. Byproducts of meaning making, such as narrative coherence, could also be measured quantitatively. The need for mixed methods that combine quantitative and qualitative methods is also another clear implication of this (Hasson-Ohayon, Roe, Yanos, & Lysaker, 2015).

The complexity that is inherent here also points to the possibility of considering outcomes in terms of networks rather than the function of individual components. In network analysis, a network is defined by a series of discrete phenomena which are understood in terms of their varying patterns of connections with one another. In a network, the specific phenomenon is conceptualized as nodes and connections as the edges of a larger structure which is the network (Epskamp, Borsboom, & Fried, 2018; Fried et al., 2017). This approach avoids a simple causal model wherein one outcome affects another and enables a visualization of how different things continuously affect one another in a way that could be analogous in a rough sense to an electronic circuit. Consistent with research on networks and resiliency (Galderisi et al., 2018), applied to recovery, it may be that the best way to think about health is in terms of a functional set of experiences whose interaction is at least as important as a specific output (Lysaker, Kean, Poirier Culleton, & Lundin, 2020).

As an illustration, in the path from symptoms of psychosis, to self-confidence, to attaining work to self-esteem, the relationship of all of these aspects may likely be affected by the kind of sense people make of symptoms, work and their decisions about how to respond to them. This pathway may also affect job tenure. Reciprocally, working can then affect the severity of symptoms, all the while the person's own interpretation of what is happening could affect their self-confidence and self-esteem. A linear model of connection between variables may thus not be sufficient, and it is only when considered as a network that the larger processes become apparent. This is consistent with a recent network analysis that indicated that metacognitive self-reflection, along with cognitive disorganization, were the variables that most often connected social cognition, neurocognition and other symptoms to one another (Hasson-Ohayon, Goldzweig, Lavi-Rotenberg, Luther, Lysaker, 2018).

Limitations and future directions

Kierkegaard in his *Concluding Unscientific Postscript* (1846/1980) reminded us that nothing can be understood without a consideration of the subjective. In this volume subjectivity has been a fundamental focus and the chapters have presented a range of approaches to respond to issues of meaning and self-experience in the treatment of psychosis. While there is great promise in this emerging body of work, there are limitations. Perhaps foremost, the voice of the recovering person needs to be more prominent. As illustrated in this volume there are many notable systematic efforts underway which are informed by an appreciation of the experience of psychosis but more research by recovering persons needs to be deeply and prominently incorporated into this evolving work. There is also work needed from a broad range of international settings including developing and non-industrial nations and indigenous non-Western cultures. The data supporting the treatment approaches in this volume are also largely in their infancy and quantitative and qualitative studies of the effectiveness of these treatments are needed as well as examinations of their applicability to broader groups of persons.

Concerning future research, as noted across this volume, there is a need for the further development of methods to assess meaning making and the formation of the kinds of understanding which support human beings' sense of self. As theoretical work on subjective experience in psychosis becomes more nuanced, the research questions multiply along with a demand for more sophisticated methodologies. Work is also needed to explicitly examine mechanisms of action. For example, are there common processes across the treatments in this volume that are responsible for change? Are there different factors which more prominently affect outcomes in different treatments but not others? Are some elements of a given treatment more prominently related to certain outcomes, for example therapeutic alliance, than others? Work is needed to explore how these emerging treatments are related to others. Are they rightfully described as novel or as iterations of previous work? What is their place alongside other approaches to psychosis?

Turning to the therapist, work is also needed to further develop and explore methods for training in these approaches and the assessment of their fidelity. An important question remains concerning who is best suited to this work. Are certain personality traits or values, for example, intrinsic to those therapists who prove most effective? What are the experiences of therapists providing these kinds of services? What kinds of hurdles exist for persons trying to learn these methods with different backgrounds and orientations? As any significant attempt to understand and respond to human suffering, the work here naturally has generated more questions than answers and hopefully will spur on many more years of fruitful research and debate.

References

Bakhtin, M. (1981). *The dialogic imagination* (C. Emerson, trans.). Austin, TX: University of Texas Press.

Beebe, B., Knoblauch, S., Rustin, J., & Sorter, D. (2005). Forms of intersubjectivity in interpersonal/relational perspective. *The International Journal of Psychoanalysis, 90*(2), 347–361.

Buber, M. (1970). *I and thou; A new translation, with a prologue and notes by Walter Kaufmann.* New York: Simon & Schuster.

Buck, K. D., Buck, B. E., Hamm, J. A., & Lysaker, P. H. (2015). Martin Buber and evidence based practice: Can the lion really lie down with the lamb. *Psychosis, 8*(2), 156–165.

Carroll, L. (1923). *The adventures of Alice in wonderland.* New York: Holt Rinehart and Winston.

Chien, W. T., Leung, S. F., Yeung, F. K., & Wong, W. K. (2013). Current approaches to treatments for schizophrenia spectrum disorders, part II: Psychosocial interventions and patient-focused perspectives in psychiatric care. *Neuropsychiatric Disease and Treatment*, *9*, 1463–1481. https://doi.org/10.2147/NDT.S49263.

Cortina, M., & Liotti, G. (2010). The intersubjective and cooperative origins of consciousness: An evolutionary-developmental approach. *Journal of the American Academy of Psychoanalysis and Dynamic Psychiatry*, *38*, 291–314. https://doi.org/10.1521/jaap.2010.38.2.291.

Epskamp, S., Borsboom, D., & Fried, E. I. (2018). Estimating psychological networks and their accuracy: A tutorial paper. *Behavior Research Methods*, *50*(1), 195–212.

Fried, E. I., van Borkulo, C. D., Cramer, A. O., Boschloo, L., Schoevers, R. A., Borsboom, D., (2017). Mental disorders as networks of problems: A review of recent insights. *Social Psychiatric Epidemiology*, *52*(1), 1–10.

Galderisi, S., Rucci, P., Kirkpatrick, B., Mucci, A., Gibertoni, D., Rocca, P., . . . & Maj, M. (2018). Interplay among psychopathologic variables, personal resources, context-related factors, and real-life functioning in individuals with schizophrenia: Network analysis. *JAMA Psychiatry*, *75*(4), 396–404.

Hasson-Ohayon, I., Goldzweig, G., Lavi-Rotenberg, A., Luther, L., Lysaker, P. H. (2018). The centrality of cognitive symptoms and metacognition within the interacting network of symptoms, neurocognition, social cognition and metacognition in schizophrenia. *Schizophrenia Reseach*, *202*, 260–266.

Hasson-Ohayon, I., Kravetz, S., & Lysaker, P. H. (2017). The special challenges of psychotherapy with persons with psychosis: Intersubjective metacognitive model of agreement and shared meaning. *Clinical Psychology & Psychotherapy*, *24*(2), 428–440.

Hasson-Ohayon, I., McLeod, H., Gumley, A., & Lysaker, P. H. (2020). Metacognition and intersubjectivity: Reconsidering their relationship following advances from the study of persons with psychosis. *Frontiers in Psychology*, *11*, 567.

Hasson-Ohayon, I., Roe, D., Yanos, P. T., & Lysaker, P. H. (2015). The trees and the forest: Mixed methods in the assessment of psychosocial interventions' processes and outcomes in psychiatry. *Journal of Mental Health*, *26*(6), 543–549.

James, W. (1890). *The principles of psychology*. New York: Henry Holt and Company.

Kierkegaard, S. (1946/1980). *Concluding unscientific postscript*. Princeton NJ: Princeton University Press.

Kierkegaard, S. (1949/1980). *The sickness unto death*. Princeton, NJ: Princeton University Press.

Leonhardt, B. L., Huling, K., Hamm, J. A., Roe, D., Hasson-Ohayon, I., McLeod, H. J., & Lysaker, P. H. (2017). Recovery and serious mental illness: A review of current clinical and research paradigms and future directions. *Expert Review of Neurotherapeutics*, *17*(11), 1117–1130.

Levant, R., & Hasan, N. (2008). Evidence-based practice in psychology. *Professional Psychology: Research and Practice*, *39*, 658–662. https://doi.org/10.1037/0735-7028.39.6.658.

Lysaker, P. H., Glynn, S. M., Wilkness, S. M., & Silverstein, S. M. (2010). Psychotherapy and recovery from schizophrenia: A review of potential application and need for future study. *Psychological Services*, *7*(2), 75–91.

Lysaker, P. H., Kean, J., Poirier Culleton, S., & Lundin, N. (2020). Schizophrenia, recovery and the self: An introduction to the special issue on metacognition. *Schizophrenia Research: Cognition*, *19*, 100167.

Nietzsche, F. (1886/1966). *Beyond good and evil*. New York: Random House.

Noorani, T. (2013). Service user involvement, authority and the "expert-by-experience" in mental health. *Journal of Political Power*, *6*, 49–68.

Stern, D. N. (2000). *The interpersonal world of the infant: A view from psychoanalysis and developmental psychology*. New York: Basic Books.

Zalzala, A. B., Gagen, E., & Lysaker, P. H. (2018). Diagnosis, personhood and recovery in diagnostic formulation in the treatment of serious mental illness: A commentary on Pavlo, Flanagan, Leitner and Davidson. *Journal of Humanistic Psychology*, *59*(3), 356–367.

INDEX

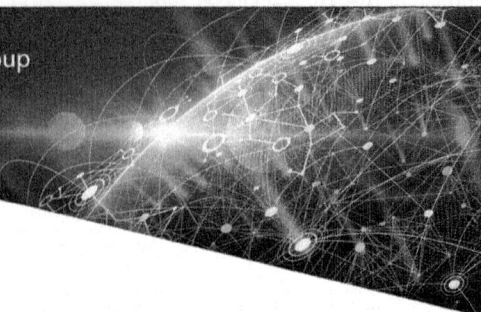